Enjoying Dog Agility

From Backyard to Competition

by Julie Daniels

Doral Publishing
Wilsonville, Oregon
1991

Published by Doral Publishing, P.O. Box 596, Wilsonville, Oregon 97070. Printed in the United States of America.

Copyedited by Luana Luther
Book Design and Sketches by Tracy Warren
Typesetting by Pioneer Graphics, Wilsonville, Oregon 97070

Library of Congress Card Number: 91-70231
ISBN: 0-944875-16-5

Daniels, Julie, 1951-
   Enjoying dog agility : from backyard to competition / Julie
Daniels. --
   p. cm.
   ISBN 0-944875-16-5

   1. Dogs--Training.   2. Dog sports.   I. Title.

SF431   636.7'088
                                    QBI91-61

This book is dedicated to Jessy, the unlikely agility dog who won't settle for less than an all-out effort at anything. When Jessy chose Agility, our fate was sealed. She chooses her friends carefully, sticks with them for life, and makes them live it to the fullest. I couldn't ask for more.

INTRODUCTION

I would love for you to meet one of my favorite activities-the sport of Dog Agility. Agility training begins as simple confidence-building exercises with ordinary obstacles around the house. From there your interest can take you and your dog all the way to precision skills and strategies for national competition. At any level, this sport invites you to develop a closer bond with your dog than you may ever have imagined.

Like many sports, dog Agility is open to anyone who wants to participate. But this sport requires that you enlist the cooperation of a dog, any dog, who also wants to participate. From the moment you decide that you would enjoy running around a large obstacle course to direct your dog over, under, around, and through various challenges, think of Agility as a team sport. This book is for helping you learn the joys and requirements of the sport, and for helping you nurture that same combination of fun, athletics, and teamwork in your canine partner.

ACKNOWLEDGEMENTS

I am grateful to Sharon Morris for countless hours of help with photographs for this book. Sharon coordinated daughter, husband, dog, pregnancy, and camera at every opportunity. She took nearly a thousand photos to capture the work and progress of many dogs and handlers during a year. I want to thank the many students in my classes and seminars who allowed us to photograph dogs in all stages of training. Several students and teammates gave extra hours and energy to photo sessions in all sorts of weather, especially Brenda Buja with Bach, Max and Tiger; Carol and George McLaughlin with Missie; Monica Percival with Hannah; Corene Edwards with Stoner; Hope Godino with Dizzy; Amanda Schaltenbrand with Sidney; Linda Desmarais with Nadia and Spuds; Bob and Audrey Leet with Chen-yu; Carol Rigattori with Blade. Special thanks to Brenda Buja for the story of her adoption of Max (Ch. 2), and to George McLaughlin, Ron Pitkin, and Monica Percival for turning good ideas into good equipment.

My neighbors helped with this book. Thank you to Jim and Marie Albrecht and to James, Bobby, Nicole and Amy with Astro; to Nancy, Megan and Colton Gwinn with Lynn, and especially to Brian Hutchins with Fluffy. I am also grateful to Nancy Gwinn for drawing the "Basic Dog Anatomy" picture. Several professional photographers contributed photos to this book, including Brumfield Studios of Danville, VA; Frank Corden Sr. of Northwood, NH; Melissa Lee Harris of San Francisco, CA; Steve Hooper of Keene, NH; and Maria Kalmring of Putney, VT. The Vizsla jumping across the front cover is Jessie, owned by Marilyn Belli of North Carolina and photographed by Brumfield Studios. The little Yorkshire Terrier in the insert is Abbee, owned by Rae Tanner of Illinois and photographed by Frank Corden Sr. The back cover photo of my Rottweiler Jessy is by Sara Nugent of Houston, TX.

Thousands of photos were submitted from all over, and I very much appreciate the effort and fun that went into each one. From California to Maine, from Minnesota to Texas, from Canada and England, the pictures showed dogs and their people Enjoying Dog Agility! Special thanks to those whose work and whose dogs are included in this book: Chuck Akerman, Pat Alford, Sharon Anderson, Alaina Axford, Mary-Jo Baldwin, Becky and Chris Barrett-Healy, Tina Bayer, Margaret Beauharnois, Kevin Belcastro, Marilyn Belli, Karin Bleecker, Scott Brown, Vicki Bush, Pat Cook, Judy Davis, Dan Dege, Jay Demeritt, Tina Dow, Paula Eldridge, Maria Elliot, Eileen Fernandez, Diana Fielder, Chris Frado,

Bev and Burt Franklin, Hollie Frost, Cynthia Gillette-Fox, Paul and Heather Girard, Sally Glei, Sue Haase, Marion Hardy, Wendy Hey, Fran Hoffman, Martha Hoffman, Barb Hustings, Pierre Lalonde, Paula Lavallee, Debbie Lightfoot, Kate Locke, Jody and John Lorenz, Honey Loring, Luana Luther, Jean MacKenzie, Bob and Sandy Madden, Ruth McAlindon, Shirley Menendez, Pat Miller, Barb Monroe, Jessica Morris, Lorraine Nichols, Hazel Olbrich, Lorri Oliver, Shirlee O'Neill, Lillian Pineo, Ron and Cheryl Pitkin, Sherry Reel, Deb Sargent, Linda Schindler, Doris Smith, Sandy Swanson, Kenneth Tatsch, Larry Tehero, J.C. Thompson, Tom Thompson, Pam Trevor, Beth True, Kara Underwood, Janis Wason, Mike and Bev Weaver, Gwen Weisgarber, Art Weiss, Judy Wilson, Sandy Zandlo, Lori Ziemba, Ester Zimmerman.

I am indebted to my publisher Al Grossman and editor Luana Luther, and to Tracy Warren for the sketches. Thank you to Pagey Elliott, Catarina Haag, Marion Hopkins, Helen Maginnes, and Kenneth Tatsch for assistance. Special gratitude to Bardi McLennan for all her support, and to Helen Maginnes for entrusting to me her loveable, zany puppy Arrow. Most important, I want to thank my husband Dick and my daughter Heather. Heather posed for pictures, traveled with me, shared my office, listened to dog talk when she needed girl talk, and went without lots of important things so I could work on this book. She and Dick kept the dogs fit and happy when I spent days at the keyboard. Dick also handled many a thankless task. He helped with scheduling and kept the computer and me on friendly terms. He provided invaluable insight by reading each chapter with a novice's eye. I did not make it easy for him to offer suggestions, but he was usually right. Without the cooperation of Dick and Heather this book could not have been written.

FOREWORD

Above all else, Julie Daniels is a compassionate guidance counselor. She recognizes our shortcomings, and guides her students (two-footed and four) on a steady path to mutual understanding, acceptance, and success. The author's insight into the human-canine relationship becomes increasingly clear as we delve into the complexities and the ramifications of her special method of learning-teaching.

Mrs. Daniels gives us all the "parts"- a lucid definition of Agility, the kind of obedience training and physical conditioning needed for agility training, how, when and where to begin, to continue, and how to appreciate the smallest success. She guides us through the nitty-gritty and even the ho-hum, and makes it fun!

The author's definition of "TLC" (Trust, Leadership and Confidence) spells out exactly how to reach the level of understanding that makes dog and owner become a team, which is the same ultimate goal whether the exercise at hand is walking the dog or entering an agility trial.

There are chuckles, too. No sooner do we get caught up in the explanation of a problem situation, than the author gives us an amusing variation gleaned from her own vast experience. It keeps even the "armchair agility" person turning pages - and learning.

For beginners, even the previously inactive dog owner, this book will amuse, guide, cajole, bolster your confidence and get you involved in a new activity that is fast becoming a most popular dog sport. Even if you never get beyond a less challenging version in your own backyard, you and your dog will have developed new bonds. I bet you'll be among the cheering spectators at an agility trial in your area, too.

One thing is certain. Anyone reading this book and following Julie Daniels' step-by-step method will realize that the right way to "beat the clock" on an agility course is by teaching good habits for accuracy along with speed.

So many "how to" books are one dimensional. They only explain the right way to do something, making no allowance for failure. Working with a dog is *always* like operating under Murphy's Law: If it can go wrong, it will. The author meets this challenge head-on with "Hints" added to each training segment in Chapters 5-9, to assure the reader that problems are solvable, and then possible solutions are given Throughout the book, photographs show the right way and, to keep right and wrong separate, illustrations show what is incorrect. A positive energy flows from the author's words, even when discussing setbacks. She consistently guides, explains, nudges, and encourages.

By the end of the book the reader will understand what agility competition is all about. It's fun, but precision training entails hard work too; it only looks easy when the pieces fit together perfectly. Perhaps the most important thing the reader will have gained is a realization of what goes into teamwork training, including fun, and the benefits that accrue from being a team with your dog. You'll soon know why this book is entitled *Enjoying Dog Agility*. Read, learn, and ENJOY!

Bardi McLennan

CONTENTS

SECTION I–This Is Agility

SECTION II–Regulation Obstacles

SECTION III–Agility for the Very Young

SECTION IV–Appendices

SECTION V–Bibliography, Index

SECTION I

This Is Agility

- A Contest of Fun

- Getting Started

- Elements of Agility

- Teamwork

A full-size agility course needs an area of about 10,000 square feet.

Brumfield Studios

1

A CONTEST OF FUN

Money will buy a pretty good dog, but it won't buy the wag of his tail.
                                                                    –Josh Billings

Welcome to an exciting young sport begun in England as an extra entertainment to fill time between events at the world-famous Crufts International Dog Show in 1978. It was such a success with the spectators and the participants that a new dog sport was born.

There's a whole new possibility for fun and teamwork with your dog. A fine agility course is an impressive and irresistible sight; it looks like a super-playground for dogs. The colors are vivid, bright and shining, the hefty equipment just calls out for playtime, and there's plenty of room for you and all your friends. Agility in action draws spectators from out of the woodwork. Everyone seems to love it vicariously as the dogs tear around the field, working the course with tails wagging and muscles rippling. The handler's job is to direct the dog and help him do well. It is certainly the dog who is in the limelight during competition.

Dog Agility thrived as a sport in England due to the hard work and dedication of several key players and training organizations. Needless to say, many people contributed a great deal of time and effort to build equipment, instruct newcomers, and literally bring the sport to new locations. For every person who appears in the spotlight, dozens more have worked hard behind the scenes. Thanks to all these people and to their unified goal of developing Agility as an athletic sport with the emphasis on fun, Agility in England now has such a large following that it draws capacity crowds of spectators and competitors all over the country.

Agility has gained steady popularity around the world, with England remaining at the forefront. Many variations on the theme have sprung up, and some of them, in Europe and in the U.S., are quite far removed from the original intent and guidelines. Any new sport is vulnerable to interpretation. Fortunately, international standards are now being adopted based on the English organization. This is the sensible thing to do, as it will ensure for the sport an international terminology and a consensus of interpretation. International competition in Agility is on the way.

The United States Dog Agility Association (USDAA) was established in 1985 and incorporated in 1986 to promote Agility in this country as the English recognize it. Coincidentally, the two first enthusiasts to build English-style agility equipment and begin organizing its introduction were both from the state of Texas, though they did not know of each other. Sandra Davis from El Paso and Kenneth Tatsch from Dallas began using their English experience to build proper equipment in the U.S. Each continued communicating with English experts in order to remain true to the sport as it was intended, and it was through that avenue that they were made aware of each other.

In a country as large as the United States, nothing short of a major campaign would be enough to promote a new sport at the national level. Without central guidance and regular communication with agility authorities in England, there would be no hope of maintaining the integrity and focus of the sport as word and interest spread. With the help

Max works the Pedigree finals course in Houston, 1990.

of underwriting from Pedigree dog foods (also called Kal Kan in the U.S.), Kenneth Tatsch set about organizing a national tournament which would attract the best agility competitors from all parts of the country.

This event, known as the Pedigree Grand Prix of Dog Agility, made its debut in 1988 in conjunction with the prestigious Astro World Series of Dog Shows held at the Astrodome complex in Houston, Texas. The intent was to promote and update Agility in all corners of the country. Because travel across the U.S. can be prohibitively expensive, it was the practice from the beginning for Pedigree to pay the expenses of regional winners to travel to Houston for the national semifinals and finals.

The Grand Prix tournament has been highly successful and made many friends for Agility. In 1990, the number of regional qualifying trials was increased to 16 (up from 10 in 1989), in order to help meet the increased demand while keeping the rapid growth under control. Perhaps the real growth of the sport in the United States is best measured by spectator interest at the nationals. There was some interest in 1988, although most spectators did not know what they were watching. In 1989, nearly 2,000 people watched the finals competition, which was taped for national TV. In 1990, Agility had extensive TV coverage and more; it had an overwhelming command of the crowds. Stands on both sides of the agility arena were packed with an estimated 4,000 cheering fans.

As Agility's popularity continues to explode across the U.S., the leadership of USDAA must also expand. In 1989, Kenneth Tatsch chose four qualified individuals from four sections of the country to serve with him as the club's first Board of Directors. These were John Cortwright of Illinois, Jean MacKenzie of Rhode Island, Matt Mantz of Texas, and Sharon Nelson of Idaho.

In 1989, again following the English lead, it was decided to introduce Agility at a major U.S. horse show. Kenneth Tatsch, again sponsored by Pedigree, invited five of the northeast's top agility dogs. These were Bach, Brownie, Jessy, and Val, all major prizewinners from the New England Agility Team, and the fifth was Cooper, a national finalist from Pennsylvania. Their handlers agreed to put on full demonstrations and offer limited one-on-one instruction for the many thousands of horse and dog enthusiasts at the Radnor Hunt International Horse Show in Pennsylvania.

As a result, Brenda Buja with Bach, Cheryl and Ron Pitkin with Val, and I with Jessy combined forces to transport a complete first-rate regulation agility course 400 miles to the show site. We also brought a great deal of introductory equipment for training newcomers. Jean MacKenzie with Brownie joined us in New York, and Alaina Axford with Cooper met us at the show site, along with Kenneth. There we all worked four long wonderful days outdoors in the rain, sun, wind, and chill that are Pennsylvania in October. The overwhelming success of that week's work put Agility on the program at several of the U.S.'s top horse shows for 1990.

A forum such as a horse show, so spacious and athletic, seems quite well suited to this sport. Agility was originally developed by combining the challenges of stadium jumping in the horse world with different challenges unique to dogs. These included many from the canine obstacle courses used by the military. Some of these, such as the "wall" shown in the photo, were modified for Agility in the interest of safety and smaller dogs.

This six-foot "wall" used to train police dogs has been modified to produce the A-frame in Agility. This is nine-year old Lasso.

Other obstacles were made more difficult and additional ones added to emphasize specific skills such as balancing, flexing, tunneling, and jumping. Agility courses are designed to test a dog's fitness, flexibility, and responsiveness. Obviously the jumps inspired by the horse world had to be adapted for dogs. Nonetheless, the two natural parents of Agility, stadium jumping and military K-9 courses, can both be clearly seen in the sport today.

Dog Agility combines a fast pace, an athletic challenge, strategy and teamwork. Everywhere the sport is introduced, dogs, handlers, volunteers and spectators alike are all falling in love with the crazy, fun-filled games that give Agility its name.

This sport invites each dog/handler team to negotiate an obstacle course. The handler serves as team captain, navigator, and chief strategist. The dog does the hard part. Each course challenges the team to get from start to finish through an array of open and closed tunnels, weave poles, dog walk, crossover, seesaw, tire jump, A-frame, pause table, pause box, and many different jumps. For clarification, we can group these obstacles by the type of challenge they represent.

The first group requires the dog to put his whole body through an obstacle. These "go-throughs" include open and closed tunnels and the tire jump. The open tunnel consists of a long tube, often bent sharply in competition. The closed tunnel begins with a rigid opening, but the dog must then push his way through a long collapsed chute of canvas or nylon. The tire is an aperture raised up in a strong framework, and the dog must jump through.

F.L. Corden Sr.

Stoner runs from the open tunnel to tire jump, with A-frame in foreground.

The next group of obstacles requires the dog to climb. These are the "go-ups," including the A-frame, dog walk, crossover, and see-saw. The A-frame is comprised of two nine-foot ramps, leaned and secured against each other to form an obstacle more than six feet high. The dog must go up one side, over the top, and down the other side.

The dog walk consists of three, narrow 12-foot planks going up, across, and down. Technically, it is a catwalk, but, as that name was incongruous with this sport, the English originators of Agility settled on the nickname dog walk, and dog walk it's still called today. Agility dog walks are four feet to four feet six inches high.

The crossover is a newer variation on the dog walk requiring a greater degree of control. It consists of a small square table, raised on legs to a height of about four feet, with four ramps, one on each side. The handler directs the dog to the particular ramp he's to go up and which ramp to come down.

The seesaw is just that, a teeter-totter, and the dog must go up far enough to tip the raised end down, then continue down the plank to dismount.

Each of these go-up obstacles is designed to have us teach the dog to ascend and descend safely. This is measured by whether the dog touches the specially painted areas called contact zones on each end. The dog walk, crossover, and see-saw have contact zones of 36 inches on each end. The A-frame, being steeper and taller, has contact zones of 42 inches at each end. Contact zones are normally painted yellow.

Dog walk is on the far left, closed tunnel in foreground, and pause table is on right.

The pause table and pause box test the dog's willingness to stay in a designated spot in a certain position until the handler says otherwise. The table is a raised platform, three feet square. The box is a low platform or marked area of about four feet square, anywhere on the course. The dog must get onto the table or into the box area, lie down, and stay there for a count of five seconds. The judge generally counts backwards from five to one, then says "go," at which point the dog may leave. Most handlers have to keep reminding their dogs to stay put during the countdown, since the dogs have been running and working hard up to the sudden interruption and know that another charging effort is next. They are usually like coiled springs during the pause. It's the epitome of "hurry up and wait."

F.L. Corden Sr.

Spectators love to see how fast a dog (this is Arrow) can do the weave poles.

The weave poles are probably the most difficult obstacle in Agility, because the dog has no approximation of this exercise in his everyday life. He must travel just so down a single row of poles, flexing left and right around them, slalom style. The row consists of five to twelve poles, made of metal or PVC pipe or wooden stakes. Poles are usually about 21 inches apart, and can be set into ready-made bases or anchored individually to the ground. The dog must enter the line of poles from right to left and may not miss a single one. The speed at which some dogs can accomplish this feat, sometimes pushing three poles at once in different directions, leaves spectators shaking their heads.

Jumps are a major part of an agility course, and they come in all kinds. There are hurdles with brush underneath, some with wings on each side,

Robby sails across a jump which has decorative side supports called wings, reflecting the influence of the horse world.

single bar jumps with nothing underneath, solid walls with any kind of decoration, spread jumps both deep and high, long jumps which are low and very deep, and almost anything else. The height of the jumps is determined by the height classification of the dog.

In agility competitions, also called agility tests, courses are not generally duplicated, so sequences cannot be trained by rote. Participants do not know until shortly before start time just what obstacle layout and sequence will be assigned. A standard course time (SCT) is set according to the length and difficulty of each particular course. Standard course time describes the number of seconds deemed to be the maximum amount of time a team should take to complete the course without penalty. It may

Competitors gather for judge's briefing. This course is set for small dogs.

range from a brisk two yards per second, seen in poor conditions, very intricate courses, or beginners classes, up to five yards per second, a very quick pace considering that the dog is negotiating up to 20 obstacles along the way.

Each dog/handler team is timed and judged individually. Course faults are assessed for incorrect performance on any obstacle, generally in increments of five faults. Time faults accrue against each team taking longer than the standard course time to complete the run, at the rate of one fault for each second over SCT. Depending on time and other constraints of the day, the judge usually sets a maximum course time (MCT), no less than half again as long as the SCT, after which a dog/handler team will be eliminated. Other causes for elimination may include aggressive behavior, soiling the course, poor sportsmanship, leaving the course area, or excessive assistance by the handler or from outside the ring. In some classes, elimination also results from other factors like accruing three refusals during a course run, taking the wrong course route, skipping any obstacle, or exceeding a maximum fault limit.

Particulars of the course and the judge's intended scoring of the class are explained to the assembled competitors during the judge's briefing, after the course has been set up for the running of the class. An informal map of the course layout is generally posted. A numbered marker is placed at each obstacle to help everyone learn the required order in which the course is to be run.

Immediately before or after the judge's briefing, handlers get the chance to walk the course without their dogs in order to plan the strategy of their individual runs. Then the test begins, with each dog/handler team taking a turn at the course, one height division at a time.

In a sanctioned test, each dog competes without collar and leash, as much for safety's sake as for the challenge of it. The handler may not touch the dog or the obstacles without incurring course faults. But the handler is free to signal and talk to his dog nonstop, repeating commands and encouraging all he wants. The crowd often plays an important, noisy role in keeping the excitement level high.

Some competitions call for each dog/handler team to compete in two rounds over two different courses, with either the better score or (usually) the cumulative score being taken. Other contests, and often when the field is down to the finalists in the event, are a one-shot run. A perfect score is zero, called a clear round. All else being equal, the fastest time wins. But trying to work the course as fast as possible often causes the dogs to make mistakes, such as missing a contact zone or knocking off a jump bar. Each is penalized by five course faults. A round completed without course faults but taking four seconds longer than the SCT receives four faults. A round completed 15 seconds faster than SCT with one missed contact zone receives five faults. So faster is not always better. Speed is commonly a tie-breaker among clear rounds, but the clear round is first priority.

Most countries have in place or are developing a system for offering agility titles to competitors who meet certain standards. But agility tests are a lot more than titles. Competitions usually feature various beginner and novelty games classes in addition to the more competitive advanced classes. Many participants enter more than one class at a day's event, and many novelty classes are apt to draw more entries than the advanced classes. Some of these games classes are fairly universal and so popular that they warrant individual descriptions.

Probably the most popular of all the theme classes is jumpers. A jumpers class consists of an extensive series of jumps but no go-up obstacles. Eliminating all the obstacles with contact zones makes for a fast course time, and consequently the SCT is usually very fast in jumpers class. Some judges include a tunnel or two and even weave poles in their jumpers course designs, but many feel a jumpers class should be nothing but jumps, and plenty of them.

A good jumpers course will be designed in a fluid but complex pattern and will contain all kinds of jumps. It should also test the handlers' ability to direct their dogs from either side, to use signals effectively, and to send

The first USDAA Agility Dog (AD) titles were earned in Virginia in May 1990 by six dogs. From left, judge Sue Henry; the author with Arrow and Jessy; Fran Hoffman with Ali; Alaina Axford with Cooper; Marilyn Belli with Jessie; and Sally Glei with Sophie.

their dogs ahead without losing control. With the quick pace of this class and the excitement many dogs feel about jumping, it is very easy for the dog to take the wrong course with so many tempting jumps in proximity. At the U.S. nationals in 1990, one excited and talented whippet even jumped the arena's five-foot retaining wall and landed in the stands above, right in the lap of a spectator.

Pairs Relay is one popular novelty class, with two handler/dog combinations to a pair. The course for pairs relay may or may not be symmetrical. The first handler and dog take off at the start and complete their half of the course as fast and accurately as they can. Being a relay, a baton is carried, and so far in Agility the baton has been carried by the handler. We shall see what the future brings! Once his dog has completed his course, the first handler passes the baton to his partner, and that handler/dog team commence the second half of the course. The clock stops when the second half of the pair returns to the finish, and the score is the total of time and faults accumulated by both halves of the pair. When time and faults are added together rather than separated in the scoring, the door is opened for dogs to work very fast with less attention to accuracy, since a five-fault penalty would be counterbalanced by a five-second faster time.

In addition to being great fun, pairs relay competition is great for young and up-and-coming dogs and handlers who aren't yet ready for the prolonged intense effort of a full individuals course. The shorter distance generally required in the pairs class is a good way to get them accustomed to an all-out effort without overtaxing an inexperienced competitor. For physical reasons, pairs relay can be just as good for older dogs and handlers.

Many competitions are still informal enough that participants could enter the pairs class and count on finding a partner at the show. Some clubs have even offered a "draw pairs" class, with entrants being paired by numbers drawn from a hat. As agility trials become more crowded, it has also become common for a club to stipulate that both dogs in each pair must be from the same height division, which makes for fewer interruptions to change equipment and simplifies administration of the class.

Nickie is doing the "gamble," which requires the dog to complete one or more obstacles at a distance from his handler.

Another popular agility class is the gamblers competition. Each dog/handler partnership has the same number of seconds (generally from 30 to 50) to accumulate as many points as possible on a random course, with no requirement as to choice or order of obstacles taken. With no penalties for the dog's independent decisions about which obstacle to perform, it's a wonderful class for dogs who are not completely under control.

In gamblers, each type of obstacle has a stipulated point value, depending on its difficulty and position on the course. After the specified seconds, a signal sounds and the competitor proceeds to the finish to stop the clock or attempts the gamble, a certain sequence of challenges prenamed by the judge which must be completed in a short timespan.

The gamble includes some element of handler control from a distance, such as sending the dog ahead to complete one or more obstacles without the handler going past a certain point. If the team completes the gamble successfully before the second signal sounds, bonus points are awarded commensurate with the difficulty of the gamble.

A deduction is made from the score if the gamble is failed, and sometimes the team is eliminated if the gamble is not completed or the finish reached on time. Gamblers class reverses the usual agility scoring of "lower is better, zero is perfect." In gamblers, the team with the highest net point count wins.

A teams class can be run separately or scored along with the individual competition. The class called team competition refers to a group of four preselected handler/dog teams whose scores will be added together. It's an opportunity for one training club or group to engage in friendly rivalries with other agility groups.

Snooker is a take-off on the versions played on pool tables and in equestrian events. Each obstacle is assigned a color, and a corresponding number from one to seven which indicates its point value. Each competitor must first complete the three mandated jumps which are designated red, or one, alternately with any three different colored obstacles, for a maximum of 24 points accumulated. This is called the opening sequence. It's very difficult to get the full 24 points on the opening sequence, since the highest pointed obstacle, number seven, is always positioned furthest away from the reds.

After completing that opening sequence of six obstacles, the team must complete a closing sequence consisting of the obstacles numbered two through seven (yellow through black), for a maximum total of 27 points. Color-blind competitors can go by the numbers on the snooker flags posted at each obstacle. The colors are only for fun, to mimic those used in pool.

The teams accumulate points with every correct obstacle completed, as many as possible in the alloted time of 60 seconds. A perfect score is 51 (24 from the opening sequence and 27 from the closing sequence). As in gamblers class, highest point total wins, and fastest time is used as a tiebreaker.

Other novelty classes in Agility are limited only by imagination. A class called knock-out calls for running two dogs at once on identical courses. A jumpers pairs relay class combines two of the most popular classes. Where Agility is well established, there are special classes for new dogs and young handlers, so important to the future vitality of the sport. Veterans classes are also being discussed. Where Agility is just getting started, classes for inexperienced dogs and handlers are more important

Dancer heads for the black during a snooker demo.

than the advanced ones. Special classes for first-time exhibitors are also a great idea. More new games classes are always appearing, often quite imaginative and always great fun.

Keeping in mind that this sport has a lot to offer anyone, whether competition is of interest or not, it's fun to speculate about just what makes a good agility partnership between a handler and his dog.

Every Dog Can Benefit

There are many people today, both kids and adults, who have a close, active relationship with their dogs. These people and their pets have much of the physical and mental tuning characteristic of a first-rate agility team. Whether they ever join dog agility classes or enter competitions, Agility is part of their way of life. And a rich life it is, whether their dogs are purebred or mixed, large or small. The sport of Agility offers many new twists, even if you think there's nothing you and your dog don't already know about camaraderie.

I see many dogs who desperately need a place to put their energies, and many owners, young and not-so-young, who would like to be able to enjoy a better life with their dogs. Agility is a positive thing to do, a step in the right direction. And it just might give you the extra motivation it takes to tackle your mutual problems, so you and your dog can learn to understand and appreciate each other.

As for physical characteristics of a natural agility dog, it is usually assumed that a relatively lightweight, lithe body type is the choice for Agility. As different jump heights for shorter dogs are adopted, the height of the dog becomes less important, but different countries define their

Missie has found a natural "dog walk."

height divisions differently, so obtain a copy of the agility regulations which affect your dog. Because the sport is still young, there will be many changes still to come, involving jump heights, obstacles, rules, and judging parameters. The only way to keep abreast of the changes which affect you is to join your national agility organization and read the newsletters.

How much does your dog weigh? How tall is he at the withers? An easy way to determine this height is to stand a yardstick next to his front leg and lay a ruler, or paint stick or level, across the top of his withers (see photo). My own experience is that a weight to height ratio of less

Jessy is being measured at home with a yardstick.

than 2.5 to 1 in pounds per inch is good for Agility. Of course, other factors can tip the scale in favor of enjoying competition with a dog who doesn't fit the ideal picture. Many dogs who are big, or short, or heavy have provided some surprises for the agility world.

If you are out to choose a dog for Agility, one who has the right stuff going in, look for a nimble dog and choose one who is sound, curious, confident, and likes people. If you're looking at puppies, think in terms of his maturing at a height and size that will be comfortable for competition. Right away, join your national agility organization in order to keep up with this fast-growing sport. You may also find a local club or class you would enjoy, and that would be a good source for regular work on regulation equipment and news of local agility events.

Regulations will dictate whether you may compete with smaller dogs at lowered jump heights, and that makes a great difference in the dogs many people will choose for agility competition. If you already have a dog who is healthy, active, likes to jump, and can be taught to take direction from you, don't rule out Agility. It combines athletics with lots of casual fun.

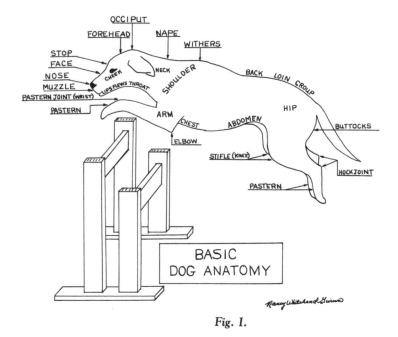

Fig. I.

Competition aside, agility training is for all dogs, but you need to make use of what is good for your dog and avoid putting him to challenges which are unsuitable for him. There are some very large dogs who live very active lives and have bodies that can stand rigorous agility work. A giant dog who is very fit may do well on less strenuous courses, and you can have

All sizes of dogs can enjoy Agility, as demonstrated by Fluffy, Anchor, and Arrow.

a lot of fun in many beginners and novelty classes (gamblers is great; not jumpers). But most extremely big dogs are not at candidates for advanced agility competition. For them, the value of Agility is in learning to use and enjoy their bodies more fully.

I have a large male Rottweiler, trim and strong and confident at two years old. He is in terrific shape and has always enjoyed Agility. His weight to height ratio is more than four to one, into the danger zone. Like all big dogs, his body is slow to mature, still broadening at this age, so I have done all his jump training at low heights. He sails over full-height jumps on his own given the chance and, like many agility dogs, he can put his coordination to his own use now and then. While waiting his turn in the back of my parked pickup at the agility field, he would sometimes hop out between the closed tailgate and the raised hatch of the truck cap.

Once when I saw him do this I yelled at him, and he spun around and easily hopped from the ground over the raised tailgate to get back in. It seems with a dog like that I might as well go all out, but I believe it would take a nasty toll on his body over a few years. The agility title classes are difficult by any standards, and downright pounding on a big dog. It's a difficult decision, since he loves the sport.

Does your own dog have any physical characteristic that should make you think twice about competing in Agility with him? A dog who has a long back and short legs is at risk from back injury. Any dog who has a chronic soreness is at risk, and don't think that giving pain killers protects from injury; quite the opposite. A dog who is out of shape is at increased risk from all sorts of injury. Weigh the risks and benefits, and consider carefully. Any dog should be pronounced sound and healthy by an expert before beginning a training program.

Agility is a sport that gives as good as it gets. You don't need to have your eye on competition, or even a complete agility course, in order to enjoy basic agility training. All dogs can benefit. For example, a high level of confidence is a plus in Agility, but agility training itself can be a wonderful confidence builder for timid dogs.

Your dog needs to be controllable to compete in Agility, but basic agility training can help you establish that control in a positive way. An agility competitor must be strong and brisk and flexible, but any dog can learn some introductory agility exercises and come out stronger, faster, and more supple than he started.

How about your dog, or a dog you know? Dog Agility is for purebreds and mixed breeds, young people and adults, beginners and the more experienced. If you and your dog would like a little more exercise, a little more fun, and a bit of a challenge, then just try this terrific sport, and see where it leads you.

Fun and Games

The sport of dog Agility calls for a dog and handler who can work independently and together at the same time, and have fun doing it. If you can't yet control your dog in a positive way, you will get help on that in several chapters of this book. You may also want to find a good basic obedience class. If you are used to exercising a great deal of control over your dog, you may need to loosen up a little in order to help him think faster for himself.

There are many things you can do with your dog to have more fun together. The best games for you to play with your dog every day are those that emphasize both Agility and fun. Would you like your dog to jump into your arms? That improves coordination and timing for both of you, and jumping confidence for your dog. Teach him by patting your leg and getting him to put his front paws there by invitation so you can scoop him up. As he gets more eager, encourage him to jump up, offering your leg as a landing pad at first (see photo). Be ready to catch and help him.

Can your dog play catch? Teach him on leash at first, to make sure you can get the toy back to try again. No corrections. No reprimands. Just keep tossing gently, and go inside out with delight when he succeeds. I have taught this game even to dogs who seemed hopelessly uncoordinated with it at first. It improves their reflexes and Agility, and it helps them

This is the ready stance for inviting your dog to jump into your arms. Max obliges his handler.

Nougat uses his speed, timing and coordination to outrun the disc and nab it in the air.

learn to watch you and concentrate. The talented ones can learn to catch from quite a distance. If your dog is very confident about this, make sure you use something he cannot get lodged in his throat by catching it too aggressively. I like to use a small stuffed toy, but tennis balls are great for many dogs. Though not usually the best choice for early training, the flying discs are wonderful for dogs who love to catch. A determined dog can outrun the disc and adjust his position to nab it in the air as it drifts down.

For early catch training, use a toy that is easy to grab and toss gently from just a few feet away. If your dog is not a natural and doesn't succeed in catching after a maximum of five or six tries, just say "OK" and put the toy away until next time. It breaks your heart not to give it to him, but he'll catch it one day, and he'll be motivated to keep trying if you keep a positive attitude. It's the most delightful thing when the hardworking student finally grabs the toy in midair and you both become ecstatic over it. Don't take it away from him.

The harder he's worked to accomplish the feat, the more you should let him strut. Having the leash on him, you can prevent from the beginning any tendency for him to run away with the prize. You can understand why he'd want to do that, since you haven't let him keep it whenever he failed to catch it. This way, he'll soon learn that you won't take it away when he succeeds, and the glory is to strut the victory for you and eat up your lavish attention.

It's fine to practice playing catch with food, as long as your dog is willing to have you pick the food up off the floor rather than have him scoop it up without catching it. For many dogs, popcorn is a good first food for catching. Beware of junk food because it can have harmful effects.

Whatever your home environment, you can find fun and games that will help you and your dog understand and enjoy each other. First, you must make the commitment to work and play with your dog.

How about some obstacles? Use what you find and invent your own challenges. The best way to prepare for unexpected quirks on an agility course later on is to get used to as many unusual situations as possible from this moment on. It's important to introduce these challenges to your dog in a constructive way. If you let him feel insecure on first introduction then you have made it much harder to build his confidence.

Start with what is easy for your dog, and never mind where any other dog's training should begin. Is your dog willing to walk over unusual surfaces, like rustling plastic or slippery linoleum? Get out the cookies or his favorite toy, and make sure he associates the new surface with something pleasant. Use that same approach on the next new encounter, such as a wide plank you've set up securely on cinder blocks.

I often use morsels of food in this work to prevent the new encounter from causing the dog stress. This is not a moral statement about whether to use food or not in all your obedience training. Any training tool can be abused, food included. You will certainly teach your dogs to run an agility course without stuffing treats at them throughout. But that is then,

Maria Kalmring

"We did it." Athena *and her trainer* celebrate.

and this is now. You will also teach them to run the course without collar and leash, but that does not mean that collar and leash are not good tools for early learning. As with food and any other enticements, gradually use them less blatantly, and then less often.

Your first job is to make sure your dog has pleasant experiences on introduction to each obstacle. Some dogs seem to be more careful on the equipment if no distraction is offered until the obstacle is completed, but remember that accuracy is not the dog's first job. It's the handler's job to keep the enticement in the right place to keep the dog where he's supposed to be. You may want to use a strong enticement at first even when it makes your dog super eager, because it also ensures that he is delighted to be on the equipment.

Once that attitude is established, offer enticement less often, until the next new task. Use your own judgment, but don't get locked into a mindset that won't let you see when the dog's confidence would be enhanced by goodies. Your dog will learn to handle the stress and the details of the sport as he gets used to it, provided that he enjoys himself early on. Just keep your mind open, and don't categorically dismiss food, toys, leash, collar, tummy-rubbing, play training, or silly antics from your cache of training tools. You just might need them all, and they just might make it lots more fun.

It would be quite possible to instruct your dog on the various regulation agility obstacles without giving him a sense of fun about it all. And what a shame. If you incorporate obstacles of all kinds into the fun you have with your dog every day, and incidentally introduce specific agility equipment as part of an interesting day, then you are appreciating Agility. It becomes part of your way of life, not just another task in your life. Whether or not you have any interest in competing in agility trials, the sport offers you and your dog another dimension in good, clean fun.

Improve Your Dog's IQ

When you add a dog to your family, the quality of that pet's life depends on you. To help your dog reach his potential, you need to be caregiver, companion, teacher, and friend. If you want a smart dog, keep his life happy and stimulating. If you want a smart dog who is a pleasure to live with, then you must also educate him. It's not your dog's job to be human, but if you will accept the responsibility of teaching him the rules and manners of his human family, you can enrich your family life a great deal. There's no substitute for the work this entails, but the rewards last forever.

Happily, one of the most effective ways of teaching your dog to use his brain constructively is also lots of fun for both of you. Agility training puts obedience to work in a whole new way. It's so much fun that dogs and handlers love to practice, and practicing the fundamentals of Agility improves basic obedience at the same time.

The basic obedience commands (sit, down, stay, come, and heel) are not just challenges for the dog; they are mind/body challenges for each dog/handler team. For the past several years, I've used agility obstacles to help get this perspective across in all my obedience classes. Agility work helps us look on obedience lessons as physical and mental effort combined, and it accelerates the building of trust, confidence, and teamwork into our human/canine partnerships. In my opinion, it also makes the dog smarter because he learns a lot about problem solving, taking unexpected challenges in stride, working with his handler (you), and coordinating his body with his mind. It is bound to improve some of these abilities in you, too, so you can expect to become a smarter dog handler.

In learning to encourage and reward your dog, you will begin to develop a stronger rapport with your pet, and to see a challenge from the dog's point of view. For example, when you introduce a tunnel and know that it's your job to inspire your dog to go through, you begin to appreciate the dog's work as well as your own. What is more, you must rise to the task of motivating your dog. And who among us, human or canine, is not interested in a new twist now and then? That's what keeps our brains in gear. If we don't give ourselves something creative to do now and then, it is only a matter of time before boredom gets the better of us.

No doubt about it, if your dog's environment is boring, and your dog is a bright dog, sooner or later he will come upon a pastime that is interesting to him but unacceptable to you. The first thing you must

A helper appreciates Dizzy's point of view.

Every mutual accomplishment strengthens the bond. This is Willie.

promise yourself in agility training is that you will take the time to vary your dog's environment in a positive way. That doesn't mean locking him in the garage instead of the cellar every other day. It really requires you to introduce him to novel stimuli every day with you on the other end of the leash. Remember, what is novel to one dog is old hat to another and terrifying to another. So choose your novel situations with your own dog's personality and experience in mind.

The perfect new encounter is something that challenges your dog to accept something different, but not so different that he cannot succeed readily. If your dog is extremely active and outgoing, you might begin by having him walk politely on leash. If your dog is terribly shy, you might have him watch with you from an appropriate distance as children play. In both cases, the best initial distance between you and distraction depends upon your dog and you.

You can work up to more interesting challenges by building a firm base of incremental successes. It's most important that each new introduction go smoothly, so your dog can steadily gain experience and confidence without being a nuisance.

Agility training can be part of this gradual widening of your dog's world. My favorite first agility obstacles for this work are various tunnels and A-frames. In Chapter 2 you will meet several versions of these obstacles which you can easily fashion at home to start improving your dog's IQ. At the same time, you'll be improving his Agility Quotient (AQ, of course).

You probably know at least a couple of bright dogs who are wasting their brains on behavior problems and who could probably be channeled into happy, positive pursuits. Many of the best known canine movie stars, police drug-search dogs, hearing ear dogs, etc., were rescued from animal shelters where they would otherwise have been just another statistic in the ever-growing problem of owner unpreparedness and misunderstanding. It warms my heart to know that some dogs are graduated from backyards or animal shelters and are given an education, which some of us take so much for granted. It hurts to know that millions more dogs never find a fulfilling life, yet some humans keep breeding puppies after puppies, never accepting responsibility for the quality of their lives.

Perhaps more people nowadays feel unsatisfied, and that makes them less sensitive to the needs of other animals. But if you tune in to your own dog and bring fulfillment to his life, he will invariably give fulfillment back to you. It's good to understand your dog's outlook, so basic and honest and different from your own. And what a bonus that your dog readily accepts your looks and quirks and imperfections.

For many of us, dogs are members of the family in a full sense. We raise them, educate them, work and play with them, and enjoy a family life all the richer for their being with us. We have the privileges and opportunities to broaden our lives when we live with dogs.

Is your dog healthy, strong, and clean? He deserves to be. Does he enjoy doing things with you? Why not start his education today? Get help from a dog obedience trainer with a philosophy compatible with your own. And look through the many good books available, again choosing what is comfortable for you and meets your goals. Dogs are wonderful and complicated companions. The sport of Agility is just one more way for us to work and play with them. You may decide as you and your dog improve that you are interested in agility competition. Then again, you may never care to participate in competition. You don't have to compete in order to enjoy the sport. Its greatest value is in strengthening your bond and giving you and your dog something new, active, challenging, and fun to do together.

2

GETTING STARTED

If a man neglects education, he walks lame to the end of his life.

—Plato

A is for Attitude

There is nothing more important to education than a positive attitude. Your dog's attitude toward new things has been shaped to some extent before now. He may approach physical challenges with delight, he may brave some novelties and fear others, or he may view anything new with misgivings.

In any case, you can do wonderful things for him by introducing agility training. Agility can help shy dogs feel proud and give active dogs a welcome outlet for their energies. It can boost self-confidence in the insecure dog and can sprinkle confidence with common sense for the independent dog. But what it can do for you and your dog together depends on you.

Your dog's attitude is the first thing to consider each time you pick up the leash. What are your goals in this sport? What are you trying to accomplish with your dog today? How can you break that intermediate goal down into manageable progressions so you and your dog will become a better team for the day's lessons?

If you don't feel relaxed about a certain lesson neither will your student, the dog. Either review a previously delightful lesson or introduce an easier version of the work you planned. Or train some other time, but don't let an introduction go badly.

Here are three basic guidelines for developing the positive attitude you and your dog need to get the most from your mutual education, and from Agility in particular:

1. Attitude comes first, before the task is mastered. Like it or not, you

are shaping attitude with guidance, correction or reward, and with the feeling you project.

2. Begin your dog's training with challenges easier than you think he needs and progress only when your dog needs more challenge, not when you do. A positive attitude toward the first agility obstacles comes from quick early success. When you hit a real snag later on, leave that lesson alone for a week or so while you go back to those delightful basics.

3. Choose your training times, enticements, and challenges according to what will best strengthen your dog's educational foundation. Don't let someone else's timetable for progress dictate your own. Every dog learns unevenly and needs your help differently.

So think positive. It will make you a better handler and your dog a better partner. And take your time. Humans are always in such a hurry. A big problem with rushing any training, particularly an active sport like Agility, is that it puts on pressure too soon, which undermines the happiness your dog feels for the basic work.

Without a positive attitude toward the introductory levels of training, your dog has limited happiness to fall back on when you have training problems later and need to review the basics, as we all do. When you rush through the first steps, or skip them and get right to the hard part, you are building a weak foundation. Even if you have a brave, outgoing dog

Natural agility in action! Fluffy is not under any command; he just found a polite way to get a better view.

Difficult challenges can be taught step by step...

...and the positive attitude sustained as the job gets tougher...

...when the foundation is pure delight. This is Arrow.

who seems able to handle it at the time, sooner or later you will be teaching your dog to fail.

Instead, introduce your dog to obedience and agility tasks that he can master quickly and enjoy these first successes thoroughly. You will see a wide variety of native abilities in Agility. Some dogs need more time at introductory levels on tunnel obstacles, and other dogs can progress quickly on tunnels, and more slowly on inclines. The important thing is to ensure early success, which builds a strong and willing spirit. Your dog learns to succeed, likes to succeed, and expects to succeed.

By the time you have taught your first agility dog his first obstacle, you and your dog have an attitude together. Are we having fun yet?

Fundamentals – Obedience for Agility

There are several good obedience training books which are helpful in teaching your dog manners and the basic obedience commands. In Agility you will at least need directives for having your dog come to you, lie down, and stay. These words need to be understood and accepted by your dog so well that he will obey them even in the excitement of running an agility course. For everyday living they comprise social skills required of a well-mannered pet who can be welcome wherever his owner goes. Here, as with obstacle training, the dog's acceptance of these manners along with his attitude toward them is our doing.

For agility training, your dog needs to be polite on a loose leash, yet tolerate physical guidance by leash and collar during early training. He must lie down instantly on command and stay until called away, even in the midst of a rousing run through the obstacles. He must come to the handler when called, especially when he is running the opposite way, and it's an advantage for him to know how to sit and heel. So your needs are not so different from those of basic obedience, but there are some marked differences from formal, or competition, obedience. The sport of Agility uses obedience in its own less structured way. Let's look briefly at Agility's use of leashwork, collar work, come, sit, down, wait, stay, and heel.

Leashwork

The leash is one of your most important tools for all early training. You need your dog to like the leash and to respect it. If a dog dislikes his leash, it means that he associates being kept close to his handler (you) with having no fun. The first order of business is to build a good relationship between the dog and the leash.

If your dog or puppy doesn't like his leash, put it on him immediately before his favorite thing happens, be it supper, a ride in the car, a walk, a treat, a cuddle, a game of catch. If a favorite person is coming to visit, put the leash on just before the door opens. Sometimes you may need to hold on to the leash. It does a lot of good for your dog to drag the leash without interference several times a day. If your dog is unduly stressed by having the leash drag along, then start with a short length of very lightweight line and introduce longer and heavier lengths as he gains confidence.

Most dogs quickly accept the funny thing and rarely step on it. I don't know how they become so adept at trotting around without getting caught in it, but they do, and that skill can only be a plus in agility training.

Once the leash is a friend, introduce some healthy respect. Any dog who spends his on leash time straining to get further away from you is a dog who will not easily give up his freedom for you when he's off leash. Good leashwork begins at home and then needs reinforcement away from home.

If your dog is very active, you can do this first exercise standing still. If your dog is more passive, you may want to start out walking, with frequent stops. Use a leash of about six feet long. The idea is to teach your dog to stay close enough to keep it slack at all times. A few gentle dogs accept this job readily if you pull them back or sound a sharp *Enh* as soon as they begin to stray, and then praise them for staying close.

It's not usually this easy. Most dogs quickly decide that whoever pulls harder gets to go where he wants. These dogs need a different approach. You must jerk the leash as soon as he begins to take up the slack, and yank fast and hard enough to change his mind. Then you can say nice

Give a sharp leash correction early, before the slack is gone.

Pretty soon, Arrow is paying attention.

things when he's paying attention again. You don't want to chastise the dog. If you jerk the leash early and strong enough to interrupt him effectively when he tries to charge off, you can quickly praise the dog when he's back to minding his manners. You are not angry with him; you are trying to help him decide to stick around.

To see that he learns to make this choice, use the leash to make him instantly uncomfortable when he tries to take off, and use your voice to make him instantly pleased with himself when he changes his mind. It does no lasting good to hang on tight, since that causes the dog to pull away. It takes two to pull. Help the dog decide for himself to stay close so it becomes a habit and ultimately he'll not require the leash at all.

Some dogs can learn this lesson on a buckle collar, but most require the added punch of a choke collar, and a few need a prong collar. There are also halter-type collars available, which don't put pressure on the neck at all. Don't use strong tools thoughtlessly. Any tool can be abused, and the more powerful the tool, the more potential for harm in its use. It may be the right thing for a certain dog at a certain point, but you must get the help you need to use it appropriately for this particular dog. If it goes against your grain, you will not use it effectively, so look for another solution.

Don't give up. You might want to accentuate the positive by offering a treat or other quick reward when the dog is paying attention to you and staying close. Keep using your head and think about what you want your dog to do and what will help your dog decide to do it.

The goal is for the dog to walk happily along, keeping the leash slack between you and stopping when you stop. You don't need him glued to your side for casual walking, but you do need him to remain interested in your whereabouts. It's good for him to look around and be curious about the environment, but dogs can do this with one ear tuned to the handler. Their wider range of peripheral vision makes it possible for them to check on us visually even when they are slightly ahead of us. The simple leashwork exercise of walking briskly and stopping often and suddenly will teach your dog to tune you in if your corrections are effective and your praise heartfelt.

Once you get good at this together, increase the challenge by running and stopping suddenly. You want your dog to respond so quickly that it becomes very difficult to fool him, no matter how quickly you stop, start, and turn. Practice first at home and then in gradually more distracting settings. Make a game of this so the sting of your correction is softened by your praise for his immediate response. His reflexes are much quicker than yours, so the game is easily won by him if he's paying any attention. A quick game of leashwork should keep his tail up and his mind busy, alert to what you might do next.

Collar Work

You will need to direct your dog by his agility collar sometimes, so he needs to have no aversion to your taking hold of it and even pulling him from side to side with it. Your dog may dislike being handled this way, but it's not difficult to see to it that it doesn't offend him.

Just as you can teach your dog to love the leash by having him associate it with things he already loves, you can teach him to love his agility collar and being handled by it. As soon as he is happy to wear his collar, begin touching the collar just prior to granting any of your dog's favorite wishes. Then gradually, depending on how your dog feels about being manhandled, increase the pressure you put on the collar as you reward him. The goal is to be able to take the dog by the collar whenever you need to help or restrain him on the agility obstacles, without your dog losing confidence or concentration.

Come

Any dog who is to have the privilege of being unrestrained needs to understand and obey when his handler calls him to come. Anything less is unsafe. In dog obedience competition, the word "come" often denotes a specific formal exercise in which the dog is expected to come straight to the handler's front and sit facing him. In Agility, you want the dog to come immediately to you, but you do not want him to sit and you may direct him elsewhere before he quite arrives.

So the two sports require different words for "come." If your dog has been taught that "come" means straight to front and sit, then use "here" or any other word to call your dog in the context of Agility. If your dog has not been taught the formal obedience exercise, you might use "come" for Agility and everyday life, and "front" for the formal exercise.

The process of teaching your dog to come to you on command is covered at length in many training books. Briefly, the dog needs to learn that he will be well received on arrival, so never call him to you to punish him. First steps in coming when called are best done on leash or in a confined area, and the dog should be greeted with a reward on arrival. Never mind if your dog knocks you down when he gets to you; he's still the greatest because he came when called. Refinements come later.

If your dog is selectively deaf when outdoors, practice first on a six-foot leash, giving an appropriate reward each time, and graduate to longer lines until your dog comes charging to your call without any tension on the line, even 50 or 100 feet away and even when he is distracted.

Your dog will respond more quickly to the recall if you trot backwards as he comes to you. Praise him as he's on the way because it's the decision to come that's so difficult. Practice surprise recalls like this: on leash, just walking happily along together, suddenly run backwards, calling your dog to come. Don't turn around; just stop and back up quickly. The dog must turn around. This teaches him to use his eyes and ears to keep track of

Surprise recall: interrupt your walk suddenly by backing up and calling your dog to come. Correct immediately if necessary...

...then run with your dog and praise him as he comes. This promotes a fast, happy recall for Astro.

you. You'll be amazed at how he can turn on a dime and beat the correction once he learns to keep you tuned in. Praise him as he pivots and hurries to catch up. You can offer a treat on his arrival, but you could also just turn and run with your dog or jump up and down with delight. Often, an active few seconds of playtime are the perfect reward for coming when called.

Sit

Sit is a good ready position, easy to teach, easy to enforce, and conducive to paying attention. Two different approaches to teaching "sit" are described here. The enticement approach is best known and well loved by most dogs. Hold the enticement at the dog's eye level, then raise it back over his head as you say "sit."

The tuck sit is done by securing one hand in the dog's collar and applying firm pressure down the dog's spine with the other hand. Rather than push down on the fanny, which can cause the dog to stiffen in resistance, stroke your hand over the tail and tuck up under the buttocks. It's a bit like folding your dog in the place where he naturally bends. After a week of 10 repetitions each day of either method, most dogs are sitting fast and pretty as soon as the word is said.

There is good use for the command "sit" in Agility, but it can easily become a command which saps enthusiasm. Agility is one of those sports in which it's usually better to have a helper hold the dog and just hang on while the dog pulls forward. Rather than order the novice dog to sit and stay put, thereby having to correct him and replace him whenever he moves, I like to see dogs straining to give the new obstacle a try. Especially when introducing weave poles and tunnels and early jump sequences off

The enticement approach allows Astro to place himself in the sitting position.

leash, it's much better to have the dog eager and thinking of dynamics, rather than having to concentrate on staying still. In fact, a good helper will try to jolly the dog up before he's called, making sure he's eager to go.

Sit is a useful tool for greeting company, waiting on leash when you stop to have a conversation, or teaching the more strict "stay." Sit has value in agility training as well, once the dog is in love with the apparatus and your training is centering on control. Even then, it's better to use the "wait" command rather than the "sit-stay" command. Let your dog move his feet and make jerking half-starts while he's getting used to waiting. Even if he breaks, it's the unusual dog who benefits from a sharp correction for a failed sit during agility training. Better to go to the dog quietly, just take him back to the original spot and remind him calmly "sit" and "wait."

For now, you should practice the command "sit" apart from the obstacles. Don't use it in conjunction with introductory work. Remember, you can compete successfully in Agility without even using the command "sit," but you can't compete successfully without that forward drive.

Down

In Agility, dogs must lie down on the pause table or in the pause box for a five-second count at any point during the course run. It's not generally what excited dogs prefer to do. The count won't start until the dog is all the way down, and it stops if he begins to rise, so he needs to be quick and steady on the down, yet maintain his enthusiasm for the rest of the run.

Training for the "instant down" is done in two steps. The first is to have the dog understand and accept the command. The second step is to have the dog throw himself into the position quickly, and that requires that you use his favorite motivators.

There are several approaches to teaching the down on command, so you should evaluate them with you and your dog in mind. And what is right for one of your dogs might be wrong for another, so don't feel that you ever have "the" method. Here we show three ways to place your dog in the prone position. Some dogs are so intensely motivated by an enticement that they will follow it down.

Other dogs need more physical help. In any case, lay your hand across the withers as soon as the dog is down, and apply pressure as necessary to interrupt him each time he tries to get up. If he doesn't succeed in rising before you say "OK," he will learn that "down" means until you say otherwise. Begin with only a few seconds at a time. If your dog needs more physical help but cannot accept it, consult a trainer for guidance tailored to your situation.

Any system for teaching the down at home will not guarantee your dog's compliance elsewhere. Practice around distractions, which may call for a bit of force in order to work through the dog's distinct impression that what is fun at home is not what he'd rather do just now. It's easy to

An enticement in one hand and the other pushing down from the top helps teach the down command to Arrow.

assume that "he knows it by now," but it is not likely to be that simple. What he remembers when he's concentrating is very different from what he remembers when he's distracted. Use your training to place your dog down on command when company comes as a prelude to working away from home. Practice often and everywhere.

Some dogs are lightning fast learning the down, but some comply with a distinct lack of enthusiasm. For the fast dogs, delay the reward slightly

Reach over the dog and gently take one pastern in each hand. Praise the dog as you lift and lower him down. This is Misty.

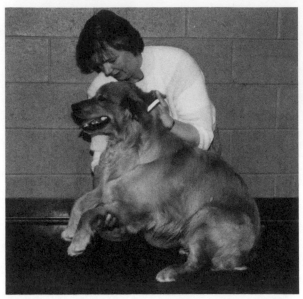

One hand in back of collar, the other behind the front legs. Praise the dog as you lift and lower him down. This is Trucker.

longer and keep their enthusiasm high. For the majority, associate this command down with favorite things, as with other commands. Take advantage of how well you know your dog. Make his favorite things contingent on your down command. You need to help him train you to give him his reward quickly. The second he's down, the reward happens. The faster he's down, the faster he wins. If your own reflexes are slow, work on that separately. Playing the two-person hand-game slapjack sharpens your manual quickness.

I will discuss the five-second down-stay required on the pause obstacle in competition later (see Ch. 8). I'm still talking immediate gratification here. Try not to practice downs on the agility table or pause box until your dog can do the instant down, because if he puts it all together while he's still slow he will be patterned for a slow down with the pause. It would then be hard to speed up his downs at the pause obstacle even when he has his speed elsewhere.

Wait

Everyone benefits from "wait training." It has many applications at home and in Agility. Canines are not designed to choose delayed reinforcement, yet it's the basis of living with humans. They have to learn to refrain from many natural things, and they have to wait for us many times a day. That's a dog's life. When you teach them to wait gracefully you are helping minimize the stress of waiting. You will use this command often in Agility, especially during early training on the obstacles.

Mealtime lends itself well to wait training. Simply hold your dog's leash or collar (you have done collar work already, so he doesn't mind this, right?) and tell him "wait" as you put the dish down for him. Then you must prevent him from getting to the food until he is no longer trying to get it. It's a Catch 22 for him, but as long as his efforts to get the food in spite of you are thwarted, he'll soon learn that when you say "wait" he must not go forward. Any other enticement may be substituted for food.

You could practice this several times a day with treats or toys, telling your dog to wait as you place the prize on the floor, then restraining him by collar or leash corrections until he stops lunging for it. When he's truly waiting, or when he has given up, as the dogs first see it, you can tell him "OK" and let him have it. Some dogs have given up so completely by this time that they won't pick up the treats when you give the release word, so for them you should tap the treat and repeat "OK" and even meet them halfway if need be.

This is not the same as "stay," which is more formal and usually means "don't move a muscle." It's easier, and generally more useful, to teach "wait" early on, and introduce "stay" as a formal exercise after the dog's training is well underway. When you tell the dogs to wait, you just want them to hold back. Once they have the idea, you can use wait training to prevent them from charging out the door or down the stairs, you can have them "wait home" when you want to leave without them, and you can help them slow down and pause where needed on the agility obstacles.

If you said "stay" for these things, you would have to correct the dog every time he moved until you released him from the command. That would not be good for Agility, and it's not usually what you mean in daily life, either. Since you don't expect the dog to stay motionless at home when you leave without him, it's better to have an alternate word that

Say "wait" as you place treat, and loosely hold leash or collar. The dog may sit, stand, or lie down...

...but if he decides to dash for the treats uninvited he is stopped, put back, and reminded to wait. This is Lynn.

accurately describes his job. Use wait training to help your dog learn to hold himself back, and you'll find lots of use for it throughout your dog's life.

Stay

You will need to train your dog separately to stay quite still on command. A five-second stay in the down position is required on top of the agility pause table or within the marked pause box area. One guideline for ascertaining if the dog is remaining in the down position is that the dog's elbows are touching the surface area. The handler may remain very close to the dog as long as he doesn't touch the dog or the equipment.

The handler is also allowed to say the command repeatedly during the countdown, and many do. But it's quite an advantage for the handler to be able to move to the next obstacle on the course while the dog stays down. It makes for faster overall time, and more important it can prevent the dog from taking the wrong obstacle next.

It's not difficult to teach your dog to stay. Many dogs just starting a basic obedience class have already been instructed at home in some use of the word, usually a sit-stay for dinner or treats. That's a fine start. However, most of the dogs who come to class already familiar with the stay command are also quite good at ignoring it when they're preoccupied and breaking it when they feel ready to leave. That part has to change in order for the command to be of any real value. I introduce this command in obedience class first in conjunction with "sit."

It's a good idea to introduce a hand signal with the command "stay," because signals require the dog to pay closer attention. An agility arena can be a very noisy place, and a signal is often stronger than a verbal command for most dogs. In Agility, you are allowed to use signals concurrent with verbal commands, so the dogs should be taught both, and you can put them together as you see fit. You may need both at once only occasionally, but it's nice to have them in your mutual repertoire.

The hand signal for "stay" is your palm presented to the dog. When you first teach this, give the hand signal before pivoting in front of the dog, not as you pivot. He needs to get the message before he's tested on it. Later, when he understands the command, you can make him sharper by moving while signaling him to stay.

The dog is encouraged to stay by applying slight upward pressure on the leash, and the hold is close enough to the collar to prevent any big mistakes. The left foot hardly moves, just twists in place as you pivot to face your dog. His head should be nearly touching your leg. If your dog is relatively calm, you may progress rapidly from a few seconds to a minute or more before pivoting back to his side.

But whether it takes you a few days or a few weeks of lessons, don't take a single step away from the dog until you both have your parts learned well. Increasing distance is not the hardest part about teaching the stay.

"Good stay, Fluffy." Leash is held taut, not tight. Only a few seconds at first, then "OK!"

Reliability is. So rather than introduce more space between you, introduce more distraction while you are still close enough to handle it. Then, when you're really ready for some distance work, take it one step at a time, literally, without distraction, before again introducing distraction.

Once the command "stay" is familiar, it's easy to pair it with the command "down" which has already been taught. For many dogs, it would be just as easy to learn "stay" in conjunction with "down." Many quick dogs assume the down naturally as a ready position, especially once you've been working on quick downs for Agility. It's a simple matter to put a hand across the shoulder blades while the dog is down and tell him "stay." Each attempt of the dog to rise is met with failure and the reminder "stay" until the dog stops trying to get up and you can quietly praise him with "good stay."

As the dog begins to understand, it's time to introduce distraction just as you did with the "down" command. Once that is handled, you can graduate to sitting in a chair beside the dog, or over several lessons you can keep him down while you stand beside him and even walk around. The trick is not to let the dog succeed in rising, so your hand must always be ready, right above the withers, to interrupt every attempt to get up. As you begin to work standing erect, you might want to step on the leash.

If your dog tries to stand and succeeds even in getting his front legs straight underneath him, you can't blame him for trying again and again. But if from the first time he's told to stay he cannot manage to get up, then the lesson is more quickly assimilated and accepted. With down-stay as with sit-stay, introduce distraction before introducing distance, and go back to quiet when you first introduce distance.

Now it's fine to be practicing the "stay" command every which way everywhere you go, as long as you don't demand what you can't enforce. But don't start inhibiting your dog's enthusiasm for Agility by overusing it in practice on the obstacles.

Heel

The dog at heel should keep pace close at your left side without interfering with your motion. Teaching him to travel short distances this way will help prevent him from taking obstacles out of proper sequence in tricky sections of an agility course. Naturally, you don't want him to lag or feel put upon by this command, nor do you want to trip over him. He needs to pay attention, but you don't want him craning to look at your face. You don't want him overly dependent and you don't want him to sit, as you'll be sending him off again right away. This is no time for formalities. If your dog is obedience trained to another set of specifications, you may want a different word for this command in Agility.

Your dog may be receiving tidbits at first for his efforts on each obstacle, and food or toy rewards are useful for early heeling efforts, too. Just call your dog to you and say "heel" as you take a few brisk steps with the lure enticing your dog to stay beside you. Say "OK" and give him the reward. This exercise is best done on leash at first. If leashwork has been taught already, you won't need to argue over whether the dog will stay by you.

The next step is to use heelwork in the dog's everyday life to precede some special privileges. You could have him heel to the car and wait while you open the door; then his reward is hopping in and going for a ride. You can think of several more ways to tuck some short stretches of heeling into his routine. You needn't concentrate overly on heelwork in Agility, but it is handy now and then, and it does help the dog learn to pay attention, which improves control. As long as you keep it short and lively, it should present no heavy discipline problems.

Once the lessons are learned at home you need to introduce more distracting circumstances, and there you might need to issue a few jerks on the leash and quick changes of direction to convince the dog to stay tuned no matter what. An agility dog needs to walk a fine line, paying attention yet aware of his surroundings. So keep your heelwork short, active, happy, and to the point. It's sound practice to go over your leashwork lessons in public before working a short stint of heeling in public, since heelwork takes the principles of leashwork that much further.

Any job is easier when you use the right equipment. Here is a simple list of items you should have for your dog before you start on the obstacles.

1. Nail clippers and grooming brush. Keep your dog's toenails short for traction. Regular brushing will improve circulation and keep his coat and skin in good condition. Your dog will work better, much better, if his body is well cared for.

2. Wide, flat collar. Your agility collar is not a choke collar, but some dogs need also a choke collar which is used when they are not on the obstacles.

3. Sturdy leash four to six feet long with no loop. This leash is for guiding the dog through the obstacles so as to prevent him from making mistakes. This allows you to praise his success while ensuring it. Loops look innocent enough but are real hazards in Agility. No matter how small, they will get caught. Even knots in the leash are to be avoided for safety's sake. Leather or canvas leashes are good choices. Nylon has the advantage and the disadvantage of being slippery. It slides easily through the equipment and sheds water, but can be hard on the hands. The braided nylon leashes are more comfortable, but loosely woven ones are not safe. Be sure to sear the end after cutting off the loop.

4. Short tab leash with no loop. This leash is for close work and for more advanced dogs who need less guidance less often. From one six-foot obedience leash, you can make both an agility lead and an agility tab.

5. Enticement. Use a favorite toy, food treats, or whatever your dog loves. The value of enticement is in preventing and alleviating stress. As the dog becomes proficient, the enticement shifts from lure to reward, that is, from before and during the work to after the work. When you use food lures, use very small pieces. Your dog should consume the treat in the time it takes you to say "What a good dog." If you use hard biscuits, tap them with a hammer to break them up into small tidbits. You want to augment learning with treats. You don't need to teach eating. The best enticements for you to use depend on what motivates your dog at the moment, so it's wise to keep a few different ideas in your bag of tricks.

Some of the best early agility training can be done with items you may have around your home. This makeshift stuff can give you a whole new way of looking around you – agility eyes – and your creations can be the basis for lots of fun and teamwork for you and your dog. If you become interested in competition, you'll be well on your way to proficiency on any regulation apparatus, and you won't be unnerved by variations in equipment from one trial to the next.

Please keep your mind on safety as you evaluate any materials. Check them thoroughly for any hazards and don't let them be used without removing potential trouble. It only takes a second for an accident to happen, and nearly all safety-related accidents are preventable.

Tires are a good warm-up for tunnels. Wrap the bottom for safety. This is Misty.

Regulation equipment is not cheap, but it has been well tested for the safety of dogs and handlers. You should make yourself familiar with the design of regulation obstacles. The following easy-to-find substitutes will not be the quality of regulation equipment, and it's your responsibility to keep dogs and people safe when working with them. With that in mind, here are some backyard items which can be put to work:
• Hula hoops, tires, swim rings
• Cinder blocks, bricks, blocks of wood
• Boxes, barrels
• Scraps of plywood, planks, doors
• Ladders
• Bales of hay
• Tarps, old sheets, plastic or fabric remnants
• Sawhorses
• Woodpiles, fallen logs
• Picnic tables, benches
• Chairs, card tables, coffee tables
• Leaves, hills, rocks, branches
• Dowels, tubing, poles, reflector stakes
• Chicken wire
• Playground equipment

• You name it. Invent your own challenges, tailored to you and your dog.

The first agility obstacles you should make at home are tunnels and A-frames. Each builds different skills, and each is easily adapted to assure the quick success of any dog. Those who find the sport delightful in itself are soon well prepared for agility classes on regulation equipment. In the meantime, these homemade obstacles provide interesting opportunities for rounding out the basic education our dogs all deserve. Here are a few ideas – there are many more – about introducing agility skills in your own backyard.

A homemade tunnel can be fashioned from just about anything, and the more different kinds you introduce the better. Just remember to design a first tunnel that will allow your dog to succeed easily. Begin with a very wide, short length of material. Some dogs, for example, are wary of slippery cardboard, so for them you could place boards or padding on the walking surface at first, or start with an entirely different type of tunnel. Some dogs are fearful of rustling plastic, so a sheet draped over a card table or coffee table might be a better first tunnel.

Some dogs prefer you to go through with them a time or two, and other dogs will enter the tunnel to greet you as you come crawling through from the other end. Some dogs want their owners right at the exit, and some need to see clearly the light at the end of the tunnel, so you need to back up some. Use an irresistible enticement to make sure the first tunnel work is great fun. You need to know your own dog, and start him on a tunnel he will master quickly. Here are some suggestions:

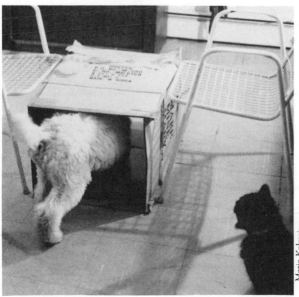

Maria Kalmring

Olympia heads through a cardboard box, which makes a wonderful backyard tunnel.

1. The versatile cardboard box should be one of your first tunnels. I have enjoyed kayak boxes, TV and refrigerator boxes, oatmeal canisters, and anything in between. I cut 'em, tape 'em, color 'em, cover 'em, to make a tunnel for any occasion. I had coloring parties for the neighborhood kids, who love tunnels as much as anyone. I got masterpieces for tunnels, and the kids' enthusiasm made the dogs most impatient for their turns to go through.

2. Fifty-five-gallon drums, in metal or plastic, are widely available and with both ends removed make good tunnels. Beware of rust on the metal drums and sharp edges on both metal and plastic ones. It may take some time with metal file, folded newspaper for padding, and duct tape to make the ends safe, but this is apt to be time well spent, since the resulting tunnel is nearly indestructible.

3. Fiberboard barrels with ends removed are useful for tunnels and are also decorated and used as jump wings and supports. Because they often come with locking lid rings, they also make excellent rigid openings for the competition collapsed tunnel. Just secure a short length of fabric chute under the ring to form an introductory closed tunnel after your dog masters the open tunnels. Fiberboard barrels will not stand up to rain without protection, but they are lightweight and usually free of sharp edges. I keep mine painted and out of the weather as much as possible.

4. Try hula hoops, anchored to the ground with coat hanger wire and attached to each other with twine. Tie end hoops to anything stationary. Two hoops, with a cloth draped between them, are fine for a start, especially if your dog started tunnel training with a single hula hoop. Add more hoops to make the tunnel longer, and even curved, as your dog gains confidence.

5. For tiny dogs and puppies, croquet wickets draped with a dish towel are great outdoor tunnels.

6. Chairs make good tunnel supports. For large dogs, begin with the chairs standing back to back and cover with a blanket-sized drape. Add more chairs as the dogs gain confidence, and curve your tunnel as you go, too. Then go back to two chairs only but lay them down with the chair backs forming the top of the tunnel. Now the familiar tunnel looks easy because of the short length, but presents a new challenge in the lowered height. Chairs can also be used to define a wide-mouthed tunnel at first. Then, by being placed gradually closer together, they can introduce that closed-in feeling.

7. Tables large and small make fine tunnel supports, indoors and out. As always, choose the size that suits your dog.

8. Culvert ends, obtainable from industry and highway departments, are good sturdy tunnels. Metal ones require some work with a heavy file and duct tape to make the edges safe, but this is worth doing, as the resulting tunnel can last forever. Be sure to get a galvanized one, for resistance to rust.

9. Flexible ducting material such as Flexaust, available in many diameters and used as heating and ventilation conduit, is my very favorite tunnel material, as it is collapsible, reasonably lightweight, weatherproof, and virtually indestructible. It is expensive, and it may take some sleuthing to locate used pieces. My secondhand pieces had to be thoroughly washed inside, a time-consuming and worthwhile task. This is the product that appears in the tunnel training photos in this book.

10. Storebought children's tunnels will not take much abuse but are collapsible and lightweight.

11. Hay bales are great for tunnel supports. You can stack them for tall tunnels, lengthen and curve your tunnel with additional bales, and make it as wide as you want. Cover with anything from clear plastic (which lets daylight through, appreciated by many beginner dogs) to horse blankets.

12. Shape your own tunnel out of chicken wire, or tubing, or define it with wooden, metal, or plastic stakes. Cover your contraption with anything and have fun. Homemade tunnels are some of the most useful because they are so diverse. Change the covering from plastic to canvas to pine boughs, whatever your environment offers, as your dog gains confidence.

Improvise with all kinds of nonthreatening inclines at home. This is Athena.

See Ch. 5 for regulation tunnel training, but don't let go of your imagination even after you start using the competition stuff. You'll be glad your dog is ready for anything, because lots of variables come into play in the world of Agility.

Along with teaching your dog at home to go through an aperture, you can also be developing his confidence about going up and over things. As for an A-frame in the backyard, the first inclines should be wide and low. Leaning wide planks against a front step is often all it takes. Or leaning plywood against cinder blocks or benches can serve the purpose. The textured plywoods sold as sheathing are good for this, as there is traction built in. I use scraps of Texture 1-11, laid sideways so the grooves are horizontal.

Picnic benches, then picnic tables make great A-frame supports, especially if you only have one side's worth of lumber. Your dog can wait on the table while you carry the incline to the other side. Or you can play with him on the table, then lead him down the way he came.

With dogs who love inclines, I like to use my stacked rows of firewood, with plywood stabilized on either side. The higher the apex, the more important it is to add traction to the climbing surfaces. It's not difficult to nail strips of wood across the ramp at about 12-inch intervals. Hinging two ramps together at the apex allows the woodpile (or barrel, or sawhorse, etc.) to provide extra bracing. Dogs who are expert climbers can eventually even learn to traverse rows of firewood, but this is only for the fearless and talented dogs with terrific balance, as the top splits of wood are uneven and unstable. Any dog who can do that will have no problem with the regulation dog walk.

Missie negotiates a ladder, which is a wonderful way for helping your dog coordinate all his feet at once in a narrow path.

When your A-frame narrows to one plank width, that is good basic training for the dog walk, but don't try narrow ramps before your dog is very confident on wide ones. A ladder can teach your dog a lot about walking on narrow planks. Just lay it on the ground and entice your dog to step lengthwise between the rungs. This is a good way to help him practice coordinating four feet at once in a narrow space.

In general, you need to use wider footing extensively, making sure your dog walks all the way on from the end and all the way off the other end, gradually building a nimble expertise at low heights and then steeper and higher heights. And there's no reason you can't use hoops or hose, or any other trick to help your dog learn not to hop on or jump off above your backyard equipment's imaginary contact zones (see Step 3 of A-frame training, Ch. 6). Good habits need to be developed early on.

A-frames can seem so easy and yet be the cause of many agility problems because so many dogs perform them inaccurately, even at expert levels of training. So spend a lot of time making sure your dog is comfortable and correct on all your A-frame and low plank obstacles at home.

Your job when you begin to introduce your dog to Agility is to broaden your dog's experience and widen his world. So the task is not to force the dog over the equipment. The real task is to design first a challenge that he can accomplish and feel proud of, and to build on that success with gradually increasing challenges. In your role as handler, you are challenged to motivate, inspire, and teach the dog in order to give the two of you a more interesting life and a fuller relationship.

MAX, A REAL SUCCESS STORY by Brenda Bruja

Max first arrived on the scene with her mixed-breed pups at a local animal shelter. Little did she know in her abused and confused state that she would be so fortunate and live to have so much fun. Not long after Max and her pups were admitted to the shelter, my phone was ringing with a message asking me if I would be able to serve as a foster home for several weeks. Well, the timing was perfect since I had the rest of the summer free, so off I went with leash and crate in hand!

Max was about 1½ years old, too young to be a mother, and she had been neglected, and worse, for most of her life. At the time she was brought to the shelter, she was nursing eight 5-week old pups which were draining the last drops of health from her. Surprisingly, she was producing enough milk, and the puppies were doing relatively well, though they needed medicine for intestinal parasites and normal veterinary care. But Max herself was a sorry sight, malnourished, with protruding bones, many skin lesions from a nasty fungal infection, scars on her face, both ears badly infected, and a painfully engorged udder.

Her adoption profile did not create a pretty picture. First and foremost, she was a "pit bull." Fortunately for Max, the Cocheco Valley Humane Society does not automatically euthanize pit bull-type dogs, as is the policy of many shelters these days. In addition to her breed type, Max had serious health problems including many allergies, was not spayed, and not housebroken. With her sparse coat of hair, infected skin, and poor health, the tough climate of New Hampshire often left her shaking with cold. Her chances for adoption after the pups were weaned were questionable at best. But that is then and this was now! And for the next several weeks, Max and her pups would live a life of luxury with me as their full-time caretaker, ready, willing, and able to give them healthy food, a home in the country, wood piles to play on, and AGILITY OBSTACLES!

Max's ticket to freedom was her adorable personality and rock solid temperament. I must admit as I drove to the shelter to pick up the bunch, I pondered where this pit bull bitch would ride home. When I approached her kennel run, she seemed as leery as any nursing bitch would be in an unfamiliar place surrounded by strangers. Within the hour, she was riding up front with me, nearly on my lap, and seemingly grinning from ear to ear as we made the trip home. Max proved to be trustworthy beyond a doubt around both people and other animals. This fun-loving creature even smiled when greeting people, which unnerved those unfamiliar with what in her was really a submissive gesture!

During her first weeks with me, Max showed me her agility daily. Despite her poor physical condition and heavy udder, she would easily scale the four-foot-high puppy pen to nurse and care for her pups only to exit the same way when her work was done. Running out in the field with the older dogs, I watched Max spring off in a dead run, then turn instantly around to race off in the other direction, to the dismay of my long-strided German shepherds in pursuit! Often in play she would jump over other dogs who got in her way. With my interest in agility nearing obsession, I became very excited about this odd-looking dog who so innocently worked her way into my heart. I was soon to find out that this was Max's nature, pure and simple and full of zest.

Long before her official adoption, I knew deep down that I would find the time and space for this dog in my life. I began introducing Max to simple agility obstacles and jumps. Max's love of food only aided her rapid progress as she tore through tunnels and strutted over ramps to receive her reward. Max showed herself as a natural jumper, a definite plus when considering agility competition. And competition had crossed my mind only a few hundred times! Soon we were working on regulation equipment and preparing for future trials.

Max's condition was improving, so I began to challenge her more, especially in jumping since she had such talent for it. I wasn't concerned with height, since she measured 20 inches at the shoulder, meaning that she would only be required to jump 21 inches in U.S. competition. She had the ability to jump much higher. We began to practice on multiple jumps in alignment before moving on to jumps situated at right angles to each other. This proved to be more difficult, since jumping ability was only part of it. Training her to accept direction would be the challenge. The tire jump proved useful in teaching her accuracy, since she had to jump through an exact area instead of cutting corners as she had on the bar jumps. The concept of the broad jump took only a few progressions, using a tennis ball for motivation.

To Max, ramps were just a part of the scenery, and she showed no fear or hesitation on the dog walk, crossover, or see-saw. This is very unusual. Her first experience on the see-saw was on her own, as she explored the ramp in search of left-over food. The board went crashing down with a bang. No problem! It ended without a mishap but surely could have had detrimental effects on her training had she frightened or injured herself! As with any natural jumper, missing contact zones and jumping off midway across an obstacle were common with Max. Using her favorite motivator (food) helped to show her more precisely what I wanted. Although a seemingly tough-skinned "pit bull," force training is not Max's method of choice!

Tiger and Max remind Brenda that dogs have the right-of-way on the A-frame.

Though Max and I still have a ways to go in our agility training, she has come a long way.* Now healthy and housebroken, Max passed her American Kennel Club K-9 Good Citizen test and is working toward other obedience titles. She now "earns her keep" as a demonstration dog in the evening obedience classes I teach each week. At home you couldn't ask for a better companion while watching TV or romping through the woods of New Hampshire (she often wears a wool sweater). But I feel I'm the lucky one here, to have found a dog like Max. She's taught me to meet life's obstacles with zest and a smile! See you on the course!

Did I neglect to mention that not ALL the pups were returned to the shelter for adoption? A dark brindle-colored pup who came to be widely known as Tiger is still with me. Prior to bringing Max and her litter home, I had made a conscious decision to adopt a mixed-breed pup for a companion and agility dog. My German Shepherd Bach was nearing six years and his career in agility was limited. After weeks of observation and interaction, I chose a small male pup that I would keep for myself. I assumed at this time that this pup would grow up to fit in the medium height division. Surprise! Tiger now stands 23 inches tall at only eight months old! The best guess is that his dad was a black Labrador retriever. Oh well.

Thanks to his mother's lovely disposition and the love and lessons with which I raised him, he too loves life and the whole world. He is a special pup and, although he's going to be a big dog, he also loves agility. He's young and gangly right now, and I don't ask anything of him that could stress young bones and muscles and concentration. But there's a lot of agility we can do while he grows up, and Tiger definitely likes to have his share of the lessons. There's no doubt he'll be part of our agility team as well as part of our family.

* Note: In April 1990, Max and Brenda won the New England Regional qualifier in the Pedigree Grand Prix of Dog Agility. In August 1990, they made it to the national finals, just one year after Brenda brought Max home.

3

ELEMENTS OF AGILITY

Today I worked with what I had, and longed for nothing more; and what had seemed like only weeds were flowers at my door. Today I loved a little more, complained a little less; and in the giving of myself, forgot my weariness.
—from *Discovery*, author unknown, reprinted in "Leaves"

Strength and Fitness

Physical fitness, at least in the dog, is an important part of Agility. If you are interested in competition, mental fitness becomes equally important, and your own mental fitness can be more important than your dog's. In this section I will concentrate on your dog's physical strength and how to improve it. The discipline and satisfaction that will accompany the increase in strength are the foundation for mental agility fitness as well.

As a universal first step, there is nothing like a good brisk walk to revitalize the mind and body when you're feeling out of shape or out of touch. The less accustomed you and your dog are to getting up and around together, the less it takes to make a difference. But don't take on the rigors of an agility course with a dog who is much overweight or unused to exerting himself. It is foolish to begin jump training, for example, with a dog who cannot spring up from a prone position on the floor.

A dog doesn't have to be big or heavy to be strong in the context of fitness; indeed, Agility would not be the competitive sport of choice for a dog who is massive or musclebound. We want the agility dog strong enough to carry his weight effortlessly. The dog who is fit enough to run full speed every which way on a course of about 10,000 square feet in size, balancing, twisting, turning, climbing, ducking and especially jumping the whole time, is a strong dog. A healthy dog can accomplish some degree of physical exertion, but it takes an athletic dog to perform well at regulation Agility.

An agility dog should be strong enough to carry his weight effortlessly. Small dogs must run all-out to make SCT. This is Tyger.

F.L. Corden Sr.

Your dog's strength and stamina are what will keep him fast and able on an agility course in spite of one obstacle after another. And just as you improve the dog's ability one step at a time, you can build his strength and fitness that way. Jogging is super for him. Inspect his feet as carefully as you inspect your agility obstacles. Trotting over rough or hot road surfaces can be as dangerous for him as splinters in your equipment. His lungs and muscles will need gradual acclimation to toughen them up, and so will his feet. If your dog leads a soft-footed life, you may need to help him develop tougher pads as you condition him. There are several salves for strengthening the calluses of dogs' feet, available from sporting dog catalogs and stores. Protecta-Pad is one such preparation; Tuff-Foot is another.

Any conditioning program you choose for your dog needs to consist of a combination of diet and exercise. You could switch an overweight dog to one of the "light" foods initially, but it's best to settle on one of the top-quality dog foods not usually available in the grocery store. There really are some excellent dog foods obtainable now, and a little research on your part can come up with one which agrees with your dog in every way. This is a far cry from the world of the highly advertised dog foods, generic feeds, and those designed to appeal to humans.

For overweight dogs, try feeding the dog about one-third fewer calories per day in a first-rate food. If you can stand it, get rid of those junk-food treats, or at least use them very sparingly. Some eager eaters happily accept nuggets of their regular dog food as treats, especially if you sprinkle them with garlic powder. Dogs love garlic, and it's in favor as a healthy spice for dogs and people. Save empty garlic powder jars for treat storage because the smell stays strong a long while, and they're a good size for tucking in a pocket. Just remember that treats are calories, too. The handfuls you might feed your dog throughout the day should come out of his allotment at meals.

Another easy way to cut down on your dog's calories is to give smaller tidbits. Many dogs swallow their delectable treats so fast they don't even taste them anyway. It would help the cause for you to break that small cookie in half, or just offer a little piece of hot dog or a teaspoon of gravy. Face it: that stuff is no good for your dog. I know people who are feeding their dogs several hot dogs a day in the name of training, or a cup of grease a week in the name of love. Even if the dog weighs more than you, that's still a huge amount of unhealthy food.

There are many dog-treat recipes that are not unhealthy and do send the dogs to food heaven. If food is love, cook healthily for him. At least use poultry hot dogs and boil them first to get most of the nitrites and salt out. Then cut them into very small pieces and microwave them until they're very dry. They'll last well, won't stick to your fingers, and a little goes a long way. Think about what you're putting into your dog and whether it will help him live longer and stronger. Spoil him with fun, healthy snacks, and a very occasional bit of junk.

Along with watching the calories, gradually begin introducing more exercise every day. For dogs who are at a good weight now and just need

Jessy's favorite no-cal treats are snowballs.

strengthening, you still need to evaluate the diet and you should probably change some of your habits about treats and exercise, but you don't need to lower your dog's daily calorie intake. And whether your dog starts out fat or thin, when he has worked up to a rigorous schedule of exercise, you may need to up the daily calories. Once you get your dog's weight where you want it, you can monitor it and adjust his daily intake up or down without undue concern.

To check your dog's weight, rely on your eyes and fingers as well as the scale. Your dog carries a certain build, either large or small, wide chested or narrow, big boned or fine, or anything in between. Most dogs are at a good weight if their individual ribs are not conspicuous but are easily felt with the fingers. You can see from the length of spine on a dachshund or a bassett hound that extra weight will translate to back trouble.

Some breeds, like greyhounds, salukis, whippets, and a few others, are healthiest at thinner weights. You can see from their fine, frail-looking bones that excess weight is a mistake for them. So begin a conditioning program by looking objectively at your pet, his coat, his skin, his energy, his weight, etc. If you opt to change his food, do so by mixing increasing amounts of the new food into his old to avoid digestive upset. It's prudent to allow a week of changeover mixing for every year that your dog has had a steady diet of the old food.

Likewise, it's sensible to introduce your dog to more physical exercise both gradually and in a way he will enjoy. My favorite is walking through the woods. As the dog gets more active, and as he learns to come when you call, you can give him more freedom on these walks. The running uphill and down, the change of footing from leaves to dirt to mud and water, jumping over and ducking under things, pushing through branches, and the general charging around will do a lot for preparing your dog for the active fun of Agility.

Once your dog is at reasonable weight and strength, you could further condition him and lengthen his stride by teaching him to trot for longer and longer distances. The trot is the gait that will do his cardiovascular and muscular systems the most good. A brisk but relaxed trot works the whole body evenly without undue strain. This is the choice for overall conditioning. After your dog is lean and strong, it's time to add "extra exertion exercises" (EEEs) to his training a few times per week.

If you have a short-legged dog, a snappy walking stride on your part may be enough to get him trotting right out, extending each leg and strengthening lungs and muscles. But be advised that very small dogs are not going to be able to run a competition agility course under SCT unless they really run, not just trot. So once your little dog is up to strength overall, adding EEEs to his workouts periodically will be essential.

EEEs are a personal thing, designed by you to condition your dog for repeated bursts of extra effort without tiring. For small dogs, an average staircase or a small steep hill in the backyard can provide all the extra workout you both need. Another great EEE for small dogs, perfect for both of you to do together, is all-out running on the flat. Work up to sprints of at least 200 yards (two football fields). Competition agility courses usually range between 160 and 200 yards. Add twists and turns to help your dog keep track of you while running, and switch to riding a small bike (mountain bikes are perfect) to get him going faster when he's ready.

With larger dogs, you need something to help you go faster as soon as your dog is ready to work at a brisk trot. If you try this using a car, you need an extra adult to drive while you hold the dog's leash and are responsible for him, and you need to keep your dog away from the car's exhaust as well as the wheels.

Whatever machine you use, work on leash, at least at first, to keep your dog near and at the proper pace. You want a strong steady trot. The piece of equipment most suited to traveling steadily at the ideal speed for your dog is a bicycle. It would be wise to introduce your dog to this new challenge while first walking the bike. I love bicycling, and my dogs are comfortable with it and well-trained in general, but I did manage to be pulled over once or twice during the teaching phase when I began with a 10-speed bike. An old-fashioned pedal-brake model leaves your hands freer. I prefer to hold the leash rather than attach it to the bike.

A child's scooter is great for when you first begin to go faster than a walk. This introduces the dog to the proximity of a contraption and a faster speed without putting you so far from the ground. A dog seems to accept the bicycle easily after that. Mountain bikes, with their wider tires and smaller wheels and frames, are also good for jogging your dog. A speed of eight mph for smaller dogs and 10 mph for larger dogs is a general guideline. Many dogs need a few weeks' practice before they are comfortable for any real distance at that speed. Some dogs work up to 12 mph. Make adjustments based on your dog.

As larger dogs become physically fit, they need EEEs in their training regimen too. Doing bike work up long hills is great, as is trotting in very loose, soft dirt. You could also teach your dog to pull a weight behind him (I use a tire, weighted differently for each dog). Steep hills and long staircases make terrific training grounds (stadium steps are perfect for both of you). If your dog likes to chase and retrieve, he can be sent up hills and steps repeatedly and have lots of fun while exerting himself much more than you. This strategy becomes an important part of good agility handling for competition.

Group play among friendly dogs is great for their muscles and their social skills. A hearty romp with friends can be the perfect EEE for any dog. Once your dog is trained to come when called, you can punctuate his play sessions with recalls for treats, then say OK and let him rejoin

Very few giant dogs are as fit as Chaucer.

the group. If you find that your dog goes deaf when involved in group play, you have an opportunity to improve his training by putting a long line on him before playtime.

There are many other activities that can put you and your dog on the active track together. Backpacking and hiking over every kind of terrain are wonderful – plan ahead – and swimming is as good for dogs as it is for people. There are lots of great games that can keep canines in shape, including fetch, frisbee, keep-away, tag, flyball and other ball games, scent hurdle racing and other games with low jumps, lure coursing, dogsledding, skijoring, and any other sport you and your dog can enjoy. Jessy swims for miles at a time in our 1½-acre pond playing her version of water boomer-ball. Anchor likes to chase the rowboat, and Arrow dives off the raft just for the fun of it.

If you want to be active with your dog, look into it. There's surely a game for you. My dogs enjoy dogsledding, and they love to accompany me cross-country skiing; I find a pace comfortable for all. Many dogs love a run at the beach or a jog around the city park (always bring plastic bags and clean up after them). Whatever your environment offers, there is opportunity for strengthening your dog. It can be good for both of you.

Flexibility

Mental and physical flexibility are both required in Agility. Mentally, both handler and dog need to learn to welcome the unexpected. That does not come naturally to many dogs nor to many people, but it is well worth developing. It's the only way to take in stride the inevitable variations in agility course design, obstacle construction, color, texture, terrain and footing, crowd and judge proximity, weather, lighting, noise, etc.

Agility would not be such an exciting and interesting test if we concentrated on eliminating the many individual differences our competitions have to offer. It's important to observe the standards described by the regulations, as they provide for safe course layout and equipment generally familiar to all. Without these guidelines, it would be hopeless for one club to compete with another. But within the framework of the regulations, a good deal of variation is a plus for Agility.

If you don't want the sport to become a perfunctory examination of a dog's rote training, you need to keep an open mind about the eccentricities of another group's equipment. Each little unfamiliarity offers a new opportunity to expand the dog's experience. To prepare for the unexpected, make it your practice to work and play in so many different environments that a variation on the theme is easily handled by your solid core of mental flexibility.

Physical flexibility is required in running any course in which jumps and turns are called in quick succession, and especially for performing the weave poles. Teaching physical flexibility means teaching the dog to bend vertically and laterally. Vertical bending can be taught with tunnels and any other archways. Some dogs not used to this may resist any opening requiring them to duck. Many such dogs, when first inspired to try going through, will actually put their heads into the aperture and become frustrated when their shoulders bang against the upper lip.

Jessy is flexing her back both vertically and laterally in catching the toy. Strength and flexibility work together to keep a dog supple.

An easy way to help such dogs learn to flex vertically is with a hula hoop or any other hoop of appropriate size. After the dog has investigated the hoop, it is tilted over his head and he is enticed to walk his feet through. He soon learns to duck into the hoop and dance through to the tune of wild praise. Once you can hardly hold him back, he's ready for a new challenge, such as a smaller hoop, a tire, etc. Make sure he's eager to go through each aperture before introducing a more difficult one (See Tunnels, Chs. 2 and 5).

For any dog, bending exercises begin gently. Later, Blade is enticed to bend himself further. It's important to let the dog control the amount of flex.

One way to develop this skill further is to teach your dog the instant down (see Ch. 2). This will greatly enhance his vertical flexibility, and so will teaching him to spring up quickly from a prone position on the floor.

Lateral bending (side to side) is practiced whenever the muscles over the dog's rib cage are compressed on one side and stretched on the other. When dogs play keep-away, tag, or any game requiring them to turn, twist, or run in circles, they improve their lateral flexibility. You can help your dog learn to bend this way by using an enticement to lead him around your leg. As the dog eats the treat or grabs the toy, put gentle pressure on his side with your leg, which flexes his rib cage slightly. For very small dogs, you can do the same thing kneeling down, using your knee.

Once your dog is used to you bending him gently, you can teach him to bend himself a little further. You should not force his body yourself. Just use your hand to brace his flanks against your leg, and lead his front end around with a treat or toy. Like any other training, you should set him up to succeed easily at first, so lead him to bend just a little, say "good" as he bends, and let him have the enticement right away. The dog controls his own front end, and thus the amount of flex. Your part is to steady his hind end and to encourage him with your voice and the reward. Repeat the bending only a time or two on each side.

You may find that your dog bends better in one direction than in the other. Some dogs also have a strong preference for turning and circling in one direction. You can help develop his flexibility by practicing quick spins and turns to both sides, especially his weaker one, using an enticement or playfulness. Though he may always have a better side, your dog will need to be comfortable turning and bending in both directions for Agility.

You also help your dogs learn to flex their bodies when you teach them to weave through agility weave poles. Competition weave poles are close together and require a good deal of concentration in addition to physical flexibility, so they are best taught in several steps (see Ch. 9) incorporating a positive introduction to both controlled lateral bending and mental effort.

Weave poles call for flexibility and concentration. Arrow learned them over many months.

Control

Successful completion of an agility course requires that your dog come when called, jump, stay, go up an incline, lie down, weave, and go through an aperture– all on command. That's a lot of control. And the dog must tackle these challenges in the unpredictable required order called by his handler, often resisting his preference for a favorite obstacle and performing the one next to it on his handler's command. To be sure, the dog must be under control. But don't make control a dirty word. Mere compliance without delight does not do justice to the sport and spirit of Agility.

A nice way to help your dog accept control with pleasure is to devise a game that allows him to train himself. Not unlike ourselves, a dog learns best what he discovers for himself. If you'd like an easy way to introduce a little positive control into your dog's daily life, try playing "no free lunch." Hold up a handful of tiny delectables, and ask your dog if he wants a cookie. Let him come over to check it out. Don't go to him. Assuming he's interested, hold up a tidbit as you simply say "sit."

Repeat the command if necessary, but leave out any extraneous conversation. No sit, no cookie. The instant his hind end hits the floor you pop a cookie into his mouth. If your dog isn't familiar with the command "sit," you can quickly teach him by beginning with the treat at his eye level – keep a tight grip on it – and raising the goodie back over his head as you say "sit." Sooner or later he'll assume the position, you'll respond at once by giving him the treat, and you're on your way. This is a fine first exercise for positive control. It gets more interesting as you and your dog get used to working together.

If your dog is currently hard for you to manage, it can be difficult to visualize him as the cooperative teammate you would like to live with. First of all, check for physical problems. Study your dog's diet and his physical and mental practices. Perhaps he needs a better quality food, one without all the junk products so common in most pet foods these days. Perhaps you should have your vet check a urine and stool sample or examine your dog in person to see that there are no parasites, infections or other physical problems causing your dog discomfort. Many of these problems require specialized diagnosis; you could not find them at home. If you have not kept up with regular shots and stool checks for your dog, the first step is a trip to the vet.

Assuming your dog gets a clean bill of health, enroll in a basic dog obedience course. And there are some things you can do right away to help your dog fit into a civilized household. Here are a few simple tactics which can help you when your rambunctious dog has trouble settling down in the house:

1. Put him on a choke collar and leash, whatever length you need so you can interrupt him without chasing him or yelling at him. Don't give him the run of your home before he knows what indoor manners are. Tie him to you if necessary to keep track of him when you're busy. A dog who is both very active and very big needs a shorter leash and sometimes even a prong collar to keep him from dragging you around.

2. Practice basic obedience exercises such as leashwork, down, come, and wait, every day (see Ch. 2). In addition, introduce a "long down" command, keeping your dog lying down beside you for 30 minutes and more at a time. This will help him learn to be with people without demanding center stage. Your long down command needs to be different from your instant down command.

3. Tell him he's good whenever he does think of something quiet to do, such as curl up with his favorite chew toy.

4. See that he gets plenty of exercise outside and practice obedience

---

work outdoors, too. Introduce random recalls into his play sessions, using treats at first if necessary. Praise him for coming, then say OK and let him go back to play. If this is difficult, you need more practice on the recall itself, and a long line on your dog at play.

Do you have more than one dog? As long as they get along, you can play a great control game called "treats in turn." Get your handful of treats and invite the dogs. When they've assembled around you and are giving you their undivided attention, say the lead dog's name, then offer a treat directly to that dog's mouth. Any interference from another dog must be intercepted calmly by your knee or ankle, depending on the size of the dog who is out of turn. Next, say another dog's name and follow immediately with a treat to that dog. Don't give a treat in response to a dog's jumping to get it.

The emphasis is on the dog's tuning in for his name and accepting a treat in his turn. There is no need to combine this exercise with the command to sit. We don't want the dog to sit every time he pays attention. It's OK if they choose to sit, but don't require it. The focus is on patience and faith.

This lesson of taking turns is hardest on your leader dog, who must learn to watch food go past him to his underling. Use your body to interrupt any rudeness, but make it a quiet lesson. There is no need to become impatient with the dogs' impatience. They will learn the ritual from your authority and from your calm, precise technique. If you have a dog in your family who is less than self-assured, it's especially important that you not reprimand any of the dogs sharply, or the underdog will feel insecure and lose confidence. It's your attitude and quiet warding off of bad manners that will make all the dogs accept the sharing situation. You must not give a treat to a dog who is being impolite or out of turn. It doesn't take more than a few one- to two-minute sessions for all the dogs to get the idea and enjoy the control game.

One of the most common control problems facing dog owners is how to handle the game of catch-me-if-you-can. It's not a bad game, but play only with your dog on leash or long line until he understands how to stop playing on cue. You can intersperse the game with recalls and instant downs (Ch. 2) to help him give up his advantage when you ask him to. I do enjoy playing chase games with my dogs–outside. It helps develop Agility and quick reflexes while enhancing our kindred sense of fun in motion. But I don't appreciate having my dog initiate such a game when we're working on some less kinetic lesson or when I am expecting him to come to me, or when I am having a quiet conversation in the living room.

I have drawn the line at our house between the game we all love and the times when we may not play it. We don't initiate the game unless we are outside and willing to play, and we don't respond to the dog's invitation to play anytime other than when we are ourselves in the play mode. Over

Mutual play-bows initiate the game of catch-me with Jessy.

time, the dogs have learned that we act like their peers occasionally (indeed we are out of our league when we play chase with them), but that the role of peer is one we assume now and then, not one that is available to them at their whim.

One very useful control command is "leave it." It warns the dog, in advance, to avoid something he might otherwise find irresistible. Set this up with the dog on leash, using any forbidden household object, like the garbage can or a bowl of snacks on the coffee table. Move toward the object with your dog. As soon as he looks at it, say "leave it." If he looks away, praise him, but be ready to repeat the command, since it will take many repetitions before he understands. When you say "leave it" and your dog does not look away from the temptation, give a sharp correction, a hard jerk on the leash. Be generous with your praise when he looks away. Eventually he will choose to walk away from an object when you tell him to leave it, and he will decide on his own to resist things that are not his.

By practicing leave-its with all sorts of inanimate no-nos around the house, you can train your dog to the level where you can interrupt thoughts of mischief with that simple order. Progress to the outdoors and gradually to more distracting circumstances, including the interference of kids, other dogs, etc. It takes tuning in to your dog to know when he's thinking about a forbidden thing, but tuning in is a necessary part of becoming your dog's agility teacher and teammate anyway. This is just good control groundwork, and it will also make your dog a better citizen.

It is always a direct challenge to the handler to be able to control the dog without sapping his confidence. In countries in which agility competition is still young, some correct but placid performances can be

Spring demonstrates an advanced, self-imposed "leave it."

enough to win, since accuracy is foremost. But in countries like England, where several hundred dogs will be entered in a day's competition and the winners will all have clear rounds and be separated in their times by tenths or even hundredths of a second, accuracy and obedience are not enough. This degree of accomplishment will come to the rest of the agility world, too. It sheds a different light on that word control. Handler strategy, the dog's work ethic and enthusiasm, and all the fundamentals are tested at once, in less than a minute per dog. The dog must be fast, bold and independent, yet take instant direction from the handler's commands. That's what we want from control in Agility. Control should mean direction and guidance, but we shouldn't be power hungry. In this sport, power rightfully belongs to the dog.

After you and your dog have accomplished some control with stationary games, you might enjoy an active control game played with toys. This game also helps your dog learn to expect and read arm signals, which you will need later in his training on regulation obstacles. Your dog needs to have wait training (see Ch. 2) before going far with this, but it can be introduced at this level anytime.

In an early control game, the ball is shown to Arrow and held while he waits...

...and he is sent with commands and signals as soon as it's thrown. This builds attitude and zest for the game.

With your dog on leash, drape the leash on the ground or floor and stand or kneel facing your dog, without causing any pressure on his collar. Tell your dog to wait as you show him the toy. Then toss the toy out to one side and point to it excitedly as you tell your dog to "get it." Use your whole arm as a signal. When he charges out and grabs the prize, let him strut with the toy as you clap your hands and praise him. If he wants to run away and hoard it, step on the leash to limit him but don't reel him in to you. Do not make him bring the toy to you, and don't take it from him if he does come to you, but pet and make much of him.

He'll soon learn he doesn't have to be defensive or take off with the prize. The purpose of the leash is to prevent him from getting the toy uninvited, to prevent him from taking off, and to accustom him to it for the fine tuning later. You should avoid reprimanding him, and you are not

As training progresses, Arrow is reminded to wait while toy is tossed...

...then he is sent on command and signal. Now he must work under control, but his love for the game is secure.

really making him wait yet, once you throw the toy. You send him immediately on throwing the toy, and exaggerate your arm signal, even though he may not notice that yet.

The real control comes later, as his love for the game grows. Begin by tossing the toy only a short distance and emphasizing your arm signal as you do so. Once he is familiar with the game in one direction introduce the other direction and corresponding arm signal. Don't mix the two until he has completely learned them both. If you have more than one dog, teach each dog separately, then let each watch from a crate or tether while you play a few rounds with the other. That makes each dog more eager to play.

Improve your dog's wait training until you can do things like toss a ball and send him five seconds later without having to restrain him physically. After that, you can safely combine the signal exercise and the waiting game. To do this, have your dog wait when you toss the toy, without giving the arm signal or "get it" command. Say wait before you toss, and again as you toss. He should be on leash for this, as described above. Since he's already used to wearing the leash for this game, it won't deter him, and you must step on it if necessary to prevent him from going too soon. Don't chastise him. Simply put him back and try again if he can't wait. After a few seconds of successful waiting, send your dog with the signal and command simultaneously. It's important that you not introduce this control measure until your dog loves the game. That way, the interruptions you occasionally need to issue will not slow him down or make him reluctant to play.

After he gets very good at this, toss two balls a short distance, one from each hand in opposite directions, while he waits. Then send him to get one or the other. Be sure to exaggerate your arm signal at first. Step on that leash if he goes the wrong way, but don't dampen his enthusiasm. As he gets more reliable, try sending him with your signal alone. Your dog's proficiency and happiness with these control games will serve you well in Agility. On the course, keeping your dog's attention without impeding his run depends on getting him to accept your instructions with zest and fire. The best control training improves your own timing and accuracy as well as your dog's. It's a two-way street.

TEAMWORK

God summoned a beast from the field and He said...'I endow you with these instincts uncommon to other beasts: faithfulness, devotion and understanding surpassing those of man himself. Lest it impair your loyalty, you shall be blind to the faults of man. Lest it impair your understanding, you are denied the power of words....Speak to your master only with your mind and through honest eyes...

So be silent, and be a friend to man....This shall be your destiny and your immortality.' So spake the Lord. And the dog heard and was content.
                    –From the motto of the American Dog Owners Association

Teamwork = TLC

What makes a good team? What does it take to get that harmony of effort, so pretty to watch, that makes the work look easy and the job go smoothly? And why do even the most solid teams, whether dancers, baseball players, or agility nuts, have days when they trip over each other's feet and can't find the rapport they had only yesterday? Whatever teamwork is, it sure takes work to maintain it as well as work to build it.

We can all recognize the special communication that sets some relationships apart from the rest. The partners respond to each other's thoughts, seemingly without a clue. You and your dog can become a more responsive working partnership if you develop the TLC of teamwork: Trust, Leadership, and Confidence. As you learn to use and coordinate these skills, they become an inextricable part of your interaction with your canine teammate. Eventually, you live by the rules of TLC as naturally as you breathe, without having to concentrate on them. But you must tune in to your dog to find them, and it takes adjustment and effort to develop them. Trust, Leadership, and Confidence are the intangibles that

Agility is a team sport.

distinguish the finest agility performances, and they stand out just as clearly in the most harmonious human-canine bonds at home.

Trust

The trust that evolves in a great team cannot be demanded. You must earn it and it's a fragile thing at first, becoming stronger with the nurturing you put into it. When your dog fully trusts you, he'll give a great effort just because you ask for it. He has faith that what you ask is OK and that he can do it if you say so. Conversely, if your dog does not trust you, his positive attitude has little to sustain it when the going gets tough. Don't blame your dog for not giving a wholehearted attempt at a new task. Instead, set about earning your dog's complete trust in your daily life, and then bring that trust to bear in agility training.

Does your dog trust you? First of all, does he know you well? Your dog cannot trust you if he can't predict your reactions to the everyday situations of his life. A trusting relationship requires consistency in your household rules and corrections your dog can understand. Dogs study the ones they live with, and dogs are masters of body language, so it is likely that your dog can read your moods. His trust depends on how those moods affect him personally. So the cornerstone of trust is predictability. Each action you take with your dog affects his ability to predict you. You can earn your dog's trust, one action at a time.

If a certain action on your part is followed by another particular action

---

time and again, your dog learns to predict that second action. You pick up the car keys and he expects you're going for a ride. You pick up his leash and he predicts that you're going to take him for a walk. It's that predicted action, what he expects to happen next, that determines his feelings when you do what you do.

Your dog's predictions can strengthen or weaken your relationship. If you are prone to screaming at him when you arrive home, he predicts this and feels insecure when you come home. That does not mean he connects your coming home to the mistakes he made some time ago. It is much more likely that his insecurity on your arrival is due to his prediction that an unpleasant encounter with you is coming next. He need not know why. These feelings are confusing, and they foster insecurity and poor self-image. They do not foster trust.

If you expect your dog to get into trouble while you are gone, teach him to sleep in a crate in a favorite spot in your home so you can leave him alone without worrying about damage, both to your home and your relationship. Prevent the unwanted behavior from happening in your absence, and concentrate on improving your dog's manners when you are home. Since canids are by nature den animals, it is usually not difficult

Helping a dog feel secure is an important part of earning his trust.

to help them associate the crate with comfort. You can learn a lot about positive crate training from obedience training books. For many dogs, this is the beginning of a better relationship with humans.

It's very important that you and your dog are happy to see each other when you come home. If you want to trust your dog, see to it that he learns what you need him to know. He can't do it without you, and he can't trust you until you can approve of him. The job of earning his trust and his earning your trust falls entirely to you. It can be a lot of work at first, but it gets much easier as you keep at it. So get to know your dog and learn to bring out the best in him.

You have already earned a certain important trust from your dog if you are reliable about seeing to his basic needs, including food, water, grooming, exercise, and love. Those come first. Then, to develop a stronger bond, teach him the manners he will need in your family (see Chs. 2 and 3). These become the ground rules between you. Without them, neither of you can trust the other because you don't know what to expect from each other.

Once you and your dog have learned to get along well in your daily life, you can further develop the trust between you with agility play sessions on backyard equipment such as that described in Ch. 2. Your dog learns to trust your judgment as you offer him a new challenge and help him master it. Be sure you choose a time, environment, and task all suited to quick success, and be properly prepared with agility collar, leash, and enticements. It's fine to assume your dog will have no hesitation or problem, but be ready to help at once if it doesn't turn out that way. Your dog's trust in you will be given a boost for every success you celebrate together, and will be set back commensurate with every problem.

It will do your trust factor more good if you introduce your dog to a challenge with you right beside him, encouraging as necessary, using food or a toy to keep his spirits up. During these first stages, don't worry about your dog's accuracy on an agility obstacle, but do put some study and effort into your own handling technique. It's important for you to develop good training skills because that will help you establish correct agility habits in your dog early. It will also develop your eye for safety and help you protect your dog. Your dog's trust in you just quietly grows. But be patient with both of you. You will find that you can't work on everything at once, especially when you're just starting out. Take your time and avoid putting pressure on the dog. Sit in the tunnel with him if he's uneasy. Let him lean on you while he walks up a ramp. By being beside him, steadying him and sharing your confidence and patience, he will learn to trust you. In time he will feel that he can do anything you ask, and that life is grand when he gets that chance.

Does your dog trust you? Will he tune in to you? Does he tend to settle down if you think quiet thoughts and settle down yourself? What if you

Although the A-frame is flat, when Dodger needs extra encouragement he gets it right away. This develops his trust.

massage his shoulders, thighs and legs? Will he let you handle his feet? It takes trust for a napping dog to remain relaxed while you rub his limbs and particularly while you touch his feet.

Does your dog know your touch from anyone else's? Two of my dogs will all but purr with pleasure if I touch them while they're stretched out, but their eyes will pop open to check out the same interruption from anyone outside the family. It's easy to build trust in a dog who loves everyone, because he has a trusting nature to work with. You just need to take the time to let him settle himself down while you remain calm. This takes tuning in, for you and for the dog.

Can you relax your dog when he's feeling nervous and insecure? That takes a higher level of trust. If he reacts with fear to something which is not dangerous, can you convince him to check it out and accept it? Start by approaching and touching the new thing (or person) yourself, then put that hand on your dog's muzzle, then on the object again, but do not pull your dog to it. Use any enticement and encouragement to teach him, perhaps over several exposures, to approach in spite of his insecurity. Say nonthreatening things like "What is that?" or "Wanna say hi?" and just a well-timed, quiet "good" as he takes each tiny step or reaches out his nose. Use what you know about your dog to help him keep trying when he's hesitant.

This work is not a matter of obedience per se. Ignore his failures. Don't force, and don't inadvertently reward failures by petting your dog when he hides behind you. The dog's willingness to reach out and smell the object of his uncertainty stems from his own curiosity once he trusts your judgment that all is OK.

These trust exercises will help to build your dog's faith in you. It will damage that faith if you punish him for noncompliance or inaccuracy now. First find a challenge at which he can easily succeed, and use that as your starting point. You can even work on your own accuracy as a handler by using a stuffed animal instead of your dog. That way, you are free to make many of the mistakes you're bound to make without having them shape bad habits in your dog. One advantage to starting with simple makeshift obstacles at home is that you and your dog can build a good working relationship which will help you progress that much faster when you get to regulation agility equipment.

Don't take your dog's trust for granted. The more timid dogs need to trust you in order to give new challenges a try. See to it that they view every attempt as a success. The more independent dogs need to trust you to take your advice. See to it that they are rewarded for listening.

Your dog's trust begins with the basic obedience commands and household etiquette. He learns that you say what you mean and mean what you say. You introduce basic agility skills in a low-pressure environment, teaching the dog that the two of you are a team and can accomplish things to make you both proud. And you build upon that trust when you tackle more challenging situations, distractions, and agility exercises. Your dog learns to trust you even when it's more difficult to do so.

Kate gets down to Akema's level to make her feel more comfortable about first attempts through the tire.

The next level of trust requires that you never order an impossible task. It's fine to call for an effort that requires your dog to stretch his abilities a little, either mentally or physically, but don't ever demand what you can't help him accomplish, and above all don't push his education too fast. Even a mature, well-trained dog occasionally needs your conservative guidance to keep him from biting off more than he can chew.

It's often tempting to skip the introductory levels of training on any one obstacle, but don't do it. The risks outweigh the benefits. Most of my agility students fall for that trap. Usually they get carried away by the dog's apparent initial confidence. They become interested in a challenge for which the dog is not fully prepared, and they try it anyway.

Sometimes the dog seems to take to the obstacle immediately, performing the regulation dog walk or the see-saw or bar jump on the very first exposure, without working up to it. Suddenly, on the next attempt or even sessions later, the dog seems to have lost all confidence on that obstacle. Since, commendably, the handler has taught his dog to expect success, he often does succeed on the first try. But the stress he feels during that unprepared initial effort can create a strong negative impression of the obstacle which soon overtakes him.

I had a wonderful collie for 13 years, and he was a very accomplished citizen by the time he was retired. His new career as chief house pet needed supplemental work to keep his spirits up, so he chose to help with certain chores. I took care of several farm-fulls of animals on a regular basis, and on one job I carried two five-gallon jugs of water to the chicken house every day and brought the jugs back empty. "Spring" was proud as a peacock to carry an empty jug. But he wanted also to carry the jugs when they were full; it seemed all the same to him. I never told him "NO," but always kept the full jugs away from him, then gave him an empty. So I often walked to the chicken house with an elderly collie gentleman dancing at my heels, trying to wrest a jug from this hand or that.

Friends suggested: "Why don't you just let him try and he'll see he can't lift it?" But I felt he wouldn't trust me so completely if I let that failure happen. I knew him well enough to predict that if he grabbed a jug expecting to hoist it and strut with it, and met absolute failure, he would not quite trust me enough to try the next new task with the same vigor. I chose never to offer him a job he couldn't do. For all his life he expected to work and succeed, and he did so with gusto.

This was my personal judgment call, based on a long, close relationship with that individual dog. Certainly many dogs could be handled differently, but in general that philosophy has stood me well. Don't give your dog a task he cannot perform, or even one that he feels he cannot do. As you get to know his weak spots, you can strengthen your dog's trust in you by improving these areas very, very gradually and by being right there beside your dog to prevent a shaky mentality from letting failure set in. And by the way, the more your dog takes his confidence from you rather than from himself, the more damage it will do to his trust in you whenever he feels insecure about your demands.

I have seen many a good handler decide to "see if" his dog will do something, and so order a task more difficult than what he has prepared his dog for. Sometimes the dog balks. The dog trusts his own judgment and questions that of his handler. Smart dog, I suppose, since the handler showed a lack of sense by demanding a quantum leap above the dog's readiness. It also leads me to expect the dog to mistrust his handler's judgment more readily in the future. Time and again, even an excellent handler will push his dog too hard, then pay the price for weeks afterward by having to rebuild the dog's confidence at a level which he had previously surpassed. The test has cost a good deal of the dog's trust, a heavy price.

One person I know couldn't resist testing his beloved and very talented dog on a whopping 15-foot-high arched playground ladder. He climbed up himself and straddled the top, having told his dog to wait. When he ordered her up, she sprang with all the strength of her faith in him, and struggled to where he caught her by the buckle collar and helped her over the top. She had no experience climbing down such an obstacle either, but she gamely made the attempt until gravity called her to jump the last several feet. She landed safely and was congratulated and hailed a great success, but that was the last time she would consider it. He tried to repeat the feat, but she absolutely refused. That utter trust was gone.

She was that rare dog who could have learned to handle such a difficult obstacle if worked up to it, so I can't help but think he sold that strength short. It was beautiful to see in her first try the power of her perfect faith. It seems that strong-willed people who themselves handle pressure and stress well are more apt to apply heavy pressure to their dogs than are people who are more intimidated by stress.

Your dog is not a simple creature, although his needs and demands often seem so. You shouldn't assume you always understand him. Each of us can learn from other people who tackle things differently. Study the positive thinking of adventurers if you're shy; watch the preparation of careful people if you're impatient. Balance your own natural tendencies with the inspiration of other people who show you something you admire. You will understand your dog better and develop your potential as a team if you explore many ways to look at a situation and bring home a new bit of insight with every outing. It helps you appreciate your dog, and can show you new ways to help your dog appreciate you.

Leadership

A good agility leader inspires confidence in himself while also enhancing his dog's personal confidence. He brings out his dog's strengths, heads off the dog's weaknesses, and motivates his dog by word and action.

Olympia feels proud, safe, and loved. A good leader expects, inspires, and appreciates effort.

His energy and confidence are contagious to his canine teammate. He exudes assurance and great expectations without making his dog a victim of high pressure.

Sound like you? Me neither, but I'm working on it. Some of us are great leaders in the classroom and in the backyard, and that's a good place to start. I have some fine students with no interest in formal competition who enjoy Agility just as much as I do. Your dog doesn't need competition to complete his life. If you don't either, that's fine. Your leadership skills are still important to you and your dog.

Your more stressful challenges will arise from maintaining that leadership around distractions, without the added pressure of competition. It's challenge enough to work well with your dog on a crowded street or on a familiar agility course. It's extremely difficult to bring that talent unchanged to the nationals. There's nothing like a national title, a TV crew and several thousand spectators to test your leadership skills to the limit. Many good handler/dog teams stay home.

Like all the intangibles, leadership has to begin at home. Daily living habits and simple obedience lessons can help your dog view you as a leader, but leadership is more than telling your dog what to do. The dog who really accepts you as leader will accept massaging the back of his neck, hugging him, hovering over him, and handling his body. It's necessary for your dog to be able to relax and enjoy these overtures from you rather than to fear or resent them as dominance gestures. Obedience and control games help your dog recognize and welcome friendly attentions from his leader.

Many dogs have adopted another dog as their leader. When the lead dog gets going, the follower wants to be right behind. Your agility dog will be a superior teammate if he is that interested in what you do. To help him relate to you as his leader, make an effort to lead him in a way he can understand. Try setting up a situation that will be interesting and fun for your dog and put you in the leader's role. Going for a ride in the car is an everyday example for some dogs. Going boating is another, or jogging or biking. For dogs who love water, swimming and even watering the garden can present leadership opportunities for you.

Now and then, initiate an activity that is distinctly "doggy." Chase a squirrel with your dog and throw a stick up in the tree after it. Jump up against the tree a few times, or climb partway up. It's important to take charge at the tree, showing command of the situation from the dog's point of view. Many dogs love to chase flies, good practice for quickening reflexes. Every now and then I invite my bug-nabbers on a fly chase. They are always quite impressed when I get a fly, and they don't seem to mind that I cheat by using a flyswatter. I also miss the best part by not eating the fly, but they know better than to raid the waste basket for it because I'm the leader.

I have one dog who likes to watch TV, so we can enjoy animal scenes together. Dogs who love to dig should have a designated digging area, and you should be chief excavator now and then. The possibilities go on and on, guided only by your dog's favorite doggy activities.

We all know that bonding with your dog includes showing affection, but many dogs need a leader they can respect on their own terms, too. So get down and doggy sometimes. Many great canine agility prospects are dogs who don't love to be cuddled. Take a good look at your dog and let yourself relate to him as his leader in action as well as someone who pets him and feeds him.

Everybody has different goals in Agility. Whatever your goals, every dog and every handler has personal character traits that make agility training a challenge. Granted, some have more than others. I prefer to look on these traits as "qualities." There is a positive side to every character trait, and it is the leader's job to develop this quality and use it to the team's advantage. My dear Rottie Jessy has a mind as hard as they come, and more than once she has disagreed with my choice of obstacle and told me so. In one competition she even pushed me aside to get to the one she preferred, thwarting my attempt to anticipate her reaction and block the tricky spot. It is a humbling experience, and it short circuits your leadership in a hurry. How can teamwork come of this? How can you feel like a leader when your dog's personal confidence seems stronger than your own?

Start by evaluating you and your dog individually. You can pinpoint many of your own motivations and habits which will help you learn the ropes of this sport. Start by listing these. Now dig deeper and list habits that might cause you problems in agility training. In a separate column, list helpful characteristics that your dog brings to the partnership. Include his intrinsic motivators and then the traits you recognize as potential problems in his agility training. It will help you design effective approaches to training if you know your strong and weak areas. And, most of all, you can see which of your traits is apt to conflict with your dog's traits. Each agility dog you train will require a separate interaction sheet. You will need to modify your approach many times in order to bring out the best in each dog and, in turn, emerge as a handler with good leadership qualities.

Your dog is who he is, a canine, a certain breed or breed mix, and a particular individual. These facts determine much of his interpretation of the world, and you can't change that in a basic sense. But you can work with it. Depending on many factors, such as his age, the time and effort you invest and the quality of that time and effort, the compatibility of your approach with his personality, and on and on, you will be able to shape your dog's outlook and his abilities to an amazing extent.

Doe negotiates a low, dog walk while her leader stays tuned in. Keep your eye on the dog.

Begin by working with your dog, not against him. For major training problems, make note of what you ultimately want and where you are now in relation to that. Then design intermediate goals which are the steps to get from here to there. It would not be fair to your dog for you to expect quickly what he is not yet ready to give. A written goal sheet will help you plan and monitor the training on that problem, and keep you from avoiding it. Believe me, if you bury it now it will surely resurface when the pressure is on. Whether this particular goal requires a few steps or many steps depends on how far from it you are now.

That hard-headed independence of Jessy's became the same tough-minded persistence that took her jumping ability from inadequate to good. Along the way she worked through some tough agility challenges that would have weeded out most heavy-set dogs. Her stubborn ways can be a plus. It's up to me, because I'm supposed to be the leader. If I can't always be smarter than she, at least I have to be the better manager.

A few years ago I kept an agility training diary to monitor the progress of young Jessy. I lasted about a month with it, and it was very useful. For the first week, the entries read like a how-to text, beginning at a logical step one and making slow but steady progress. Then comes week two. The first entry announces a setback, and the next day's entry is just AAAAGH!!! The following day is blank, the next says we're going to try again, and the next day reads much like step one.

It helps, especially when you're working out a snag, to keep track of progress, uneven though it might be. You will easily see if a pattern develops, and you will think more clearly with your deeds in writing. Although I haven't yet done so, I would like to keep a diary of a dog's entire training regimen for a year or more. It's impossible to remember even most of the important details. Trials and errors, quirks and breakthroughs in one dog's training can provide some insight for another day, another dog, or another handler.

After all, we can't be brilliant every day, and writing down our work and ideas gives us access to that much more information and experience next time. If you like to write, try keeping a diary to help you manage your dog's training, especially if you don't train every day. If a dairy is not for you, at least try one goal sheet to help you solve one training snag between you and your dog. I think you'll find it very useful, both now and later.

You should always work on simple things with the more difficult things in mind. Choose a starting point at which you both can succeed. Choose intermediate goals which will challenge your dog – but not too much. This philosophy will make it easier to back up a little whenever you see yourself going too fast or pushing too hard, and it will help you and your dog accomplish goals you didn't think you could reach.

Leadership is the connecting thread that is woven back and forth through the work you and your dog do together. It's an invisible thing, and it doesn't remain strong without your steady efforts to enhance it. Without your attention, slowly but surely the thread loosens and begins to unravel. Look at it this way: Every day, your fabric gets stronger or weaker, according to your work. The best dog/handler teams, like the best marriages, have great days and terrible days. A good leader knows, and surely his dog knows deeper, that the relationship is what it's all about.

Confidence

Confidence is such an elusive intangible, and to do your best on an agility course you need to feel confident in yourself, in your dog, and in the strong relationship between you. Your dog needs confidence in his ability and in you as his leader. Bringing out and channeling the dog's confidence is your job (as if you didn't have enough to work on just developing your own). A lapse of confidence anywhere undermines the strength of the team.

In order to develop confidence as an agility team, you need to be emotionally bonded with your dog. Without that, you can still do your pet a big favor by introducing him to Agility and basic obedience, and you can use these tools to help develop his confidence and tractability. But unless you and your dog tune in to each other and find a mutual affection, you will not be able to make the most of Agility.

Agility is certainly a means as well as an end. I have used agility training with more than a thousand dogs as a training aid and confidence-builder. As you embark on the first tunnel and A-frame lessons, you are beginning agility confidence work. Think of your pet being pushed and dragged into a regulation agility tunnel or up a steep, narrow dog walk plank, and imagine what his first impression would feel like. For most dogs, even though they may have come to the lesson with superior aptitude for Agility, a first experience based on aversion met with force is disastrous. It represents the opposite of teamwork. This approach does lasting damage to the dog's trust in you, your image as his leader, and above all to his confidence.

The dog who is introduced first to a hoop or tire, then to a short tunnel, and then to gentle inclines is a dog who has maximum opportunity to develop agility confidence. Praise, enticements, and rewards should be judiciously offered to minimize the inevitable stress of the new demands.

Some dogs get so excited over treats that they are slap-happy about details like where their feet should go, but for first introductions I prefer to permit the dog to work that way in order to cement that go-get-it positive attitude. The careful work of keeping the dog properly on the apparatus falls to the handler.

In all probability, the dog who is so food crazy that he's careless is also a dog whose confidence on the equipment is quickly assured, and then it's fine to back off a bit and have him think about his performance a

Agility dogs can assert their confidence unexpectedly. Dizzy leaped into the bleachers... just to say hi.

little more. But no harshness from you is called for even if he's jumping up and down. Just steady him quietly and let him figure it out. Give as much guidance and enticement as the situation warrants. It's your judgment. Your dog's delight in the first lessons translates into confidence, and it's this generalized confidence that will keep you both succeeding as the lessons get more demanding.

We all know dogs who come on like maniacs, so enthused about everything that they want to charge here and there, jumping on everything and everyone. Remember that because a dog exhibits manic behavior does not necessarily mean that the dog is confident. In fact, many active dogs display an even higher level of energy when they don't know what to do. So don't rush ahead with excessive levels of agility challenges with very physical dogs. Keep your own body position steady and your handling techniques in order because you won't have a lot of time to correct them if your crazy friend gets himself into trouble. Follow a logical progression in your work sessions with every type of dog, and don't go on to the next level of challenge prematurely.

Many times a dog will rush through an obstacle because he lacks confidence and wants to get to the end. The dog may be carrying his tail up and his head high, seemingly showing all the confidence in the world, but be quite unsure of himself inside. When this is the case and you respond by introducing a tougher challenge, you could be setting up a serious setback in confidence later on.

Let the dog demonstrate his acclimation to an obstacle by performing it willingly with you at his side a few times. One way to tell if the dog is rushing from lack of confidence is to have him wait partway along. The dog who is truly comfortable on the obstacle will be glad to eat a cookie or two along the way, or stop for a belly rub. The dog who is manic and insecure will be quite stressed about stopping. In that case, go back to square one and develop confidence with the dog's favorite motivators at that first level, then proceed more slowly. Remember, food and toys can be used to slow your dog down as well as to speed him up and keep him in the middle.

Don't automatically assume that a crazy dog is simply one with a very high energy level. It could be, but hyperactivity can also indicate a medical problem, anything from a genetic imbalance or a thyroid condition to a food allergy. Certainly, the behavior calls for investigation, along with basic education, healthy diet, proper socialization, and lots of exercise.

Now is the time to begin proper training practices as a handler, especially since you're avoiding putting any stress of accuracy on the dog just yet. For example, hold the food down low and in the middle of the plank, or you'll be enticing your dog right off the incline. As you learn to stand beside your dog, extending your food arm properly and using the agility collar effectively, he is free to feel safe, happy, and brave. You are

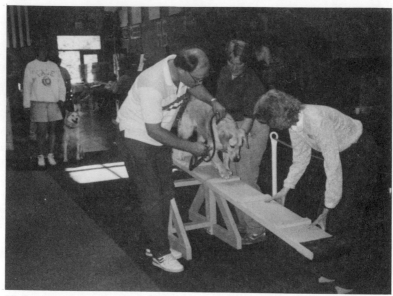

Nickie likes lots of support when she tackles a new step.

fostering trust, establishing your leadership, and developing confidence. Teamwork is coming.

In the further interest of long-term confidence, keep each lesson short and sweet. Don't keep working until your dog is tired. End the lesson early while he's eager to do it again. That way he's sure to welcome the sight of the equipment when you come back to it. For the same reason, always control the level of difficulty in the lesson, so your dog emerges with feelings of accomplishment. By following these guidelines, practicing agility skills can turn confidence-building into pleasure for both dog and handler.

A dog who approaches the introductory agility obstacles with trepidation, tail tucked and body low, needs extra time to check out the equipment before being asked to work with it. This kind of dog can benefit from being an observer at a more outgoing dog's lessons for awhile, and he needs the opportunity to sniff everything to his heart's content. But don't assume that Agility is not for this dog. Many such dogs have begun slowly and become agility nuts in time, as long as their training is conducted with their confidence always in mind. Some people do not have the patience to develop competence in this kind of dog, but lucky is the hesitant dog whose owner does.

Your dog need not be a socialite to be a good candidate for Agility. Many dogs who cannot make friends easily have forged a strong bond to one special human. If you have a special dog who is undersocialized, you might be surprised how much you can do for his general confidence by adding some agility exercises to his life. As long as you are willing to be the dog's big buddy, you can develop great teamwork with that dog. As you practice and your skills improve together, your insecure friend will become confident as long as you are there to keep up his self-esteem. When you are absent or distracted or unhappy, he won't have the emotional strength to sustain his ability. He takes his confidence straight from your heart.

If your shy dog has real aptitude for Agility, and isn't nasty-tempered, Agility could even become a good competition sport for you. No group work is required in an agility competition. You and your dog will be tested by yourselves against the course and the clock, and your dog need only go about the work at hand and ignore a nearby judge and the commotion outside the ring. If that is too much hassle for your dog to bear, you can still do his confidence a world of good by introducing agility challenges in a familiar environment. And one thing leads to another; you may one day decide your dog is ready for gradual acclimation to the big wide world, with Agility as a common denominator. This sport will surprise you. I have seen a very introverted dog jump onto a picnic table smack in the middle of lunch with a group of strangers. Picnic tables make great agility training aids, and this dog invited herself to hop up even though she would normally shy away from people.

Every dog has little agility gremlins that come up and grab him from time to time. They seem to hold his pasterns and make him hit the jumps, or they wobble his feet on the planks and make him unsteady. Above all, they whisper in his ear that he can't do it, and with that they toss his confidence out of his head. Dogs have different ways of communicating to us that the gremlins have taken their confidence. Until you know your own dog very well and can recognize the various ways he has for worrying about the gremlins, don't ever punish your dog for failing.

I have a very good dog who meets the gremlins head on: when in doubt, barge ahead. Tackle something. It's her way. It took me a long time to figure out that she charged the equipment even harder and listened less to me when the gremlins had her confidence. I thought she was displaying brazen confidence and lack of teamwork. Things started going a lot more smoothly when I realized that she really needed me to slow the lesson down and review easier work until she got her confidence back.

I have another very good dog who handles the gremlins quite differently: when in doubt, circle tightly to the left. This is sometimes harder for me to bear, but at least it's easy to tell when the gremlins have his confidence. Again, the answer is to slow the lesson down and review an easier version of the same task.

In addition to his own gremlins, your dog can be the victim of your nerves also. Your dog will be more free to feel confident if you let him feel your pride in him. Most dogs have an Achilles heel in Agility, so we seldom run a complete course without holding our breath here and there, even with our teamwork well in place. Try to balance your dog's problems with positive energy. By working with an eye to the dog's confidence you can often prevent a tough spot from breaking his concentration.

In planning your training sessions, you need to think forward to your dog's personal problem spots and plan a strategy to help your pet overcome his shortcomings gradually. Succeeding quickly at a task designed to be mildly challenging for him will bolster his confidence. Pretty soon, over weeks or months of steps toward your goal, your dog becomes confident about challenges that used to get the better of him. Remember, your dog needs you to work with him in mind when you train. Never mind how high the book says to send him. You are the one who knows his weaknesses and must work gradually and patiently to overcome them. As he progresses in ability, you must still maintain control of situations that are personally difficult for your dog.

There's no way around it, the dog's confidence in himself and in you, and your confidence in yourself, your dog, and the relationship between you, all falls to you. As you work at it all, you'll get to know yourself better than you ever have, and you'll learn much about what makes you and your dog tick in harmony. It's worth the effort because, on those days when it all comes together, the two of you can jump the moon. That unbeatable fit is what people notice when they watch a great team. The rarity of it is what makes great teamwork shine so bright.

Confidence is the result of developing skills and attitude. Thanks to her handler's patience, Akema decided the tire was fun.

SECTION II
Regulation Obstacles

- *The Go-Throughs*

- *The Go-Ups*

- *The Jumps*

- *The Pause*

- *The Poles*

- *Bringing it all Together*

A well-trained tunneler goes through on cue at a run, and exits ready for the next cue. This is 12-year-old Spinner, a 1990 national contender.

5

THE GO-THROUGHS

He that can have patience, can have what he will.

–Benjamin Franklin

Teaching Yourself, Teaching Your Dog

Up close, all that agility equipment can look forbidding. Heights seem higher when you picture your dog up there, and a jump looks more imposing when you look around the course and see 10 others just as high, some broader, and some downright strange looking. There isn't much room for error on those planks, and how on earth can a dog be taught to weave so fast through those silly poles?

This section is designed to make agility training logical, fun, and almost painless. Its goal is to bring you and your dog from introductory work to full competence on the regulation agility obstacles. If you keep up with the fundamentals and complementary exercises of the earlier chapters, you'll continue to improve your dog's AQ.

The regulation obstacles described here are those recommended by the United States Dog Agility Association (USDAA). Some differences between this interpretation and that of other national organizations are noted in the introduction to each obstacle.

In this section, the obstacles are divided into five different chapters by the different skills required. It's a good idea to become familiar with each chapter before beginning to instruct your dog. But it's not necessary to gain complete competence in one category before beginning work in another. As long as you start at the beginning in each chapter, your dog will probably benefit from working in two or more areas. Just keep track of your dog's progress in each area because he may be quick to learn some skills and slow to learn others. Use this section as a guide, but let your dog dictate the timetable.

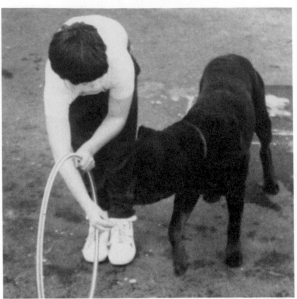

*Basic to all tunnel and tire work is a simple go-through.
"Hey, Anchor, want a cookie?"*

*"Good boy." A well-manipulated enticement can help a
dog get it right without stress.*

Go-through obstacles require the dog to enter an aperture and go all the way through in a specified direction. These obstacles include the open, or pipe, tunnel, the closed, or collapsed tunnel, and the tire jump.

Where agility competition is more advanced, judges stipulate that any deviation from a clean performance here on the first attempt results in faults being assessed – sometimes elimination.

Where agility competition is newer, and especially in beginner classes, judges are more lenient and allow the dog to correct his mistakes to some extent.

So a flawless go-through for each of these three obstacles is universally interpreted, but you will still see some variation in leniency from class to class.

Open Tunnel, Introduction: *Also called pipe tunnel*

The dog must go through a tunnel of about 24 inches in diameter. Tunnel lengths range from 10 to 20 feet, and they are generally constructed of spiral wire covered with nylon, cloth, or special coated materials.

Most agility dogs love open tunnels and perform them readily. This is a mixed blessing in competition, as it is not uncommon for the dog to prefer the tunnel and enter it even when the handler is trying to direct him to a different obstacle nearby. Competition courses usually include an open tunnel next to the A-frame or dog walk for this reason.

Your dog can begin tunnel training right away, perhaps with a hula hoop (see Ch. 2) if the dog has any hesitation about going through an opening. Hoops, rings, and tires are available in various diameters. Too big is OK for starters but too small is not. After a thorough investigation by the dog, the hoop can be tilted over his body and the dog encouraged to walk through, preferably with a cookie to his nose in order to minimize stress. Once the hoop presents no threat, introduce a smaller aperture.

If your dog is very small, you can cut off the rim of a properly sized bucket, cut an arch out of a cardboard box, stretch out a coathanger, use an embroidery hoop, styrofoam swim ring, or any suitable material you find at home. Make sure you examine your creation for sharp edges. You'll get quite a bit of use out of it, so don't hesitate to put some effort into selection and preparation. When the dog is eager to go through something snug, it's time for a tunnel.

The very best first tunnels are compressible, so you can start with them very short and gradually lengthen them as your dog gains confidence. But a perfectly good tunnel can be fashioned from a cardboard box sized for your dog. I know some tiny dogs who love their tunnels made of round oatmeal boxes and some who can't yet tolerate anything smaller than a washing machine box. And if your tiny dog needs a huge box at first, so be it. Many dogs who start out wary of tunnels are soon charging through regulation tunnels with every bit as much confidence as the dogs who loved them from the first introduction. It depends on the patience and ingenuity of the handler.

Most of the national agility organizations are using regulation tunnels made from flexible ducting conduit manufactured for industrial use. Flexaust is one such manufacturer, with three plants in the U.S., one in Canada, and one in Germany. The model owned by USDAA and ADAC is a 15-foot length of 24-inch diameter model SD-W. Contact Flexaust Corp., 11 Chestnut St., Amesbury, MA 01913, telephone 508-388-9700 (U.S.), or P.O. Box 536, Whitby, Ontario L1N 5V3, telephone 416-668-8818 (Canada), for distributors closest to you. Another source for this kind of tunnel material in the U.S. is Peabody ABC Corp., P.O. Box 2928, Grand Jct., CO 81502, telephone 303-242-3664.

It's advisable for agility clubs to purchase such a tunnel if possible, partly because the dogs will surely see this type of tunnel in competition, and also because the tunnel's durability makes it a good investment. Because of its flexibility, the material also lends itself well to group work. It's easily shortened, lengthened and bent.

Flexaust is compressible at a ratio of 5:1. It is impervious to extremes of weather, portable and practically indestructible. It is also available in other diameters. I use a 32-inch diameter piece as an introductory tunnel in class, and I use several short lengths of smaller diameter conduit to keep the advanced dogs sharp and fast.

You should find that the hard part about teaching your dog to go through an open tunnel is already accomplished before you get to the regulation tunnel. Check some of the backyard ideas in Chapter 2, especially if your dog is uncertain. In introducing your dog to the real thing, just take it one step at a time and keep his confidence up and the pressure down.

Open Tunnel, Progression

STEP 1. Tunnel is completely compressed. Helper holds dog while you go to the other side. Coax your dog through and reward.

HINTS: Many dogs will be much more willing if you stabilize the tunnel from side to side to minimize rolling. Strong elastic stretch cords (bungie cords), passed through the tunnel and hooked together, are good for holding it tightly compressed and the ends wide open. Two cords per tunnel suffice.

If your dog needs extra reassurance, experiment to find out whether he prefers you to come into the tunnel toward him or hold a treat into the tunnel, whether he wants to see your face in the tunnel or whether he needs to see more daylight. Do whatever makes him comfortable, and don't spare the praise for each forward step he takes. Do not order him to come. Coax him but don't set him up for correction.

Some dogs do best when their handlers go through the tunnel with them a time or two, as they have you near for security and can still see

Fig. II. Don't work alone introducing your dog to tunnels...

Fig. III. ...or you can expect him to take the easy way out.

Carol restrains Tiger yet encourages him to pull toward the tunnel. Owner makes eye contact through tunnel aperture.

Tiger is intent on his handler and the cookie, so he doesn't balk at the strange feel and sound of the tunnel.

the light at the end. Entice and reward your dog's forward progress as necessary, and reward immediately upon his completion of the tunnel.

If your dog is looking at you over the tunnel or around it, the helper can touch the dog's nose with a finger and then point into the tunnel. The dog will often follow the finger and then see your face at the other end. The helper could cradle your dog from behind if he is hesitant but not really afraid.

An indecisive dog might go right through on the tail of another dog, so tunnels are great for group work. Often an obedience-trained dog will go through at once if his leash is draped through and then you call, but under no circumstances should the dog be pulled into the tunnel. Some dogs charge right through and some need to stutter-step a bit first. Let your dog work this out. If the dog is fearful, go back to hoops and tires, then very short lengths of wide makeshift tunnels until your dog is fast and fearless. Let the fearful dog watch confident ones go through and have fun.

As soon as your dog enjoys the obstacle, give it a name, such as "tunnel." This will become his command to go through any tunnel. Don't introduce your tunnel word while your dog is hesitant. Begin as soon as he likes the game.

STEP 2. Use longer tunnel. Same game plan, just more tunnel between your dog and you. Use your tunnel word each time. Work up to 8- to 10-foot tunnel length.

HINTS: Increase the length of the tunnel gradually. *Flexaust* tunnels are quite cooperative about posing in stages of partial extension. Others may need to be secured or at least may need the end held upright as you call your dog through.

Your helper should let your dog go through as soon as you give your tunnel command, such as "Tunnel" or "Go through" As your dog becomes bolder and pulls toward the mouth of the tunnel, the helper should let him go from slightly further away. Don't rush this, because some dogs who are zeroed in on the aperture are still dependent on the helper's hands and will go around the tunnel if the guidance is suddenly removed. The helper needs to read the dog's intent and give just enough help to ensure that the dog chooses to go in.

Some dogs need to remain on leash for this work, but it's nice to work off leash as soon as possible. Once your dog is trained to run to you when you call, you won't have to worry about trying to catch hold of his leash when he exits the tunnel. You'll be able to run and play with him as a reward for coming through. Food and other enticements are great motivators, but many of the best agility dogs are also motivated by pure fun, so you may not need treats for every trip through the tunnel any more.

Even when your dog is delighted with longer tunnels, do a very short one now and then to keep his speed and confidence up. Make sure to switch ends often, so your dog is comfortable from either direction.

STEP 3. Send your dog. As you approach the tunnel, give your dog a signal and his tunnel word, and get him started yourself. Then run around to greet him at the other end.

HINTS: It's prudent to shorten the tunnel again for this step. And, since you won't be there to steady the end, it's a good idea to secure it at the new length, or use your stretch cords with one hook attached to the mouth of the tunnel and the other end hooked to the exit. This way, 30-inch cords would secure a tunnel to a length of 30 inches, etc. You could also hook cords end to end to control longer tunnel lengths. Hooking the ends of a tunnel insures against an end falling forward flat on the ground, blocking the exit. That can be a real disaster for the dog who is less than brazen.

With helper in position, Brenda guides Tiger to short tunnel...

...sends him through...

...and quickly greets him at the other end.

Guide your dog with one hand and signal to the aperture with the other. As soon as you start your dog through, get to the exit. The helper is still stationed at the mouth of the tunnel but interferes only if your dog tries to avoid entering or turns around inside. Turning around in the tunnel happens often at this step, unless the tunnel is very short, because suddenly the handler's face is not there to greet the dog when he expects it.

When this happens, it's best if the helper simply blocks the opening when he tries to come back the way he went in, while you call out the tunnel word from the exit end. For repeated offenses, the helper should issue a matter-of-fact NO at the dog as well. It's better for you to remain the cheerful party motivating success rather than a disciplinarian.

Sometimes you should be on your dog's left side and sometimes on his right when you send him and greet him. He needs to get accustomed to being handled and taking direction from either side.

STEP 4. Gradually extend tunnel to full length. Begin by calling dog through as at first, then send your dog.

HINTS: After your dog is very reliable, begin to work without a helper, with the tunnel shortened again at first. Exaggerate your signal at first, pointing directly to the aperture. As the dog gets more and more sure of himself, begin to run several steps past the tunnel exit before rewarding him. If he's not fast, that will help speed him up, and if he's very fast that will help him keep an eye on you.

Fluffy acts on tunnel command and signal from a short distance.

Run past the exit to speed your dog up and teach him teamwork.

To keep him fast, remember to send your dog zipping through a short tunnel occasionally even after he's learned to do long ones. This also helps prevent dogs from getting into the habit of turning around in the tunnel. Some very small dogs even love to spin a few circles in there. Dogs who have time to dance around in the tunnel are not being challenged enough. It happens most often to handlers who are too slow getting to the other end, but that's not always the case.

Some dogs just take the time to turn a circle or two even with fast handlers. Either go back to shorter tunnels and concentrate on forward speed again by using a helper and enticement, or go immediately from the tunnel to another active job, an agility obstacle or any other job enjoyable to the whirling dervish. Reward the dog on completion of the subsequent activity. And you'll have to mix up these activities, or change the second agility obstacle regularly, or your little dynamo will become patterned to it. That could be a tougher problem. At any rate, it's easier to keep your dog's mind on getting out the other end of the tunnel if he has something exciting to do next.

Begin to introduce some lengths of tunnel in narrower and wider diameters and in different materials. This helps keep your dog's confidence high, too. It's surprising how many dogs who are fine with narrow tunnels are then afraid of large-mouth tunnels. To us, it seems that if they can get through a small one the large ones will seem easy. But some dogs seem to feel they're about to be eaten by a monster, and other dogs are more apt to turn around in large tunnels. It's a good idea to introduce as many different kinds of tunnels as you can to minimize the chance of your dog being fooled by someone else's choice of tunnel in an agility test.

Don't be ashamed to go back to short tunnels to work on a specific problem. If you don't own the tunnel that is giving your dog trouble, you can create one of your own (see Ch. 2) that will introduce the element of difficulty in a nonthreatening way.

A small tunnel keeps dogs fast and accurate. Dizzy is stopped as he emerges from an 18-inch-diameter.

STEP 5. Use full-length regulation tunnel. Gradually introduce tunnel bends. Then send your dog.

HINTS: From the tunnel entrance, check the amount of daylight coming through. Until you've done this many times, it's not easy to predict what your dog sees with the various bends. You need to let only part of the exit be out of sight at first. It often helps to shorten the tunnel when first bending it. Using a helper and calling your dog through from the other end can also remind him that it's the same job. And of course, the more unsure your dog is, the more gradually you should bend the tunnel.

Once your dog is confident with hairpin turns (which completely eclipse the exit hole) in both directions, then start introducing S-curves and extreme shapes. I like to secure two or more tunnels together. It's great to have a helper again when you first do this, so you can be waiting

*The dog gradually learns to go on signal from further away
and from more angled approaches.*

at the exit and calling your dog to an immediate reward. As his confidence is heightened, resume running past the exit and having him catch up to you.

It also improves your dog's tunnel confidence and his ability to scrunch down while running if you teach him to wriggle under things. Just coax him to crawl under with a cookie to his nose. You could call this a tunnel, or "under," or "crawl," etc. If he doesn't seem to understand, have him begin by lying down to get him low enough to see what you want.

Remember to review all sorts of tunnels, both short and long, wide diameter and narrow, to keep your dog fast and confident with the unexpected.

*Jinx heads for the open tunnel during the 1990 Pedigree final. This run made her the
U.S. national champion.*

Open Tunnel, Summary

Use your dog's favorite enticement every time at first to alleviate stress. As the dog becomes more comfortable and proficient with each step, use enticement less often on that step. Always praise your dog's first efforts and keep training sessions lively and fun.

Use a signal whenever you send your dog. Switch sides with your dog regularly to keep him accustomed to taking commands and signals from either side. Switch ends often as well, and move your tunnels to different locations, so your dog can get used to variations.

STEP 1. Tunnel is compressed. Helper holds dog while you go to other side. Coax your dog through.

STEP 2. Gradually lengthen tunnel. Use helper. Use your tunnel word. Work up to an 8- to 10-foot tunnel length.

STEP 3. Send your dog. Use helper to assist if dog turns around.

STEP 4. Gradually extend tunnel to full length. Using helper, begin by calling dog through at first. Once he's confident, begin sending him yourself.

STEP 5. Gradually introduce bends in the tunnel. Use helper and shorter tunnel length as necessary.

Closed Tunnel, Introduction: *Also called collapsed, or soft, tunnel*

During competitions, performances of the closed tunnel draw laughter from the crowd. People love to see a dog enter the open end and then watch the lump of dog as it travels down the length of chute and pops out the other end.

The dog must enter a rigid opening of approximately 20 inches in diameter and 30 inches in depth, often a fiberboard barrel with a locking lid ring. (Also popular in England as a rigid opening is a semicircular apparatus made from thin plywood or pressboard, flexed over a two-foot wide x three-foot long wooden base.)

Whatever the composition of this open end, the closed tunnel gets its name from a long cylindrical chute of fabric which has been firmly attached to the opening. The chute is about 12 feet long, generally made of canvas, plastic, rip-stop nylon, or even tough nylon net, gathered and secured to the rigid portion of the tunnel. It lies closed on the ground, and the dog is required to burrow through to the exit.

In competition, I have seen more problems with the integrity of collapsed tunnels than with most other pieces of agility equipment. One of my dogs is a large, rough competitor, so I have to spend extra time checking out closed tunnels for her sake. The staked rigid portion of a closed tunnel has come up off the ground, a seemingly well-secured chute has been ripped off its mooring, and a chute's anchored exit has been pulled out from the ground.

In each case, no one was negligent. The equipment looked fine, felt sturdy, and was properly set up. These things happen. A heavy dog slamming against the entrance at full speed will put much more strain on the obstacle than the handlers testing it prior to the competition.

Nowadays I try to test a closed tunnel by rocking the top of the entrance with both hands to try the anchoring. If the back of the entrance is also braced, so much the better. I also pull on the exit fabric to test the anchoring at that end, and straddle the chute just behind the rigid opening and pull on the top of the fabric with both hands. It has become common for clubs to leave the chute portion unstaked in some cases, a good practice in calm weather as long as it's straightened after every dog.

If the tunnel is reasonably secure but still not as strong as your dog, you may decide it's best to slow your dog and send him through carefully. You must also be ready to step in and get your dog out of trouble if he runs into course problems he can't solve. How to score such an intervention is the judge's problem, and should depend on case-by-case particulars.

If the closed tunnel is used indoors, care should be taken to secure the base to the matting with generous amounts of duct tape at the entrance and exit. It also helps to secure a nonskid surface, such as sponge matting, to the underside of the tunnel base to minimize slipping. The heavy closed tunnels, like those made to look like doghouses, are much more stable than open barrels and flexed plywood entrances. Even so, handlers of large aggressive tunnelers should plan to slow the dogs before sending them in because the closed tunnel indoors cannot be made especially stable.

The accepted materials for construction of a closed tunnel are extremely varied, so this obstacle requires that your dog be well versed in dealing with wood, metal, plastic, pressboard, and many weights of canvas, nylon and plastic tarp. The dog whose handler has not invented a few different closed tunnel games around the house may well take exception to some of the ones he finds in competition.

Many clubs invest in a high-quality regulation chute made of rip-stop nylon or coated canvas. Nylon is lightweight, but sticks to itself when wet. Direct sunlight eventually weakens the fabric. Coated canvas is heavier. It repels rain, but can concentrate heat, so choose a light color. Net materials are lightweight, non-stick, and cooler, but more prone to tangles. Each material has its advantages, so what is locally available often determines a club's choice. A chute is not difficult to sew (use very tough thread), and sailmakers, banner makers and larger fabric stores often stock suitable materials. One good source for ready-made chutes is Texas Canvas Products, 728 South Beltline Rd., Irving, TX 75060, telephone 214-790-1501.

Provided you can control your dog, tunnel confidence helps make an agility course run fast and fun. One way to help your dog become a bold tunneler is to develop his speed and confidence on all sorts of open tunnels before introducing the more claustrophobic closed ones. When your dog is ready for closed tunnel work, begin with a lightweight chute and graduate to heavier ones. Introducing a heavy chute too soon can slow your dog's pace.

He might think of a trip down the long heavy chute as a labor instead of a game unless you work him up to it in the spirit of fun and goodies. You can do some perfectly good introductory work using a sheet. Stay on Step 1 until you have found the trick to getting your dog through as fast and happy as he can go. The faster he goes, the more he'll like it, and whipping through this tunnel will speed his overall course time by a few seconds, too.

Closed Tunnel, Progression

STEP 1. Chute is folded back on itself to a six-foot length maximum. Helper holds dog while you kneel at exit end, hold open the chute, and call dog through with your tunnel word. Reward. Gradually drape chute onto dog's back as he comes through but keep the end wide open.

HINTS: This is treated much like square one of the open tunnel, except that we use the tunnel command right from the beginning. Because your dog is already familiar with the tunnel word and likes the work, it will help him understand what is wanted here.

This should go quickly once your dog accepts the feel of the material on his body. If you can't use a lightweight chute for this introductory work, make sure the heavy one is very short and gradually increase the weight of it on your dog's back. Holding the chute wide open at first is also very important.

Students work together to hold and motivate each other's dogs. Tessa heads through a short chute while Golda strains to follow.

Your dog should be speeding through the chute and bursting out the exit. This habit is formed early when you begin by showing him the opening at the end and offering an immediate and delicious treat on his arrival. Stand aside for him when he's charging through. If you have a regulation chute made, you may be able to get an additional short one, four feet or so in length, made with leftover material. It's great as an introductory teaching chute.

As with the open tunnel, the helper is guiding the dog by the collar, so you will be able to dispense with the leash quickly if your dog likes to be near you or at least will come running at once when you call. An agility leash or tab won't hurt, but the eventual goal is to work off leash, so it's nice to introduce that feeling early.

Some other obstacles will require much more leashwork than tunnels. If you still need to catch your dog's leash as he exits in order to keep him around, work separately on recall and leadership exercises as well.

STEP 2. Chute is folded back to six feet. Let the middle drape halfway to ground before calling your dog. Gradually let middle of chute touch ground, then more of the chute until it lies closed.

HINTS: It's time for the dog to begin doing more of the work. Now he has to have a little more faith in himself and be willing to push through to get out. Make this a gradual process, and give him a big cheer as he plows through the draped spot.

Continue to hold the end open when you first let the chute lay on the ground in the middle. Then let the middle third lie closed, then half, etc. Don't let yourself repeat the exercise to death in trying to do the whole step in one lesson. Several times through is enough, and your dog may need many lessons before he is ready to move on from here. Rushing it will cost more time, confidence, and trust than it's worth.

Once your dog is barreling through the closed tunnel, begin a variable schedule of rewards. He should still get a special reward often, but not every time. If your dog is not yet running through the tunnel, you need to go back to Step 1 and find a more effective reward system for your dog, or he'll get slower as the chute gets longer. Many dogs speed up if you drop the end and run ahead of them just as they get to the exit or throw a ball for them as they emerge. If this step isn't associated with lots of fun, your dog will slow down.

The rewards are for maintaining top speed so your dog gets into the habit of whipping through that material like a dog with a mission. Use rewards every time until your dog has that wild enthusiasm, then begin to wean him. Each time you increase the challenge, go back to using your enticement and repeat the process of weaning.

STEP 3. Chute is about six feet long, lying closed. Send your dog. Introduce signal.

HINTS: As with Step 3 of the open tunnel, run toward the entrance

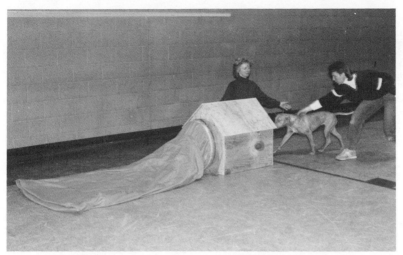

Max is sent through a short chute, with helper at the ready.

More freedom of choice — now the signal is emphasized, with handler and helper less obtrusive. Helper will block entrance once Max is inside.

with your dog and get him started yourself. Having mastered the open tunnel already, this should come easily. Remember to work both on your dog's right and his left to keep him comfortable with either side. Give an exaggerated signal with your free arm, pointing all the way to the aperture at first.

Your helper needs to be ready to block the entrance if the dog tries to turn back. Your own concern is to get to the exit end fast and greet your dog immediately with his favorite reward as he emerges. When your

Bach is eager to tunnel, so George remains ready but lets go of the collar early.

Wheee! Fast and happy is what you want.

dog is confident with this, begin to run past the exit a few strides, encouraging your dog to catch up with you for his reward. Then you could make it more interesting by darting a few strides left or right of the tunnel as your dog exits. Get him to emerge looking for you and running to catch up. This will keep your dog thinking ahead and will make it easy to go from the closed tunnel to the next obstacle on an agility course.

STEP 4. Peel chute back to an 8- to 10-foot length. Stand at exit and hold end open. Call dog and rest fabric on his back as he comes down the chute. Work up to full chute length.

HINTS: Because the closed tunnel is harder to do quickly than the open tunnel, get your dog well motivated for speed before he has to burrow through a long chute lying on the ground. You could throw his favorite toy for him as his head nears the exit. Throw the toy away from the tunnel to get your dog running out the exit and beyond. Don't throw toys and food into the tunnel. Food in the chute teaches the dog to vacuum the chute all the way down. Toys are also likely to slow him down, and often end up left in the chute. Better to fold the chute back to a shorter length and let your helper throw the toy all the way through, out the end you're holding open. Or hold the toy yourself and show it to your dog through

Brenda holds up only the end before calling. She will drop it and run when Max bursts through the middle section.

the open chute, then toss it away as he's emerging. Pretty soon he'll come flying, knowing that you're going to throw the toy.

STEP 5. Use full length of chute. Hold exit open, but stand back and drape middle of chute on ground before calling your dog through. Gradually stand to one side and let entire chute rest on ground.

HINTS: "Gradually" means over the course of one lesson for a few dogs, and over a couple weeks of lessons for others. Don't rush your dog's progress. Cheer your dog on when he pushes through, and reward often. To prepare him for tunneling the entire chute, begin to drop the fabric on him as he approaches the exit, and run away from him. When he catches up, he gets his treat.

Standing to one side helps your dog get used to not seeing you straight ahead as a target for his tunneling. He may try to take the more direct route to you, so your helper has to steady him going into the rigid opening.

Your dog may try to go around the tunnel when the entire chute is closed on the ground. Your helper has to be ready for this, too, and help the dog steer into the tunnel when you give the tunnel command.

Running past the exit can keep your dog running straight through the chute. This is Jiska.

STEP 6. Chute is at full length. Send your dog.

HINTS: Your helper's job is very important here. It's not uncommon for a dog who has been charging through a partially draped tunnel to balk or turn around when the whole chute lies on the ground and the handler is at the entrance. It's also natural for the helper to be taking your dog's reliability for granted by now, so it may come as a surprise if the dog changes his mind. A bad habit will quickly be formed if the dog is allowed to cut out. The helper should block the entrance if the dog turns around, and you should pick up the exit slightly and command again, followed by lots of praise as your dog makes his way through.

An exaggerated arm signal can help the dog decide to go through. Even so, as you taper off on your physical guidance a snag at this step should not be a big surprise, so don't be alarmed and don't let it get away from you. Review easier steps for a few days if it seems to be giving you too much trouble, but don't punish your dog. It's quite unlikely that your dog is trying to give you a hard time. Some dogs have a bit of trouble with confidence at this step and need extra time and remedial practice to get it all together.

STEP 7. Use full-length chute, preferably anchored. Begin angled approaches and then wind interference.

HINTS: When your dog has become very strong with the closed

tunnel, introduce an approach that is slightly less than straight on. The ultimate goal is to send your dog through the tunnel by calling the tunnel command and giving an arm signal toward the entrance. It would be foolish to go from a clear approach to an advanced oblique sendaway all in one step, so break that goal down into a gradual progression.

Just as you spend many lessons with the open tunnel going from straight to sharply bent, you need to take a comparable amount of time introducing the dog to an eclipsed entrance to the closed tunnel. You can't bend the rigid opening, so change your start point instead and send the dog from slightly off to one side, then the other, until he understands how to find the hole for himself from anywhere. Start with a clear approach. When that is fully learned introduce angles in the same step-by-step manner.

Sooner or later your dog may get tangled in the chute of a closed tunnel. Yank the exit wide open fast. Don't let him work it out for himself because his confidence could be damaged badly in a matter of seconds. Quickly show him out and give him a jolly greeting, jumping and playing with him to let him work off the stress of the ordeal.

I find that if the dog gets way off track in the chute, he can't usually make it right again just then. The dog gets used to accomplishing the closed tunnel in a certain way, charging straight ahead, so solutions which require finesse are not likely to occur to him in there. First, get him out

Steve Hooper

The advanced tunneler will need to handle angled approaches and flapping chutes, like Bandit is demonstrating.

and congratulate his efforts. Just for good measure, your next work should be with the chute shorter and your enticement ready.

Later, you may want to set up a tunnel lesson to introduce complications in a controlled way. Wind is a common troublemaker, and it can wreak havoc even with a chute well anchored at the exit. In competition, the judge should position the closed tunnel to minimize conflict with the wind, but it can still be flapping and canted off center as your dog goes through. It's so common to have the closed tunnel affected to some degree by wind that practicing for it should be considered standard preparation for outdoor competitions. Even chutes that are anchored by tabs all the way down both sides can still flap and make a lot of noise.

When your dog's training in a calm, closed tunnel is complete and he is delighted to run through without a helper and from any angle, you are ready to practice for wind. If you have windy weather, just position the tunnel to be mildly affected at first and begin with the chute short.

If you need to simulate wind problems, begin by having the dog wait at the entrance or using a helper to hold him. Hold the exit yourself and flap the chute as your dog comes through. Alternatively, let your helper flap the chute and you send your dog through normally, on the run. You could also anchor your chute offcenter or pull the top to one side as if the wind had sent it slightly off course.

The complications should not be practiced until your dog is brazen through a normal closed tunnel, but they can be quite a lot of fun and add a new dimension to your confident tunneler's ability.

Closed Tunnel, Summary

Use a favorite enticement every time at first to alleviate stress. As the dog becomes more confident and proficient with each step, use enticement less often on that step. Always praise your dog's first efforts, and keep training sessions lively and fun.

Use a signal along with your command whenever you send your dog. Switch sides with your dog regularly to keep him accustomed to taking commands and signals from either side. Move your tunnel to different locations so your dog can get used to all kinds of variations.

STEP 1. Fold chute back to six feet, or use introductory chute. Helper holds dog while you kneel at exit end. Hold chute wide open. Use tunnel word. Gradually drape chute onto dog's back as he comes through.

STEP 2. Chute is six feet long. Let middle drape halfway to ground before calling dog. Gradually let more and more of chute drape and touch ground.

STEP 3. Chute is six feet long, lying closed. Send your dog. Play games or throw a toy to keep the dog running through.

STEP 4. Chute is 8-10 feet long. Hold exit open. Call dog through and rest fabric on his back as he comes. Work up to full chute length of 12 feet.

Hannah charges through a 12-foot nylon chute. The exit was left loose; the entrance is held by the locking lid ring of a barrel bolted inside of the "dog house."

STEP 5. Use full length of chute. Hold exit open, stand back. Drape middle on ground before calling your dog through. Gradually let entire chute lie on ground, and stand aside.

STEP 6. Use full length of chute lying closed. Send your dog. Play catch-up games and throw toys to keep him running.

STEP 7. Use full length of chute, preferably anchored. Gradually introduce angled approaches and wind interference.

Tire Jump, Introduction: Also called hoop or tire

The tire jump is a combination of go-through and jump. The dog must jump through a tire or ring with an aperture of 15-24 inches. The tire is suspended in a frame to which it is secured top and bottom. In the U.S. and Canada, the bottom of the tire aperture is stationed at the appropriate division jump height. The tire's surrounding frame is generally constructed of wood, but metal and PVC pipe are becoming more popular. The most important feature must be sturdiness. The supporting framework must be very strong, with long "feet" to prevent tipping if the tire is hit hard from either direction. The rules also specify that the tire must be wrapped securely to prevent a dog from getting a foot caught in the gap. Some regulation tire jumps do not use standard tires, but use dryer venting hose and reinforced styrofoam circles.

U.S. regulations describe a minimum rim width of four inches all around the aperture of the tire, so a simple hula hoop would not be acceptable, nor would a narrow bicycle tire. A very popular tire for tire jumps is a motorcycle tire.

Most regulations do not specify that the dog must jump through the tire cleanly, and many smaller dogs do use the tire to push off with their hind feet. This actually takes slightly longer than jumping cleanly through,

It's not regulation equipment, but a stepladder can help Chips learn the basics.

and it's not less strain on the dog. Many big dogs have the opposite problem of rapping their feet on the tire when passing through, or hitting the top of the aperture with their backs. Add to that the problem, all too common among dogs of all sizes, of passing between the tire and the frame instead of jumping through the hole, and the simple tire jump presents its share of challenges.

Tire Jump, Progression

STEP 1. Tire is touching or nearly touching ground. Helper holds dog. You entice dog from other side and reward when he comes through.

HINTS: If you did not use a tire in your preliminary tunnel work, you may want to begin without using the frame. Just hold the tire between your knees, or have a helper hold it, and entice your dog through. If your dog really doesn't care for the thing, spend a good deal of time coaxing him back and forth through all different kinds of hoops and tires, until he can't help but associate this with good things. One person even attached a tire to the entrance of her dog's beloved crate, and soon he was going through tires without a second thought.

Improvising a tire jump frame can be done in the backyard. Your dog will need to be introduced to a regulation frame in order to become completely reliable about how to handle it, but a simple stepladder can be used to familiarize your dog with the basic job. Even hanging your tire from a tree limb and staking anchor ropes to the ground can serve to teach the fundamentals.

Whether you are using a frame or not a helper can be useful, just as in early tunnel training. It also often helps to have your dog on leash and drape that through the aperture before coaxing your dog through. Do not pull the dog through. If he's already proficient with leashwork, he will see where it is and will accept that you want him to go there. It's the enticement from the other side that makes it seem like a great idea, and your enthusiastic praise as he comes through will tell him he was right.

When you start using the tire suspended in the frame, let the tire rest on the ground for small dogs and raise it several inches for large dogs. If your dog is uneasy about this new contraption, put your face to the opening from the other side and clap your hands through the hole to encourage him to come there, or let him nibble a cookie during his forward progress. The goal is to minimize stress, so don't just order him to come to you. Do use a separate tire command as soon as your dog accepts the thing.

Some people use a tunnel command, such as "through," for the tire jump, but it's advisable to call it a separate name, like "tire." The tire jump is easily distinguished on the course and the dogs quickly learn to pick it out on command. Your dog can learn many individual obstacle names over time, and it's not unusual for a tunnel to be placed near a tire jump, which could be confusing if they are called by the same name.

The ready position is much like that for tunnels, with the handler enticing and making eye contact with Max through the aperture.

STEP 2. Tire is raised an inch or two higher for small dogs, three or four for large dogs. Helper holds dog. You entice dog through and trot backwards as he comes.

HINTS: Your helper can line the dog up and point to help him focus through the aperture instead of around it. The faster your dog comes through the tire, the faster you need to run backwards to keep his speed up. He'll probably get to you even faster if you fall over backwards. Dogs think that's the funniest trick in the book.

If you don't have a helper, you should be keeping your dog on leash for tire lessons for some time yet, using longer lengths as he learns. You and your dog must have wait training down pat in order to avoid frustration if you have no helper, since you must leave your dog on one side while you go around to the other. Drape the leash through. I much prefer the command "wait" rather than "stay" for this use, since you don't want to inhibit your dog by forcing him to hold still. It's better for him to be at the ready, just holding back in his own chosen position. If you tell him "wait" while he's in the sit position and he wants to pop up to stand in anticipation, that is fine if you've said "wait," and it lets the dog take an active part in his own preparation without disobeying you.

Even with a helper, the leash can still be a big help in these early stages. The tire jump is one of those things that people are apt to take for granted from the start, and that attitude can get your dog into big trouble. The job looks clear enough to us, but the dog often gets other ideas. It could save a lot of time and aggravation to begin at the beginning here. If your dog takes to the tire quickly, then these first steps don't take very long. Let your dog show you the timetable.

If your dog is very sensitive or very independent, a helper can be worth his weight in cookies by preventing early misunderstandings. It's a fine line the best helper must tread, getting the dog focused on the aperture and holding him back while keeping his forward enthusiasm strong. But if problems arise in spite of these efforts, neither of you should come down hard on the dog.

To give a helpful correction to the dog who ignores the leash and tries to go around the tire, hold tight to bring him up short before he gets by the apparatus, but do not scold him. Keeping the lead tight, go to the tire hole and stick your hand through from the exit side, even stick your head through if necessary, and encourage your errant student to approach the hole from the entrance side. Then use your charm and whatever else it takes to cajole him through the hole, and praise him with great enthusiasm for hopping through.

Handling a correction in this way, rather than by admonishing the dog, will actually improve his attitude about taking your directions. You come across as the trusty guide who teaches the dog his way out of a jam instead of the ogre who adds to the stress when things don't go right.

A little bit higher. Max decides to pick up two feet at once.

STEP 3. Tire is at same height as in Step 2. Send your dog. Begin to introduce signal.

HINTS: Your first send-throughs should be done from right in front of the tire rather than running by. Just pass your arm around the tire and hold a treat to the exit side if necessary. Entice him through and let him have his reward. If enticement is not needed, just run around the tire to meet him as soon as he hops through, to prevent his coming back to you between the tire and the frame. Start switching sides now, working on your dog's right sometimes and running around the right side of the jump, and other times working the same exercise from his left. He needs to be "ambidextrous" in Agility, and it comes more naturally if you start right away.

After perfecting this from directly in front, begin to stand back a little bit so you and your dog can run to the tire. Having your dog on an agility tab for this step makes it possible for you to increase gradually your hand's distance from the collar without losing your ability to guide the dog. It also makes it much easier for the helper to catch your dog if he tries to dart around the aperture as you do.

You could also perform this step on leash as long as you're holding it up out of the dog's way. You can guide him without pulling him. As your

Fig. IV. Pulling the dog through the tire results in the dog's bracing himself against it, mentally and physically. It's better to lower it and entice him through. The leash is to show him the correct path and prevent him from running around.

Fig. V. At this height the helper should start further back. To encourage a longer stride, your hand should back up as dog jumps through.

dog gets more eager and reliable, it's good to use a leash rather than a tab so you can give him that much more space between you without completely giving up guidance. The signal is given with either arm. Signal directly into the aperture.

As with tunnel work, the helper works with you to prevent your dog from changing his mind at the last instant when you run around the obstacle. You should greet your dog immediately with a reward when he completes the tire. As he gets comfortable with the job, begin to play the catch-up game like you did with the tunnels as a means of delaying the dog's reward and keeping him watchful and fast. Pretty soon, your running past becomes part of the reward, and that's to be encouraged.

Get this progression well in hand before raising the tire any higher. The bottom of the aperture is only several inches off the ground for the very small dogs and up a foot or so for large and jump-happy dogs. The exact height should be higher or lower depending on your dog, but not more than half of his eventual full jump height.

Whether your dog is a jumping fool or a timid jumper, this gradual progression is for helping the dog learn to enjoy going through the hole in the tire, and to get used to it. This develops his pleasure and general understanding of the obstacle before making him do the hard work of putting everything together.

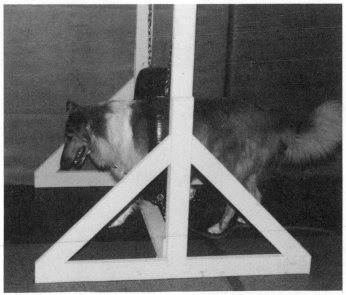

Casey practices from further away. This skill is begun early, positively, and with tire low.

Phoebe is one step back from the tire at 16 inches. She is confident at 14 inches, but unsure of herself about this.

Sherry's praise and backwards motion keep Phoebe coming forward, quite pleased with herself.

STEP 4. Raise tire another inch or two for small dogs, another two to four inches for large dogs. Start dog further back.

HINTS: This step is designed to teach your dog to jump a little higher, from a little further away. It is best to use a helper and/or a leash at first when you raise the tire height, since that is the easiest way to prevent mistakes. At this step, continue to drape the lead through the tire first, but stand your dog back a little further. Position yourself right in front of the exit hole, and run away or trot backwards as your dog comes through. Reward him when he catches up. Review the leash correction described in Step 2, as you are apt to need it a time or two before your dog decides to go through the tire every time.

After your dog is reliable about jumping through the aperture with you close to the tire, begin to position yourself back further, just a step or so. Use your agility leash draped through at first to remind your dog where to go. As he accepts your increased distance, gradually let the leash dangle more and stand back a bit further still. Now you have much less control, so you need a helper to make sure the dog goes through correctly, or you must be prepared to stop the dog with a sharp voice correction if he puts his nose between the tire and the frame.

If your dog is sensitive or not ready to take a sharp correction in stride, don't set him up for a possible mistake yet. Use a helper or a leash for many lessons, and send him through only a few times each lesson. As before, run away when the dog jumps through and reward him when he catches up to you. Also practice running to the right or left as he jumps through so he learns to come out of the tire prepared to change course. It may take weeks to bring your dog this far. Take your time.

After your dog is happy and reliable with all that on leash, go ahead and work off leash with the helper holding your dog near the tire. Some dogs need to be quite close to the tire at first, but the helper should gradually back away a bit as the dog learns, to improve his take off. You don't want the dog to come to a dead stop right before jumping the tire, as that will accentuate any tendency to hit the tire or step on it. As soon as the dog is reliable about jumping willingly through the tire, the helper can begin standing back a bit to give the dog another step to the tire before jumping. This is usually the most difficult step to master. Don't hesitate to lower the tire while you work on any reliability snags.

STEP 5. Tire is at same height as in Step 4. Send your dog.

HINTS: Use your dog's agility tab for this step, which is for teaching your dog to choose to go through the aperture on command no matter where you are. Exaggerate your arm signal and hold the signal all the way to the aperture at first. You could use a helper to hold the dog by the tab close to the tire as you stand to one side and send him through without touching him, or you could start a few steps back holding the tab and run up to the tire, then run around as he jumps through. As with tunnel work, the helper can prevent the dog from changing his mind at the last instant as you run around the frame.

Some dogs work better with one method than another, so you might like to try both, and add any variation that improves your dog's understanding. Either way, greet your dog quickly on the other side to prevent him from returning to get you. As he learns the job, work on either side of him and run around the jump one way, then the other.

As your dog becomes reliable with this, gradually give him more freedom to choose his own path. The helper stands back further and begins to let go sooner and sooner, or you start back further and let go sooner. Make sure you are giving the command by the time the dog is released. The faster your dog, the earlier he will need to be commanded and given the signal.

Now is when you might expect to see a few more mistakes happen if

Willie practices teamwork and turns at 20 inches, which is two-thirds of her regulation jump height.

the dog hasn't yet got it all together. Don't raise the tire any higher until you have taught your dog thoroughly about choosing to jump through the aperture rather than going around. You may have to issue some verbal corrections during this step, but if you've done your groundwork positively and thoroughly it should not upset your dog or confuse him. Don't hesitate to go back on leash or lower the tire and begin again directly in front of it.

Even though it seems unnecessary by now to tell your dog to wait while you drape a long leash through the tire and go around to call him through, it can prevent problems. Limiting the dog's margin of error at first is a means of showing him he can do it and putting him in the habit of doing it correctly. Otherwise, it's awfully tempting for him to follow the path you take or to pop between the tire and the frame without jumping through that little hole. Preventing mistakes initially at these lower heights is part of building your dog's tire confidence.

STEP 6. Raise tire gradually over many lessons to full height. Gradually eliminate leashwork, and send your dog.

HINTS: How quickly you increase the height of the tire depends on how correctly your dog performs the obstacle and how much he likes to jump. There is every reason to raise the tire no more than an inch per week with many dogs. Better to spend the time now than to find yourself months later with a dog who'd rather go over, under, or around the tire than through it. At each new height, use a helper whenever possible to

The important details of signals, sending the dog, and angled approaches are perfected at lower heights...

...and reintroduced from either side each time the tire is raised.

help guide your dog until he's ready and eager to hit that hole every time. After an introductory lesson at the new height, you and your helper should make your influence less and less obvious as the dog takes over the job.

You need to get your dog reliable about being sent through the tire on the run before you approach full regulation height. It's usually not good to have a large dog set up to hop through from a standstill once the tire is more than two-thirds of his full jump height. You don't want him to pop the tire jump rather than stretch out to get through it cleanly. A big dog who stops and hops through at full height is apt to hit his back on the top of the tire and land too sharply on his pasterns. A small dog is apt to jump onto the tire instead of through. So any reliability problems at this point should be met by a return to lower tire height for remedial work.

As your dog gets more sure of himself, begin to run past the tire frame and then turn sharply right or left for several strides. When your dog catches up to you, reward him. Also practice working him on your right as well as your left. Begin to give him blatant freedom of choice on your command to take the tire jump. Either congratulate your dog for jumping through or issue a reprimand the instant he begins to go incorrectly. It's bound to happen sooner or later.

Chances are, if you have been conservative in your earlier training and have taught your dog to enjoy the tire jump, he will not try to get out of it very often. That may not make his later mistakes any less frustrating, but you'll have fewer of them, and be well equipped to offer remedial training. You could review the exercises you know at lower tire heights, or even drape a long leash from your dog through the tire and back around to you. If he jumps through, great. Just let go and meet him.

If he tries to go around, pull him up short the way you would have in Step 2, even though you're now starting from the same side as your dog. Without scolding, just hold tight to the leash to prevent your dog from feeling too pleased about the alternate route. Take him by the collar and quietly put him back where you started, and repeat the opportunity. Greet a correct performance with extra enthusiasm.

If he chooses incorrectly a second time, correct him as above. But instead of repeating the exercise, now have him wait on one side while you go to the other to review. For persistent cases there are ingenious tricks like wrapping invisible fishline between the tire and the frame or putting a piece of plexiglass or cellophane across. But before you resort to countermeasures like these, ask yourself if you have really done enough of the basic groundwork. It may be that you should go back to an earlier step and work up more gradually.

If your dog hasn't had much experience with different kinds of tire jumps, now is the time to introduce him, at low heights initially, to all kinds and colors. The tires he meets in competition will vary greatly in

A helper and enticement are used again for early full-height work, keeping the job familiar and the dog relaxed.

size of aperture, size of tire, wrapping arrangement, and even framework. Just as a large tunnel opening might make a dog ill at ease, a wide tire-jump aperture can give him second thoughts too. And if your dog was trained using a wide hole you will certainly need to acclimate him to narrow ones.

The more variety he accepts, the better. For all the room for interpretation and expression in the regulation tire jump, it really is just the same task. Once your dog understands that, the variations on the theme make them even more fun.

Tire Jump, Summary

Use your dog's favorite enticement every time at first to alleviate stress. As the dog becomes confident and proficient, use enticement less often on that step. Always praise your dog's first efforts and keep training sessions lively and fun.

Use a signal along with your command whenever you send your dog. Switch sides with your dog regularly to keep him accustomed to taking commands and signals from either side. Switch the direction in which your dog is jumping, and move your tire to different locations so your dog can get used to variations.

Leashwork can be very helpful in teaching the tire, with or without a helper. See progression and photos.

STEP 1. Tire is near or touching ground. Helper holds dog while you go to other side. Coax your dog through. Introduce tire command as soon as dog enjoys the obstacle.

STEP 2. Raise tire one to two inches higher for small dogs, three to four inches for large dogs. Helper holds dog. Entice your dog through and trot backwards as he comes.

STEP 3. Tire is at same height as in Step 2. Send your dog. Introduce signal.

STEP 4. Raise tire one to two inches higher for small dogs, three to four inches for large dogs. Helper holds dog further back. When dog is confident, stand back slightly.

STEP 5. Tire is at same height as in Step 4. Send your dog. Perfect the exercise on the run before raising tire higher.

STEP 6. Raise tire gradually over many lessons to full height.

Melissa Lee Harris

The mighty Moulty is in command of the tire.

6

THE GO-UPS

The higher your structure is to be, the deeper must be its foundation.
—St. Augustine

There are four go-up obstacles: the A-frame, the dog walk, the crossover, and the seesaw. In addition to requiring the dog to go up and come down via ramps or planks, the go-ups incorporate a safety area at the bottom of each end, called a contact zone, into which the dog must step if he is to complete the obstacle without faults. There's nothing different about a contact zone, except that it's painted a contrasting color for ease of identification. The zone is required as a safety measure to prevent handlers from allowing their dogs to leap on and off a go-up obstacle rather than go all the way up and down.

The contact zones on the dog walk, crossover, and seesaw are each 36 inches. The steeper A-frame has contact zones of 42 inches. The more Agility courses the dogs run the more important the zones are, for soundness as well as scores. The cumulative effect of ignoring this safety measure would be broken-down dogs. There are two contact zones on each piece of go-up equipment, and five course faults are assessed for each one missed. Since there are at least three and sometimes four go-up obstacles on a competition course, the faults for jumping over the zones add up quickly.

It's important to think about zone training even when you're working on downscaled or backyard go-up equipment with no painted zones. Your training techniques should instill in the dog the habit of getting onto the go-up from the end rather than hopping on from the side or leaping from the end to the top. The basic stance suggested for introduction to inclines is shown here.

The handler stands beside the dog, ready to serve as a leaning post whenever the dog wants one. One hand holds the flat collar, reassuring

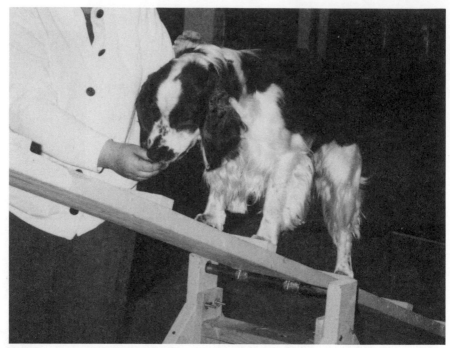

Handler reassures the dog with voice and body, and uses enticement to keep him relaxed and moving forward in correct position.

the dog without pulling him off balance. The other hand offers an enticement, held low and in the middle of the plank. The hands are quiet and relaxed, ready to help but not interfering. This basic position fosters confidence and accuracy from the start. As the dog gains proficiency he is gradually given more leeway, and thus more room for error.

If you concentrate on guiding your dog so he is comfortable going all the way from end to end, he will accept it and form correct habits, but if you grant zone responsibility to your dog too soon don't blame him for choosing a different course of action. Going all the way up and down requires some patience, and most dogs, like most people, are in a hurry.

The sport of Agility rewards speed, but only if accuracy is not lost. So don't dampen your dog's forward thinking, but do develop certain habits to keep him safe and accurate on the go-up obstacles.

A-frame, Introduction: Also called A-Ramp, or Scale

The A-frame is constructed of two sides, each three feet wide and nine feet long. In competition, the hinged apex is set at a height of six feet three inches, making the angle between the sides approximately 90 degrees, and the ascent and descent angles about 45 degrees to the ground.

The dog must scale this obstacle, up one side and down the other, touching 42-inch contact zones at the bottom of both sides. (The Canadian group ADAC has used an A-frame with eight-foot-long sides at an apex of six feet three inches. That makes ascent and descent angles much steeper, about 51 degrees to the ground, with the angle at the apex about 78 degrees.)

For stability, each side of the A-frame must be braced underneath. The hinged ramps are secured to each other about three feet from the bottom with chain or wood. The ramp surfaces are equipped with horizontal slats of wood (for the dog to use when climbing) about every 12 inches. These cleats are usually made from 1"x2"x3' strips of lumber. The ramp surfaces are roughened, usually with a dusting of sand between coats of paint, for limited additional traction. The end result should feel like fine grade sandpaper, not smooth but not coarse.

"Put 'er there, Vallie, hit the zone, ol' pal, right here, easy, name your price, Val, put 'er there..."

A few years ago I decided to use a training A-frame with no sand at all. That ensures that my dogs, and my students' dogs, all learn to use the cleats right from the start. Though we can't use that A-frame in competition, it's good for class work. To teach your dog proper scaling techniques for the A-frame, the cleats are more important than the sand paint. If you want an easier obstacle, space the cleats closer together. I have one small A-frame with no sand in the paint and cleats just 6 inches apart.

If you decide to build a large A-frame, you might just as well build a regulation one using plans from your national organization. It will get lots of use and can be taken apart for storage. It's not that much less work to build it to lesser specifications, and, since you can adjust a good one to any height, including completely flat, there is no need to start with a down-scaled version.

Your dog, even a young pup, can begin A-frame training right away, and you don't need a regulation obstacle for the first try. A basic incline can be fashioned at home by leaning ramps up steps. (Many public buildings have outside ramps nowadays, and practicing there will improve your dog's social skills and ability to tolerate distraction. If your dog is afraid of people, you'll have to go on Sundays until he's confident.)

Used or imperfect doors or plywood can be hinged together to make a fairly stable incline by resting the apex on a sawhorse, hay bale, barrel drum, or cinder blocks (see Ch. 2). It's helpful to practice inclines with your dog in a casual way to keep it fresh and fun.

Many students like the A-frame best because it looks so difficult but is learned so easily. A regulation A-frame that is adjustable is great for learning. Start with it flat and raise it gradually over several weeks. That helps keep the dogs accurate on the contact zones as their confidence develops. Dogs who are taught early on to charge and leap at the thing develop bad zone habits.

Training on the A-frame is greatly enhanced by group work. The more confident dogs are invited to go across first and are praised wildly as they succeed. That makes it much easier for others to follow and learn how it's done.

A-frame, Progression

STEP 1. A-frame is flat or nearly flat. Let dog check it out. Use enticement to lead him over the obstacle.

HINTS: The first task is not so much to get the dog over the obstacle as to make him comfortable with the thing. Let your dog teach you what works to relax him on the A-frame if he's nervous. Find the positive inducement that motivates him to traverse the obstacle with pleasure. The dog's confidence will tell you how much enticement to use, and his personality will tell you how silly he needs you to be. Have your enticement ready, and always congratulate your dog's first efforts.

In addition to food and toys, effective enticements may include: walking on the A-frame with your dog; sitting on the A-frame with your dog and petting him while he relaxes, then walking him off; having a second person hold him while you come to the apex from the other side, then calling him to you; playing on the A-frame with a trained dog while your dog watches. Use anything to help your dog relax and anticipate pleasure while on the A-frame. One note of caution: The lower the apex of your A-frame, the more force the hinges must bear. Support the middle or put an upended cinder block under each side.

As soon as your dog is comfortable on the A-frame, name the obstacle. If you always call this "A-frame" your dog will learn the name by hearing you say it each and every time you direct him onto it. Don't name the obstacle until your dog enjoys it because you want to be sure he is happy to hear the command. As with the go-throughs, practice from the beginning and at each step with the dog on your right as well as on your left.

Using guidance and enticements, teach your dog from the start to begin in the contact zone and go all the way up and down in the middle of the obstacle. If it is your practice to start him low in the zone, steer him to the middle and keep him happy there, and it will be easier to teach

Dodger is ready for a slightly elevated A-frame. He is young and large, his muscles immature, so he should not be sent up very steep inclines.

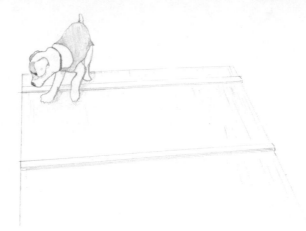

Fig. VI. What's this youngster doing unsupervised up this high? Lack of fear is often accompanied by lack of sense at this age. Don't expect him to stay in the middle of the ramp, or even on the obstacle, by himself yet.

him to do these things himself as he takes over. At first, use an enticement– whatever it takes–to get him to hit the zone and to keep his body centered on the A-frame. If you walk up with him, you must be to one side for him to have the middle of the ramp.

It's best to work at first with a helper if the work takes your dog off the ground. Your helper shares responsibility with you, but the one holding the enticement usually has more control over the dog's position. Just hold the goodie in front of your dog, and keep it in the middle of the ramp as you move it up one side and down the other. If you are much shorter than six feet, you need to develop your dog's feel for the middle of each ramp early or prepare to stand on a pause table later, as you will not be able to reach him at the apex from the ground for remedial guidance at regulation height.

STEP 2. Apex is raised gradually to about three feet for small dogs and four feet for large dogs. Raise only when dog is ready. Also practice "wait," going up and coming down.

HINTS: Remember, fast is not necessarily confident. If your dog wants to run across the obstacle, he may simply be trying to get off quickly. In that case, you need to keep the A-frame lower and spend more time building confidence. A confident dog is pleased to be on the obstacle and may easily be taught to wait at any point during his performance.

This is a good time to use your dog's wait training. Use his agility leash or collar to stop him (don't jerk him, just stop him) partway up, while he's still touching the contact zone, and command "wait." Praise him and let him nibble a treat or pet him while he's standing still.

The A-frame should still be low enough so this presents no physical difficulty for him. It's better to raise it no more than a foot each session, to make sure your dog gets a feel for the obstacle and builds his strength and accuracy along with his confidence. That will make it easier for him to climb properly when the A-frame is steeper. Also remember to keep your dog acclimated to having you work on either side of him.

With very fast dogs, or dogs with contact-zone problems, practice waiting more than once on each trip over the A-frame. As you tell your dog to wait, entice his attention down. Walk him all the way down to the ground, with your hand in his collar at first, to prevent him from jumping off partway down.

You should reward the dog while he's waiting until he is very comfortable with the new twist, and then gradually delay the reward until he's well into the downside contact zone. Don't start off delaying the treat until he's off the obstacle because it's being in the zone that you're trying to reward just now. You could also use food tidbits placed strategically on the downside and into the contact zone.

When your dog is at home with the A-frame, introduce an arm signal to direct him to the contact zones, both going up and coming down. At first, you may need to hold his collar or tab with one hand to control his accuracy while you signal with the other. Gradually give the signal from further away.

Anchor works with less and less assistance at the familiar height before the A-frame is raised again.

STEP 3. Continue to monitor dog's enthusiasm and accuracy. Gradually raise A-frame higher.

HINTS: Don't take your dog's early success as a promise that he won't have problems later. Some days the A-frame just looks more imposing than other days. When you raise the A-frame, try to show your dog how

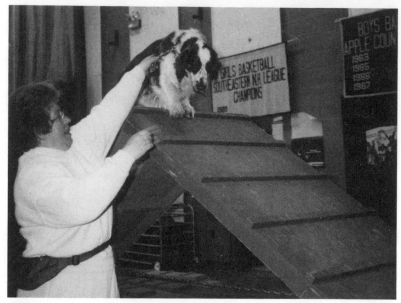

Chips is introduced to a five-foot apex. Sandy can barely reach his tab, but his good working habits are already established.

the obstacle is accomplished at that new height, either by clambering up yourself or having another human or a dog demonstrate.

If you walk over the A-frame at each new foot of elevation, you will understand how differently the obstacle needs to be handled as the angle becomes steeper. The dog needs to lean forward and use his hindquarters much more forcefully as the apex goes up. If the obstacle is raised gradually and the time schedule is leisurely, your dog will take this all in stride.

If you rush the raising of the A-frame your dog will either slip back or fear that he might fall. That unsteady feeling comes from not using his rear muscles properly for propulsion. Once he has that feeling of falling back, he will compensate by either balking at the obstacle or by jumping onto it.

Many medium and large dogs develop lasting problems touching the required contact zones because they have the habit of jumping onto the obstacle in order to feel secure about getting to the top.

For most dogs this is a confidence problem. A dog may look brave when he's leaping on like that, but it is usually accompanied by insecurity about trotting on slowly. It's good to spend extra time with the apex just high enough to require your dog to propel from the rear rather than simply walk up. The smaller your dog, the lower the apex is when this transition needs to take place.

Keep your training positive. Use enticements and focus your dog's attention low and to the middle. Large dogs should trot onto the A-frame putting a front foot in the contact zone. They need to use the muscles of their hindquarters to propel them and use their feet on the cleats to give them traction.

Small dogs should run onto the A-frame using both their hindquarters and their forequarters to push off from cleat to cleat. The very small dogs cannot scale the A-frame without using the cleats effectively. Their momentum alone will not be enough to carry them to the top, and a proper A-frame does not have a surface rough enough to afford traction without using the cleats. There's another sort of jumper, one we don't want to lean forward on beginning a go-up because when he leans it's at 30 mph. Some jump-happy dogs just plain love to jump onto anything. They are not necessarily crazy until it comes to the opportunity to fly through the air. Superdog sees the A-frame as just another tall building to be leaped in a single bound. Some of them, notably the sighthounds, can literally jump to the apex from the ground. These wonderful jumpers can rack up 30 or 40 faults per course run on contact zones alone without lacking a speck of confidence.

It is not enough just to teach these dogs to trot onto the A-frame. Their trotting strides are so strong that they often put their first foot above the zone and hop their back feet past it. They are not being stubborn and they are not afraid of the steepness. It's their natural way. They are shot from guns. They are so spring-loaded and well coordinated that they bounce from the ground to the apex without even thinking about it, so walking them onto the equipment is sometimes not enough. Even with your hand in the agility collar, some of these dogs can miss the zone.

Brumfield Studios

BB scales the A-frame at regulation height, showing the power required of tiny dogs.

If the dog is also sensitive, as is often the case, and you lose your patience or come down with a heavy correction, the dog is apt to respond with indecision or balking at the A-frame, a result of worrying about the correction he anticipates. That probably means he does not understand how to do it your way, or maybe even what your way is. You are fighting nature here, and you would be smart to use a positive approach if you'd like to keep the dog working with you.

Dogs who leap like gazelles have to be taught to make their first steps onto the contact obstacles small steps. If the dog likes food it's a simple matter to put a few well-placed tidbits in the zone and up the A-frame, or hold his agility collar with one hand and an enticement down low with the other.

Something he finds hard to resist (like a white plastic bag if he's a lure courser, or a cloth with animal scent on it if he's a hunter) can be used to get his mind off the apex and focus him down where you need him. Using one person on either side, each with a guiding hand in his collar or on a tab, can help him get the idea. Praise lavishly the mincing first steps you want him to take.

Although most contact zones are painted a bright, contrasting yellow, some color contrasts are easy for people to see but not clear to dogs, so the handler should accompany the "hit it" command with a signal aimed at the zone as well. Any trick that makes your dog happy to work well in the contact zone is fine.

Hoops of all sorts can help Zapper learn correct zone habits, which should be patterned before the A-frame is raised to full height.

Vixcie enjoys some extra wait training in the zone. This apex is set at about five and one half feet.

It's important to keep the A-frame at the dog's transition height for a long time so he will develop proper skills and habits. Make sure the dog is happy to take a small first step onto the obstacle, placing his foot on the first or second cleat up before you raise the A-frame slightly higher.

It's hard to make yourself work slowly with the A-frame when you know your dog can practically leap over the whole thing end to end already, but then that's the problem. You would pay later in accuracy much more than it will cost you now in time and pride to work conservatively.

STEP 4. Gradually raise A-frame to full height, six feet three inches at apex. Further improve control for contact zones.

HINTS: Many dogs are trained to stop at the top of the A-frame while the handler runs to the down side, then coaxes the dog down slowly, step by step. This is good for dogs who are at once extremely quick and extremely difficult to control. It's better than having the dog leap off from above the contact zone.

It's better to train your dog to wait halfway down the other side. Lots of dogs who come to a complete stop at the apex seem to freeze for the camera and spend an extra few seconds or more enjoying the view.

If your dog is well trained to wait on command, teach him to pause after crossing the apex, and come down slowly the rest of the way. Pausing at the apex seems to encourage looking up and about, while pausing partway down encourages looking down, which is better for zone training.

Extra wait training on the downside contact, from both the left and the right sides, is helpful for all dogs, but the very quick and the very independent ones need it much more intensely than others. Be positive, not punishing about it.

If your dog is not too fast or is easy to control, teach him to slow down without coming to a stop on the A-frame. Point to the zone and give your chosen "slow down" word. My favorite is "easy." I continue to use "wait" as a stronger control if the dog is especially wild on the run, but "easy" is a word my dogs are accustomed to in other sports and around the house. For us, it means either "calm down" or "slow down." It does not mean "stop."

You can teach this word to your dog by trotting with him on leash and slowing down as you tell him "easy," then speeding up with "let's go" or "OK" and repeating the pattern. When you are running an agility course, the command for the next obstacle will be your cue for the dog to take off again.

In competition, all that has to touch the zone is any part of the dog's foot. But during your practices you need to train your dog to perform go-ups all the way from end to end. In the excitement of competition you will probably get less accuracy than at home, and contact-zone penalties are costly and common, especially for the bigger dogs. Small dogs are often not trained with an eye to the zones because they so seldom miss them at home, but I have seen even tiny dogs leap off above the zones in competition, sometimes to the amazement of their handlers. Good habits are formed at home, so don't neglect zone training.

A-frame, Summary

Use your dog's favorite enticement every time at first to alleviate stress. As the dog becomes more confident and proficient, use enticement less often on that step. Always praise your dog's first efforts, and keep the training sessions lively and fun.

Switch sides with your dog regularly to keep him accustomed to taking commands and signals from either side. Switch ends often as well, and move your A-frame to different locations, so your dog can get used to variations.

STEP 1. A-frame is flat or nearly flat. Let dog check it out thoroughly. Coax dog over the obstacle.

STEP 2. Raise apex little by little; raise only when dog is ready. Apex is about three feet high for little dogs, four feet high for big dogs. Practice wait training going up and coming down. Introduce arm signal.

STEP 3. Gradually, as dog is ready, raise apex higher. Continue to encourage dog's enthusiasm and accuracy.

STEP 4. Gradually raise apex to full height. Further improve control training.

Dog Walk, Introduction: Also known as the balance beam

The dog walk is indeed the balance beam of dog Agility, made up of

Brownie trots merrily across the dog walk. Extra supports under the planks add stability and minimize bouncing.

three narrow planks and two raised supports. The dog must go up in a specified direction, traverse the raised plank, and descend the plank on the other side. There is a contact zone 36 inches long at the bottom of each side plank. The dog must touch both zones in order to perform the obstacle without faults.

Each of the three planks is about 12 feet long and 10 inches wide. They are hinged to special, tall, sawhorse supports and the hinge pins are removable for dismantling the obstacle. Two of the planks are end ramps, each secured to a sawhorse by one end and resting on the ground with the other end.

These end ramps have cleats every 12-15 inches for climbing. The top plank is laid horizontally and attached to the tops of the sawhorses, anywhere from four feet to four feet six inches off the ground. It is not cleated, but is treated with a light coat of sand in the paint for traction.

Downscaled dog walks should be practiced before introducing the regulation walk, as it is not always easy to predict which dogs will have trouble handling the real thing. The introductory materials I use most are:

• Cinder blocks
• One 2"x12"x8' long plank, sand-painted on one side
• Two 2"x10"x8' long planks, sand-painted and cleated every 12"-15"
• Two double sawhorses or other low stanchions

Dog Walk, Progression

STEP 1. Plank is set up a foot or so off the ground. Walk beside dog. Entice as necessary and reward while he's still on the plank, then walk him off the other end. Introduce "straight ahead" command.

HINTS: The first planks you use should be about 12 inches wide, set on cinder blocks, or any nonslippery support. Ideally, they should be painted, with sand in the paint to afford good traction and resemble the footing on a regulation dog walk. Be ready to help your dog with a hand in his agility collar and your body next to his midsection in case he wants to lean. Hold an enticement in the middle of the plank right in front of his nose for extra motivation. Make sure you teach him from the start to accept guidance and direction from you on either side of him.

I recommend practice on a sand-painted plank on the floor only if the dog is both extremely skittish with new surfaces underfoot and is also afraid of steps. Then you would want to practice the surface and the height separately before putting them together. If you want a lower raised starting point for any dog, a bed of bricks under each end of the plank makes a good support.

A small dog can be started just like a big one, since the planks seem a lot wider to a little dog and he won't have the weight to bounce the plank much. The hardest part of guiding a tiny dog is keeping a finger in the agility collar. He may remain steady with just a little upward tautness on an agility leash. Straight up, or you'll encourage him right off the plank. And don't pull.

If the little devil keeps jumping off, you'll need to get down there with your hands. Your forearm can also steady him instead of your leg or hip. If you can't bend down, try holding a yardstick on the other side of him and keeping your leg close to his near side. Your tiny dog needs to run up the regulation dog walk, so don't let yourself jerk him back when he scampers along. Just use the same positive inducements and guidance as big dogs get to keep their self-image strong.

Seventeen-pound Lynn and 110-pound Anchor practice on a low plank, a prerequisite for agility go-ups.

Most dogs have no aversion to trotting along the raised single plank. If your dog doesn't like the plank, start with two planks laid together. Fasten a cord or two around them, or nail them, to prevent a separation.

One training method calls for gradually separating two planks. The dog begins by walking with one side of his body on each plank, but as the gap gets wider he eventually chooses one or the other. The dog's assurance on the planks dictates the separation schedule. Some dogs put a lot of sideways pressure on the planks this way, making it difficult to keep them steady. Done carefully, so the planks don't part suddenly and leave your dog spread-eagled, this system is fine for many dogs.

Avoid initial plank supports with uneven surfaces, as this will cause the plank to wobble. Let the plank wobble only after your dog knows what he's doing and loves it. In fact, when your dog is really confident, use a hand or foot to make the board bounce while you give your dog a treat and praise him. Gymnastic mats, the ones which fold up in sections, are great for these early plank exercises. Just lay the plank from one mat to the other, and position the folded mats closer together or further apart to adjust the length of the open traverse.

No matter how confident the dog, I don't like to go straight to the regulation dog walk without introductory steps because its too easy for the dog to have a scare or a fall. It only takes a short time to give him a good sense of the dog walk down low first. And there's a lot you can teach your dog at this step, such as how to balance when the plank bounces or wobbles and to continue straight ahead on command.

When your dog is really comfortable with the raised plank, introduce a command to send him straight ahead. It will be easy for him to learn, since the plank only goes in one direction. This command will help him learn to complete plank obstacles ahead of you, thinking forward instead of holding back, and it will make it so much easier to teach him the crossover directions later. I use "go ahead" for this.

Some dogs need more practice being off the ground than others, and many larger dogs dislike the bounce of the board. The weight of your dog, the bounce in his stride, the thickness of your plank, and the distance between supports will all contribute to the spring in the board as your dog walks the plank.

The flexing is most pronounced in the middle of the crossing, so that's where many dogs decide to bail out. Better to get your dog accustomed to this obstacle down low, and introduce height a little later, when he's sure of his balance.

STEP 2. Use inclined planks with support about two feet high that holds one plank up and another down. Walk beside dog; let him lean. Use enticement, and reward while he's on the planks.

HINTS: It's very helpful to have a sawhorse with double bars at the top for this step, and it's not difficult to make one (see Appendix). Or

Fig. VII. Plank work is no place for a tight leash. It can suddenly pull the dog off balance. Use your hand in his collar and/or an enticement to slow him down, if necessary.

you could hinge two planks together end to end, and prop them over a sturdy conventional sawhorse.

To guide your dog and help him remain steady on the planks, keep your hand in his agility collar. It may take some practice to coordinate one hand in his collar, the other hand out front with your enticement, and your body beside the dog to steady him. It might help to place tidbits on the planks before guiding your dog over the obstacle.

Food helps prevent stress, which, although displayed differently from dog to dog has certain classic signs, including tail tucked, ears back, panting, averting the eyes, and sometimes avoidance of food. If your dog can make the trip up and down this downscaled obstacle following an enticement, eating goodies or playing with a toy as he goes, then you know he is not worrying unduly about the task. Use fewer tidbits as his confidence grows. Then begin using rewards to teach him to wait on command both going up and coming down, as with the A-frame. Once he's comfortable with the apparatus, begin to work on his left as well as his right.

From the very start give the dog a clear approach and guide him onto the plank from the very end. This must become his habit. Hopping onto the plank partway up and jumping off partway down is not safe and is heavily penalized in competition.

Leaping onto the plank with all fours shows confidence and is one of

Working gradually, even with confident dogs like Blade, helps develop cooperation and zone reliability.

the happier dog-walk problems to face. It should not be corrected at this time. Rather, make a mental note to issue more guidance using the collar and perhaps enticements to help the dog focus down low at the ends of the planks. This will slow the dog down for the time being but will keep his confidence high and his attitude positive. His speed will return very easily, and he'll be better able to handle it.

Some dogs have no interest in hopping onto the plank and will walk their front paws up the plank while sticking to the ground with the back feet. These dogs lack confidence on the narrow incline and need to be helped, sometimes with a lower incline at first. Introduce a variety of gentle climbing challenges in different locations until your dog is ready for the real thing.

Let him watch you serve as helper for dogs who climb well and ignore him while you make much of the climbers. Have a helper hold your dog at the bottom of the up plank while you lean over the sawhorse from the other side and entice him up. Your helper can walk alongside. His fears are not his fault, so accept them as valid and devise intermediate goals to get him to the skill level you'd like him to have.

Most dogs lose their fear if a wider ramp is used rather than single planks, especially if they've already gained proficiency on the A-frame and on the raised horizontal plank. Start by leaning a wide plank or double planks against a low stable object such as a concrete well cover, picnic bench, low porch or deck, large telephone spool, bale of hay, or folded gym mat.

Be sure to brace or stake the ends of the plank so it doesn't slip down. Using a platform can alleviate a dog's nervousness about climbing because he can see an object to get to and stand on at the top. As your dog becomes confident with this have him walk down the plank again.

Once he's no longer afraid to climb to a platform surface, then lean your planks against low supports with no walking surface, like stacked cinder blocks, a fallen log, or milk crates. Some supports will be slippery, so you'll need to secure the top and bottom of the plank against sliding.

At first, let your dog scramble up and hop off the other side until he's convinced of his safety. Next, start asking him to pause, stopping a few times on each trip up the plank until he can relax and enjoy himself. Then go back to the up-and-down planks as before, preferably with a helper for additional side support in case your dog wants to lean both ways or jump off.

A helper on the other side of your dog can make the difference for a dog who feels unhappy about going up and down these planks. The helper should position himself at the dog's midsection, be ready to support the dog's hindquarters and forequarters, and stroke the dog if that helps. Both of you should be aware of the dog's feet, since it's still easy to step off the narrow plank. Sometimes the helper doesn't have to touch the dog at all; just walking alongside may give the dog enough security. There should be no forcing, just cajoling.

If the dog refuses but does not seem overly fearful, and he's not too large, pick him up and put him on the down ramp a few feet from the bottom. Have him begin by walking off instead of walking on. In most cases, this approach helps dogs feel in control and capable.

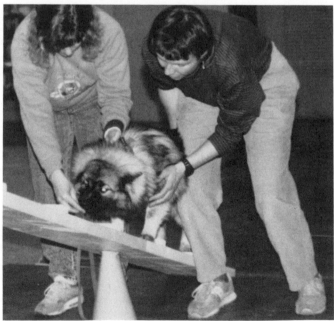

Keesha wanted extra moral support. A cookie for every step was an incentive bonus, and she quickly became confident.

More confidence deserves more independence, but still lots of encouragement. The leash is held up so as not to disturb Zak's balance.

Lift him a little higher each time until you are placing him at the top and he comes down on his own to your enthusiastic praise. Then you can usually entice him to walk the up ramp to that now-familiar spot; if not, place him near the top on the up ramp, and use that system until little by little he has mastered the contraption.

Once your dog is happy and competent with this exercise, introduce your arm signal with a command such as "dog walk." This is done the same way you accomplished it on the A-frame. Or the signal could be introduced in conjunction with Step 3.

STEP 3. Use two stable supports, from two feet to two feet six inches high, with 8- to 12-foot long planks up, across, and down. Introduce arm signal and "wait." Practice "go ahead."

HINTS: Once your dog is relaxed and capable with all your ingenious variations on Steps 1 and 2, this downscaled dog walk should present no real problems. It's a good idea at first to arrange a support under the middle of the cross plank if it's at all bouncy.

As your dog's confidence is established, lower this additional support little by little, allowing increasing amounts of bounce until the board is allowed to spring naturally. At first, continue to guide your dog as in Step 2.

Use a specific command each time now, such as "dog walk," and simultaneously signal to the up ramp with your whole arm. Make sure you point low on the incline to prepare for the contact zones of the regulation obstacle. As with the A-frame, introduce an occasional wait command

Fig. VIII. Handler's body is in good position and hand is well placed in collar, but the enticement is being held off center. Dog is following food and walking his front legs right off the plank.

Fig. IX. Although this dog seems fine, the handler is in no position to help if needed. Only after a good deal of practice down low and with the handler directly beside the dog should he be allowed this much freedom up high. A fall now could set this young spaniel back for quite a while.

both going up and coming down, to be sure your dog is confident and accurate. And work on either side of him, practicing signaling and guiding him with either hand.

Gradually use your hand in the agility collar less and less noticeably. Soon you will be able to give the arm signal and command without taking your dog by the collar. Continue to walk beside him, but don't handle him physically unless you need to.

Your encouragement will still be important, and you should continue to stay close enough to keep your dog centered on the plank. As your dog becomes confident with this obstacle, start using your command to have him go straight ahead again (see Step 1).

There are some adjustable dog walk supports that can be raised and lowered in height, much like an ironing board. Now is the time to use such a wonderful piece of equipment. If your dog is confident on a long,

Little dogs find the planks roomier, and their lower center of gravity makes them more stable, but they have to take many more steps. Caper will soon be encouraged to run on the low, dog walk.

narrow plank when it bounces up and down close to the ground, and he's also confident going up and down an inclined long, narrow plank, then he's ready to put the two together.

If your dog ever becomes afraid of this obstacle, go back to Steps 1 and 2 and find out exactly what is bothering him, bounce, height, or incline. It's much easier and more effective to work on these elements separately, then put them together when the dog is ready.

It's a good idea to sand-paint your practice planks and nail cleats onto them every 12-15 inches. Your dog needs to get used to climbing with cleats on this obstacle, although the incline of the regulation dog walk is nearer 30 degrees, far from the 45 degrees of the A-frame at regulation height.

Cubbie and John practice on a homemade bench. Rounded and irregular surfaces require better balance.

Wherever you go and whatever materials you use, you're responsible for safety on your makeshift dog walks. Your dog should be accustomed to some bounce and sideways movement by now, but plan your creations with your mind on stability. Accidents can cause injury and damage your dog's confidence and trust in you. Most dogs who need remedial help will be set back considerably by an accident.

Check your surfaces for protruding nails and prop the planks well and hold them steady as your dog climbs. You need your canine partner's trust so if you tell him to try he'll feel safe doing so.

No matter how long it takes to give your dog talent and pride with this, don't go on to the next step until your dog is fully confident on either side with your introductory dog walk.

STEP 4. Use regulation dog walk. Experienced spotter on other side of dog. Hand in agility collar and enticement in front. Reward while dog is on the planks, especially in contact zones.

HINTS: Remember to keep your hand in the agility collar. Even though it might seem the dog's head should be up, that's not the case. Even the expert dogs carry their heads low to pay attention to the obstacle and their next steps. Using enticement helps the dog focus down. The hand in the collar also helps your dog feel safer, since it tells him you're in control and reminds him of the earlier steps he mastered. Most people will not be tall enough to serve as leaning posts now, so your dog needs to perform the obstacle without leaning.

From this point, Sparky sees a long traverse and cannot see the down ramp. He has confidence from practice at lower heights, but it's important to be ready to help with this new step.

When your dog is confident and under control, like Maia, you can stop him anywhere on the dog walk.

It helps your dog feel comfortable his first time over the regulation dog walk if you prop the middle of the planks to minimize bouncing for awhile. A stout piece of lumber, metal or plastic pipe should do the trick. The length can be cut to the correct height or the excess dug into the ground. If you can lower the middle support inch by inch as your dog gains confidence, so much the better.

As the dog's ability improves, wean him gradually from enticement. He still needs rewards often, just less predictably. Your encouragement is still important, and there's nothing wrong with having your dog pause for a belly rub and a cookie sometimes. Naturally, enticements should always be near at hand in case of a setback.

When you and your dog have found harmony with the regulation dog walk, it's time to reintroduce your word for the dog to associate with continuing straight ahead on the plank. I use "go ahead" for this, but you could use any word or phrase ("straight ahead," "on by," "away," etc.). This helps your dog learn to move out in front of you and also prepares him for taking directions on the crossover, where he is not always to go straight ahead.

Issue your command to go ahead as your dog approaches the top of the up ramp. It won't seem important to him until he's done a good deal of work on the crossover and knows words for the other alternatives, but it will make it so much easier to direct him from below when he has a choice. Because of the physical structure of the crossover, it's more cumbersome to use the leash for the straight ahead option there, so it's helpful to begin teaching that command using the dog walk.

Remember to work your dog from both sides to keep him comfortable

Melody is a lot of talent in a wild, sure-footed little body. She flies over the dog walk and needs extra help in the zones.

with either. When he's ready, make your influence with the collar felt less and less until he doesn't depend on you to help at all. As with the A-frame, there are many devices and tricks that help the dog cement the habit of hitting the contact zones (see A-frame, Step 3). But you'll still need to be near him and use words and signals to keep him accurate on the ramps. That's the captain's job.

As your dog becomes proficient at the regulation dog walk and practice inclines, further his education by getting him accustomed to more unsteadiness in the planks. Many older dog walks have started to sag in the middle of the traverse. In competition, the judge should prop the plank if it's rickety, but some will bounce quite a bit as a big dog trots over them.

If you are too aggressive with bouncing practice, you'll make your dog feel unsteady and he won't trust you so readily. If you have your dog wait for treats in the middle while you use your hand to bounce the board slightly at first, he'll soon get used to it. Keep tabs on his confidence and steady him if he needs it, praising profusely and offering enticement. Many dogs can learn to lie down in the middle of the plank, demonstrating a thorough command of balance and relaxed confidence. These dogs can become real experts, ready for anybody's dog walk.

As you give your dog more freedom of choice on the dog walk, remember to use hoops, body language, "easy," or any other aids to keep your dog reliable about hitting the contact zones (see Ch. 10 for angled approaches). Make use of signals, agility recalls, other favorite obstacles positioned before or after the dog walk, all kinds of variations to keep your dog happy, brisk, and paying attention at the same time.

Dog Walk, Summary

Use your dog's favorite enticement every time at first to alleviate stress. As the dog becomes more confident and proficient, use enticement less often on that step. Always praise your dog's first efforts and keep the training sessions lively and fun.

Switch sides with your dog regularly to keep him accustomed to taking direction from either side. Switch ends often as well, and move your dog walk to different locations so your dog can get used to variations.

STEP 1. Use a 12-inch wide plank set up about 12 inches off ground. Walk beside dog, hand in collar, and let him lean if he likes. Reward him while he's on the plank, then walk him off.

STEP 2. Use inclined planks up and down on support about two feet high. Use helper, if possible, on other side of dog. Walk beside dog, hand in collar, and let him lean if he likes. Reward him while he's on the plank, then walk him off.

STEP 3. Use two supports, two feet to two feet six inches high with 8- to 12-foot-long planks up, across, and down. Introduce arm signal and "wait."

Sitting and lying down on the cross plank are tests of your dog's security with the obstacle, as Stoner demonstrates. A support brace under the middle at first, please, and lots of cookies.

This hoop, a wrapped motorcycle tire, lets Amanda head for the next obstacle while sending Sidney to finish the dog walk accurately.

STEP 4. Use regulation dog walk and experienced spotter. Walk beside dog, hand in collar. Reward especially in contact zones. Continue to improve control training.

Brenda meets Bach for the descent.

Crossover, Introduction: Also called dog cross or cross walk

This obstacle is a relative newcomer on the agility scene. It's a two-foot-eight-inch square table (in Canada, 36 inches square), raised on legs to a height of about four feet, with a narrow ramp hinged to each of the four sides. It most closely resembles the dog walk, as the planks are about the same length and width with 36-inch contact zones at the bottom. But the crossover can be quite tricky.

In competition, the judge stipulates which plank will be the up ramp and which will be the down ramp. Any other route is penalized as wrong course – from five faults to elimination. (In Canada, where the crossover table is 36 inches square like the pause table, the judge may also require the dog to lie down at the top for a five-second count before descending.)

The crossover is an interesting obstacle. If the dog is proficient on the dog walk, he does what he already knows in climbing a 12-foot plank to a height of about four feet. With the crossover he has a nice platform and view of the world, but most important he has to make a decision because there are four directions in which he could descend.

Of all the agility obstacles only the weave poles call for more mental effort. The dog cannot learn the crossover in the same rote way he can become familiar with tunnels and jumps. He has to pay attention up there and take his cue from his handler. If he forgets, chances are he'll choose incorrectly.

Because of this complication, lessons on the crossover are not generally begun until a dog is quite sure of himself on the dog walk. That approach is fine for most dogs, but I start dogs on the crossover after all introductory dog walk work (Steps 1-3) because most dogs prefer to climb to a platform they can see.

From a dog's eye level, the regulation dog walk seems to drop off to nothing. The crossover presents an obvious landing pad. By keeping a hand in the collar or on the leash and using an enticement, you can issue positive guidance and prevent the dog from choosing his own descent route.

Introducing the crossover before the regulation dog walk tends to prevent the bad habit of charging straight ahead on the crossover rather than listening for the handler's directional command. Currently, some of the best dog-walk performers are the least reliable on the crossover for this reason. Conversely, crossover-first dogs seem to transfer well to the regulation dog walk.

If you want to make your dog familiar with the crossover before becoming familiar with the dog walk, he should be thoroughly versed on all kinds of inclines and planks (A-frames and Steps 1-3 of dog-walk progression). I have found downscaled crossovers helpful because the dog is more relaxed down low, and I can physically guide him more easily. This is a convenient way to teach your dog about taking his descent cue from you. It is helpful to introduce this concept, at least down low, before imprinting the dog so completely on the pattern of the dog walk.

A downscaled crossover can be fashioned from an agility pause table by using planks six feet or longer on any two or more sides. A picnic table for larger dogs or a card table for small dogs makes a good practice crossover, using planks eight feet or longer. In any case, the idea here is to improve your dog's ability to concentrate on you and the obstacle at the same time, so use these makeshift crossovers on lead at first to prevent mistakes. And make sure your planks are stable.

Use enticement at first so your dog can pick up on the new task without stress. Guide him gently as he steps onto the platform and direct him right away to the down ramp you've chosen. If you give him time to think without giving any instruction, he will probably make a mistake. Whether you start work on the crossover at regulation height or not, you will probably need to improve your own directing skills as well as your dog's listening skills.

If you are teaching the crossover before the dog walk, begin with basic plank work covered in Steps 1-3 of the dog walk, then come back here. This section presumes that you and your dog have your basics well in hand. If your dog is not already used to heights, your hand should be in the collar instead of on the leash. You should also use extra enticement and allow less room for error for quite some time, since any correction to stop your dog in his tracks could be inhibiting to one who is still developing his confidence about being up there.

Crossover, Progression

STEP 1. Dog is on leash. Guide him up a ramp on your left. As he approaches the top, say your turn word. Turn him to his right, toward you, and guide him down that ramp, rewarding in the contact zone.

HINTS: This is the easiest turn to direct since your dog can go up the ramp at your left side and you are already in place for guiding him down, again at your left. Give an arm signal to the up ramp as you send your dog, and stay close. Try to apply just enough pressure when he's reached

First trips up the crossover should be done carefully, as demonstrated by Max, no matter how secure your dog feels.

By the time your dog gets to the platform, he should be told where he's going. Early on, prevent mistakes by guiding the dog as you instruct him.

the top to turn his head to the right. Don't hesitate; call him to the right with "this way" or "here," or any directional he may have learned in another job such as herding or dogsledding. Praise him as he walks toward you, and walk him all the way off the down ramp, pausing well into the contact zone for a reward.

I suggest a lot of control and enticement for this introduction because there are a lot of bad habits and insecurities a dog can develop on this obstacle. It's not a bit unusual for dogs to jump off the crossover table or to run down the opposite ramp as if they were on the dog walk. These mistakes usually result the dog not knowing what to do and not waiting to find out. You can prevent that by training in such a way that he gets used to listening up there and learns from the beginning to expect his handler's instruction.

Repeat this exercise a few times, working to establish cooperation. Keep the pressure off as much as possible. When the dog is comfortable with this exercise, begin to walk him up another plank, still turning to the right. Don't send him up more than a few times in the early lessons. If your dog has more than a little trouble with this work, go to a downscaled crossover and separate positive wait training.

STEP 2. Dog is on leash. Guide him up any ramp, command him at the top, and turn him to his left. Walk all the way down, rewarding in the contact zone.

HINTS: Same as Step 1, but the dog should go up at your right this time. Because of switching sides, your dog may pay more attention and this exercise may go quite smoothly. Use your "this way" command, or your dog's left turn command. Be lavish with your praise if it does go smoothly. Your dog is tuning you in.

Because you expect him to turn automatically to the right, try to head off that mistake with gentle leash pressure and an early command to turn. How much extra enticement you need here depends on how well your dog is accepting the crossover, but you should have your enticement ready in case your dog becomes unsure.

Don't practice this off leash until your dog is relaxed and not guessing incorrectly when you alternate the left and right directionals.

STEP 3. Over several lessons, repeat Steps 1 and 2 off leash. Use enticement, and reward in the zones.

HINTS: Use "wait" or even "down" to keep a very quick dog under control as soon as he gets to the top. Show him the correct way down along with commanding him, and use enticement to prevent an incorrect choice. See Ch. 2 to review the instant down.

If you have not yet introduced the regulation dog walk, now is a good time, before your dog becomes too dependent on turning always toward you when he's up high. Be thorough with Step 4 of the dog walk, and review Steps 1-3 for good measure, perhaps with a bit more spring in your planks.

Only her second time at regulation height, and Keesha is already cocky. Only the hand in her collar keeps her from jumping the zone.

Now it's time to bring your "straight ahead" word to the crossover. Your dog should always hear a directional command by the time he sets a foot on the platform. He must learn to continue straight ahead when told to, even though you may be to one side or the other when you send him.

STEP 4. Straight across.

HINTS: Review the dog walk immediately prior to this step, using your go- ahead command. Then try the same direction on the crossover.

Your dog will benefit from being on leash the first few times you guide him straight across on the crossover. You should plan to have the dog wait immediately at the top so you can go around or under the protruding plank without your dog assuming that's the way he should go.

Have him lie down if necessary to keep him from descending (and make a mental note to command him earlier next time and polish your wait training). Pick up the agility leash or tab once you're on the other side, and guide your dog down the opposite plank. It will take many repetitions for this to sink in, but it's much easier for having taught the command for straight ahead early on with all your dog walks.

Don't hesitate to use enticement as necessary to keep your dog on track, even by placing a few tidbits on the opposite plank. And you may have to do some practicing to find your own best route to the other side.

As your dog becomes comfortable with going straight ahead on command, begin to send him ahead earlier, before you quite get around to him. Gradually send him ahead without making him wait. This is a weaning process; it takes time. Your hoops and other contact zone tricks will all be necessary as you give your dog more freedom to choose his own path.

STEP 5. Random directionals. Gradually work all directions off leash.

HINTS: Before sending your dog up, decide which ramp you're going to use for the down ramp. Command your dog early enough, and make sure that your body language matches your verbal direction. The route is easier to plan in the context of a sequence of obstacles because that makes it clear on which side you want to be approaching and leaving the crossover. Make sure you don't end up standing and giving body signals to your dog's right while telling him to go left.

All the tricks for keeping your dog honest on the A-frame and dog walk are just as effective here, and your pattern of training your dog to step into the contact zones should be followed just as carefully.

Crossover competence will include sending your dog ahead of you. This is Belle.

Crossover, Summary

Use your dog's favorite enticement every time at first to alleviate stress. As the dog becomes more confident and proficient, use enticement less often on that step. Always praise your dog's first efforts and keep the training sessions lively and fun.

Switch sides with your dog regularly to keep him accustomed to taking commands and signals from either side. Switch planks often as well, and move your crossover to different locations, so your dog can get used to variations.

STEP 1. Dog is on leash. Guide him up ramp on your left. Turn him to right and guide down. Reward in contact zone.

STEP 2. Dog is on leash. Guide him up ramp on your right. Turn him to left and guide down. Reward in contact zone.

STEP 3. Over many lessons, repeat Steps 1 and 2 until well learned.

Alternate Steps 1 and 2 off leash, rewarding in zones.

STEP 4. Review dog walk, using "straight across" command. With dog on leash, guide him up ramp and have him wait while you cross. Guide him down opposite ramp, rewarding in zone. Gradually send dog straight ahead without having him wait.

STEP 5. Gradually work all directions off leash. Further improve control training.

Seesaw, Introduction: Also called teeter-totter

One of the favorite obstacles of spectators, the seesaw cements the image of an agility course as a big playground. The dog needs an extra measure of balance, patience, and practice to do well on this obstacle. He must go up an inclined plank of about 12 feet which is secured to a fulcrum about two feet high. The dog must find his own pivot point and bring the raised end to the ground, then descend.

The seesaw is slightly weighted on one end, or attached an inch or so off center, so it will return itself to the proper position for use from the

Jinx slows down for the tip.

same direction over and over. The dog must touch 36-inch contact zones both ascending and descending.

This obstacle looks much like the dog walk from the end-on dog's eye view– an 8-inch to 12-inch-wide inclined board with contact zone and cleats. But halfway up, what a surprise! This sudden instability is dreadful to the dog, and if not introduced gradually and carefully can create a lasting distrust of this obstacle. It should be introduced only after your fundamentals (Ch. 2) are secure and your dog is well-balanced and confident on long, narrow, bouncy inclined planks.

The seesaw should have a command different from that used for any other contact obstacle. Even if you prefer to use a single "go-up" command for the A-frame, dog walk, and crossover, the seesaw should be called something different to alert the dog to the obstacle that rocks. You don't want him to have to guess whether the plank he is ascending will fall out from under him. It takes time for him to learn the name, so start using it as soon as your dog is comfortable with the rocking motion. If you use the seesaw command before your dog enjoys the obstacle, the word will conjure up images of insecurity, so let your dog tell you when the time is right.

A downscaled seesaw is well worth building if your dog is not crazy about rickety planks under him. An easy-to-build version for fulcrums more than eight inches high is shown in the Appendix. For a great seesaw with a fulcrum about eight inches high, just use one of the cinder blocks with large holes, and use scraps of lumber to secure one of your eight-foot practice planks across the center. I use bits of two-by-fours in the holes to make the upright scraps stay straight up. You don't want the plank to swing from side to side, so some type of channel is important.

A puppy or small dog who likes to be cradled can get used to the unique motion of the seesaw by being on it with you, either a regulation model or a downscaled one. You can rock the plank a little at a time while loving up the dog to keep him reassured.

Seesaw, Progression

STEP 1. Review double sawhorse with two planks. Perfect wait training at top, then on down ramp.

HINTS: Before beginning work on a seesaw, your dog should be an expert at Step 2 of the dog-walk progression. Use one narrow plank up and another down. Have your dog wait on command at the top, then just a step or two (or three or four for tiny dogs) onto the down ramp. This is to prepare him for having to wait on command and feeling offbalance initially as the seesaw tilts. He will have to shift his weight to halt on the down ramp, and he will need to learn this for keeping his balance on the seesaw. Let him eat a cookie or play with a toy for a few seconds in that leaned-back position, then walk him all the way down to the ground.

STEP 2. Downscaled seesaw.

HINTS: So many dogs have trouble with the seesaw that it deserves extra time and patience. The downscaled seesaw helps dogs understand it and learn to accept and control that strange sudden motion. It can be as simple as a cinder block with a stanchion to support the cross plank, or as fancy as a regulation seesaw in miniature. This potentially scary obstacle can translate into fun in a group setting. Let the more confident dogs go first, then let a less sure dog follow a brave one.

A helper should be in charge of the plank, to make it tip gently and smoothly. You may have plenty to do in taking care of the dog, keeping one hand in his collar, enticing him, offering your leg at his midsection

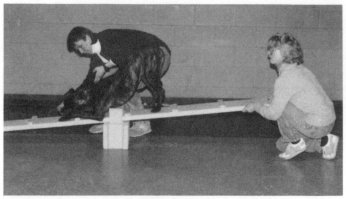

Introduce the motion of the seesaw down low. Tiger had an interesting reaction to his first few tilts...

...but he soon paid no attention. Using a helper, free the handler to relax the dog.

if he wants to lean on you, and having him wait over the fulcrum. Spoil him a bit while he waits and the helper slowly tilts the plank, and then guide him all the way down.

If you don't have a helper, you can handle this yourself if your dog is not frightened or extremely active. Just make sure you keep him steady and get him to wait at the fulcrum, and you can use a foot to tip the plank while you reward the dog. With a very steady dog you can use your enticement hand to lower the plank while he waits. Whatever is comfortable for your dog. For most dogs, a helper is the ounce of prevention that is worth a pound of cure.

Be sure to keep your enticement low on the plank to keep the dog looking down. This means that you must lower the treat as the plank tips. Otherwise the dog tries to raise his muzzle as his front feet go down with the tipping plank, and his balance is easily lost.

If your dog is not ready to handle the downscaled seesaw, he may need more confidence work with bouncy planks, or you may be able to acclimate him by putting a small block under the raised end of the plank, so it doesn't go down all the way. Your dog can dismount by walking down the slightly raised plank, a job he already knows. As soon as he's comfortable with you on one side of him, begin switching sides.

Don't go on to the next step until your dog is trotting up the small seesaw happily, waiting when you tell him to, balancing easily when the plank is lowered, and pausing comfortably in the zone area on the way off.

STEP 3. Dog learns to tip plank.

HINTS: If you really wait until your dog accepts the motion of the seesaw before you do this, it's not difficult and it's a lot of fun to see your dog figure this out. He has to learn that he can control the plank himself, and he has to want to do it, so keep it fun.

Have your dog wait at the fulcrum, reward him, and then ask him to take another step (the less the dog weighs, the more steps he has to take before the plank tips). It's best to do this with cookie to nose, so he won't just charge off. The helper remains ready to keep the operation of the plank smooth and gentle. The dog's job is to get used to causing the plank to tip by associating it with a certain forward step. Praise profusely as the plank tips, and reward your dog all the way down.

As above, don't go on to the next step until your dog is relaxed with the new responsibility and enjoys it. He should now be ready to work without a helper. He should have figured out his personal pivot point, at which the plank begins to tip, and he should be comfortable and pleased with himself for tipping the plank before you go on to Step 4.

Willie learns to take over the job. If the dog tucks his tail, give extra help and more encouragement.

Fig. X. The enticement should be lowered as the seesaw is tilted, or your dog will not shift his weight properly. He should be looking down.

STEP 4. Dog controls obstacle by himself.

HINTS: Gradually make your influence less and less felt, until your hand is no longer in the collar and you do not need to touch the dog to have him go up, wait, tip the plank, and descend. You will still want to stand near and walk along beside at the ready until he has you fully convinced that he owns this thing. After that, you can increase distance gradually until he meets someone else's seesaw, when you should again work very close to him.

You won't generally send your dog very far from you to perform any contact obstacle. It's standard practice to work him quite close, so you can have him slow down or wait to ensure his accuracy on those all-important contact zones. Although these downscaled seesaws may not have painted zones, the dog's performance habits will be formed in these early stages.

As with other obstacles, begin to use your arm signal to get the dog started, making sure that he touches the zone area getting on and off. With most dogs, you shouldn't do much running away from the contact obstacles and playing the catch-up game until the dog is both advanced and careful, because it can create such problems with contact zones.

If the dog is brought along slowly and surely on the seesaw, you won't have too many problems with your dog trying to fly over the thing without touching it. Of course, if you notice any avoidance behaviors, such as walking front legs only up the plank or trying to duck around the plank, go back a couple steps right away, and spend some time rebuilding confidence. It doesn't matter if your dog was fine yesterday. If he acts unsure today, believe him and help him.

Don't go on to the next step until your dog is completely relaxed on the small seesaw: He should trot up without hesitation; he should be balancing smoothly in harmony with the plank as it tilts; he should no longer care to lean on you; and he should no longer need a helper all before you go on to Step 5.

STEP 5. Regulation seesaw. Let dog investigate. Let him watch another dog perform it happily.

HINTS: Guide your dog through his investigation; when he's checked out the base, tip the plank a bit to show him that it moves. Don't pull him and don't rush him. Let him do everything short of walking up the plank. If he wants to walk up, distract him elsewhere rather than issue a reprimand. This investigation helps your dog realize that this is not a dog walk, but it acts like the small seesaw.

Because dogs mimic behavior of other dogs and of people, that "monkey see, monkey do" gets them into a lot of trouble sometimes. Agility lends itself well to a positive application of mimicry. It does help a new physical challenge go more smoothly if your dog can watch it being done correctly and associate that with pleasure. If you know an accomplished canine who enjoys the seesaw, let that dog take a few turns and be praised sincerely while the student dog watches from the side (it's impossible for him to see just what is happening if he has only an end-on view).

The handler of the experienced dog should command "wait" at the pivot point and reward the dog in the leaned-back position as the raised end drops, then walk the dog all the way off, praising lavishly. If you are the handler of the trained dog, tie or crate the student dog to give him a side-on view. It can make your dog more eager to perform the obstacle if it's his favorite person doing all that praising over there.

STEP 6. Student dog takes turn on regulation seesaw. Entice dog, have him wait at fulcrum while spotter tilts plank. Reward during wait, and again in contact zone.

HINTS: With your hand in the agility collar, use treats held low to

When you graduate to the regulation seesaw, use extra help again to ensure your dog's peace of mind.

Over many lessons, Stoner takes more responsibility on the regulation seesaw, but Corene stays close and keeps an eye on her dog.

Soft ground will absorb much of the force when the plank hits, but a hard surface is very jarring to a dog. Ease the force a bit to prevent hard slams while your dog is still learning.

help your dog walk up the seesaw. Your helper stands at the low end and prevents that end from rising, should your dog go too far. Help your dog "wait" near his pivot point (which is just past the midpoint for very large dogs and can be quite near the raised end for very small dogs). Reward your dog and steady him as needed while your helper slowly and smoothly raises the low end fully, then holds that end high for stability while you walk your dog all the way down the other side. Great job. Repeat this only a few times your first day.

With most dogs, it's quite important to have a helper for this step, even though you no longer need one on the small seesaw. Your dog will need to accept more height and a new pivot point. I seem to be in the minority in my preference for having the helper at the low end instead of the high end, but I choose it because I like to have a helper there if needed to get the dog started, which is usually harder than getting him to walk off. A helper from the low end can walk along to the fulcrum, so the dog is already used to having two people alongside by the time he gets to the middle, which is where many dogs start to wobble and need support from both sides.

It is the helper's job to prevent the plank from tipping too abruptly or from tipping back if the dog stutter-steps going down. At the low end, the helper can put a foot on the plank. When the plank is high, he uses a hand. Because of the importance of keeping the plank steady, the helper should not go around the fulcrum unless he can do it while holding the plank in place.

If the dog goes up willingly but is badly unnerved when the helper slowly tips the plank, take steps to make the obstacle less frightening. The most obvious is to review the downscaled seesaw, perhaps with a longer plank, and then reintroduce the regulation model with a support such as a cinder block under the high end to keep it from tipping all the way to the ground.

Many seesaw bases are not as stable as they could be and allow too much sway from side to side. An unsteady dog can set it vibrating and scare himself into jumping ship, so be prepared to lean against the plank and the dog, and hold him with both hands to steady him. Sometimes the helper can steady the base and the plank. A good base should have solid crosspieces that keep the two sides secure and parallel.

As with the downscaled seesaw, gradually have the dog take over more of the responsibility for operating the obstacle, and then begin to introduce signals and a bit of distance. Once your dog relaxes with the motion of the regulation seesaw, he will quickly take over and you will be put to work seeing that he continues to wait for the plank to drop and to hit the contact zones going up and coming down.

Sometimes problems with the contact zones develop only after the dog has become very familiar with and enamored of the obstacle. So even if

Spuds rides the tilt, already in the contact zone. Tiny dogs do not weigh enough to keep the plank firmly on the ground when it hits, so they often bounce back up before jumping off.

your dog is very correct about the seesaw zones now, be prepared to use your contact-zone tricks to keep him that way, and don't let yourself congratulate him for getting very brave and sloppy, even though you should be proud of his confidence. You've done a good job of bringing him along.

Now go back to Step 3 of the A-frame and read up on zone work, before your wonderful reckless driver gets into a habit that the crowds will love and you will hate. Some suggestions for further improving control of advanced climbers are described in Ch. 10.

Seesaw, Summary

Use your dog's favorite enticement every time at first to alleviate stress. As the dog becomes more confident and proficient with each step, use enticement less often on that step. Always praise your dog's first efforts, and keep the training sessions lively and fun.

Switch sides with your dog regularly, to keep him accustomed to taking direction from either side. Turn your seesaw often and move it to different locations so your dog can get used to variations.

STEP 1. Review double sawhorse with two planks. Perfect wait training at top, then a step or two down.

STEP 2. Use downscaled seesaw, stabilized from side to side. Use helper if possible. Walk beside dog, letting him lean if he likes. Have him wait at the fulcrum. Helper or handler tips plank. Reward dog while tipping. Walk him all the way off, rewarding in the zone.

STEP 3. Walk dog to fulcrum, rewarding in zone. Have him wait over the fulcrum. Entice dog to take a step and tip the plank himself. Helper controls smoothness of tip. Walk him all the way off, and reward in the zone.

STEP 4. Gradually encourage dog to control the obstacle. Introduce arm signal and more distance.

STEP 5. Let dog investigate regulation seesaw. Dog watches from side as seesaw is demonstrated.

STEP 6. Repeat Steps 2-4 using regulation seesaw and helper. Continue to improve control work.

Bach sails over a 30-inch triple spread. Jump cups could be placed at many heights along the five uprights, for training and regulation jump heights.

7

THE JUMPS

I can run that course in 21 obstacles. Watch her face when I take the extra jump.
—Jessy

Several types of jumps are expected on an agility course, in many different sizes, shapes, and colors. Most agility jumps have decorative markers on either side, and many have wings, which are usually wooden frameworks that extend a few feet out from either side of the jump bars. In this chapter jump training is divided into two parts: one for jumps that are tall but not broad; and, one for jumps that have considerable breadth to them, called spreads if they are also tall, and long jumps if they are low.

Every agility jump is required to be displaceable, or at least have a top piece that will fall off if a jumping dog hits it. This helps prevent injuries and indicates if the dog should be faulted. Five faults are assessed for each jump that is not jumped clear.

In addition, jump obstacles produce refusals. A refusal is marked if the dog balks or goes under or around a jump, if he goes over the wings instead of the bars, goes other than all the way from end to end across a long jump, or passes anywhere between tire and frame of a tire jump. Currently, the penalty for jumping refusals ranges from no faults to five faults apiece plus elimination after a total of three refusals anywhere on the course.

When Agility became established in England, all dogs were required to jump 30-inch hurdles and long jumps up to five feet long and 15 inches high. After nearly a decade, the sport has become so popular that another division has been added, and mini-Agility has begun to draw its own large crowds to watch dogs up to 15 inches tall compete using hurdles set to 15 inches high instead of 30 inches. Since the sport is still gaining popularity, further revisions to accommodate smaller and in-between heights are being considered.

Much of Europe adopted a 30-inch Agility jump height and added a 15-inch division in turn. In 1989, a new Canadian organization called

ADAC (Agility Dog Association, Canada) adopted a structure based on the divisions used in the United States.

On the advice of English experts, the USDAA tried to accommodate different sizes from the outset. Three jump heights have been established to allow dogs of different sizes to compete. These heights were 12, 21, and 30 inches. The long jump was no more than 10 inches high, with distances of 20, 42, and 64 inches (later shortened to 60 inches). Except for minor changes, the rules have held for several years, helping Agility become the game of choice for dogs of all sizes.

With agility fever running high in the U.S., revisions for 1991 further divided jump height categories, with two divisions for "minis" and two for larger dogs. The small dog class includes 12-inch and 18-inch jump heights, with long jumps of 20 and 36 inches respectively. The large dog class includes 24-inch and 30-inch jump heights, with long jumps of 48 and 60 inches respectively. The dog's jump height division is determined by his height at the withers, with breakpoints at 12, 16, and 21 inches.

Revised and additional height divisions have been debated all over the world, with some countries waiting to see what others decide. Hopefully an international standard will emerge. Meanwhile, current jump height specifics should be obtained from individual national organizations; see Appendix.

Jump heights will always be a major issue in Agility because jumps are such a large part of the course. A competition course of 20 obstacles will typically include about 13 jumps. Your dog will encounter jumps of widely varied colors, shapes, textures, materials, motifs and dimensions in Agility. Teach him that, no matter what it looks like, if you say the word he simply jumps it.

Some dogs are born jumpers and others are not. But even dogs who are not natural jumpers can learn to do it well. The first step is to have your dog's soundness evaluated, for if his body is not sound it will not hold up to the amount of jumping which an agility course demands.

The canine body type best suited for jumping is determined by how much weight must be carried per amount of supporting bone in the leg (see Ch. 1). In addition, the dog's physical structure and condition and his enjoyment of jumping all have an important part in determining how fit he is for jumping.

For Agility, your dog needs to be strong enough in the rear to tuck his haunches under him like a coiled spring, compressed and then powered upward by the release of that tension when he pushes off. Once over the jump, successful or not, his forequarters absorb all that pressure when he lands on the other side. The heavier your dog and the more powerful his spring, the more force his front end has to withstand on landing. That force is greatly intensified when an immediate sharp turn is required to get to the next obstacle.

The experienced dog, taking his directional cue from his handler, will actually be twisting in the air and assuming the new direction as soon as he hits the ground. That means his inside leg, the one on the side toward the turn, will absorb nearly all the force of the landing. Because the leg will be turning as it hits the ground, a great deal of lateral strain will be put on the dog's shoulder, knee and pastern joints.

No matter how much strength the dog has both fore and aft, if he doesn't know where to begin his leap and at what angle to propel himself, he will have jumping problems. So a smart jumper is an efficient jumper, one who knows how to read a jump, bothers to do so, then puts out the right amount and kind of effort to clear it properly. An efficient jumper consistently turns in a clean performance in a faster time. More importantly, he lasts longer.

Solid Jumps and Bar Jumps, Introduction (solid jumps are also called high jumps; bar jumps are also called pole jumps)

Although the first thing you usually wish for in jump training is a dog who bounds as though on springs, dogs who are spring-loaded don't always jump wisely or well. To be successful on an agility course, a dog needs good judgment about the height and depth of an upcoming jump, and he needs to take off properly and propel himself accurately to clear the jump without wasting time and energy.

The impressive dogs who come to a standstill and then effortlessly pop over a jump are real crowd-pleasers, but they are not using their gifts to the fullest. Neither are the dogs who jump much higher than necessary. Some dogs even spring straight-legged over the jumps and look to be standing in the air, usually several inches above the jump. These are very talented dogs with very inefficient jumping styles.

Teaching your dog to jump is largely a matter of helping him develop timing and strength. When a dog is more powerful in the forequarters, he prefers to pull himself over things rather than propel from the rear. This shows up markedly in A-frame training when the dog wants to hop onto the obstacle and power up on his forequarters rather than using those rear muscles extensively. Assuming he doesn't suffer from hip dysplasia or another infirmity of the rear, this dog needs a conditioning program of roadwork and stair work (see Ch. 3), A-frame (Ch. 6), and the jumping exercises of this chapter to develop his thigh muscles. His forequarters will be able to handle what he learns to put out with his rear muscles.

The more dangerous long-term situation is seen in dogs with powerful hindquarters and much weaker structure in the front. These dogs usually have rear legs with very sharp angulation of the bones and a lot of muscle in their thighs. A line drawn from the ilium to the rear foot following the major bones of the leg would be a very pronounced zig-zag. In marked contrast, the angulation of the bones of their front legs is much less pronounced, that is, a line from withers to foot through the major bones would be only slightly zig-zagged. These dogs, assuming no shoulder problem or other infirmity of the front exists, can be strengthened with roadwork, digging, swimming, and climbing.

Still, because of the structural imbalance between the front and the rear, the handler should beware of the dog's tendency to overstress his front and the damage that can be done over time, particularly to the shoulders. It's especially important that dogs of this physical type learn to judge their jumps and propel themselves smoothly with just enough power to clear the jump. All that excess push from the rear makes for extra strain on the shock-absorbing front, and it will eventually cause damage.

Jump heights are calculated to be low enough for your dog to be tested without requiring heroic effort to clear the jumps. And, because the courses vary so, your dog will turn as often in one direction as the other, so cumulatively distributing the force evenly. The most important preparations for agility jumping are to have your dog in great shape physically and to help him develop and maintain an enthusiasm and confidence for jumping as you guide his technical progress at home.

Melody issues a quick change of direction in mid-air.

Solid Jumps and Bar Jumps, Progression

STEP 1. Solid jump is set at half the height of the dog at withers. Introduce pole jump. Introduce command to jump.

HINTS: These low solid jumps belong everywhere, outdoors and in. My favorite indoor place is a doorway or hallway where the dog will have

"Did I make it?" Young Hannah's initial reaction to an eight-inch jump is extreme. A six-inch jump and cookie to nose helped her walk over, then hop over. Bar was raised very gradually.

to go over it, not around it, day in and day out. It could even be set up in front of your dog's crate or in his exercise pen. It's usually low enough to be lived with by humans, and gives the dog his first lessons in timing without any strain at all. It's all right if he trots over it instead of hopping over; that takes timing too.

A piece of plywood leaned against a doorway makes a serviceable solid jump. A tension rod designed for doing chin-ups in doorways works well too. Just drape something over it at first to make it solid; a pillowcase or small blanket should do. A piece of cloth between the rod and a wall will protect the finish.

Working outside, use the solid jump at half your dog's height for the first few jumping sessions. Your dog should be on leash and you should jump with him and carry on in delight at his willingness to hop over with you. Remember to stay to either side yourself in order to give your dog the middle of the jump as much as possible. As with all other obstacles, work sometimes with your dog on the left and sometimes on the right.

This is the same Hannah one year later, winning a tough Starters class. Jump number two is a "double bar."

Fig. XI. Here the dog leans sideways, away from leash pressure. To develop his natural ability, the dog must have his balance.

Don't pull up on the leash as you jump, and don't interfere with the dog's jumping. Let him figure it out. If he's insecure, lower the jump. At this point, jumping is just simple fun, more for the attitude than for the muscles.

If jumping with your dog is not for you, use a helper to hold the dog on one side while you go to the other. If possible, step over the little jump rather than go around, since that helps your dog expect to go the same way. Do use enticement to help your dog decide to make the effort, but don't order your dog to come or to jump unless he loves those commands. Instead, use the same sort of cajoling you used for the first step of open-tunnel work.

It's great to have a helper for early jump lessons. The helper holds the dog's collar (or leash at first), keeping him tuned in to you across the jump. When you call the dog, the helper lets go when the dog is committed to the jump. You could even call the dog back and forth between you, rewarding him at each station. Whatever approach you choose, keep it filled with fun and praise.

If the dog has a problem doing what you want, change your approach to give him more enticement and less freedom for error, but don't blame the dog. This step is for attitude, and it's a critical one. His accuracy falls to you and your helper. Review and revise, but don't criticize.

Start using your jump command as soon as your dog thoroughly enjoys the jumping. It would be a mistake to issue the command while he is nervous or unhappy about jumping because the command would continue to conjure up insecurity long after his ability has progressed. Better to wait until you've helped the dog overcome any initial mental blocks. Then name the job while the jump is still very low. Various commands are used to tell the dog to jump, including "jump," "over," and "hup."

After everyone is accustomed to the solid jump, it's time for a single pole. The height is low enough that your dog doesn't decide to go under instead of over the jump in your doorway, where he'll be off leash and on his own for the most part. If he does wriggle under, either add a second pole below the first, or lower the pole an inch or two, or block off a portion of the space below the pole, or go back to a solid jump in the house for awhile longer. It's also good to change the jump often, to get your dog accustomed to different textures, shapes, and colors of jumps, both solid and bar, with bar jumps now comprising most of your arsenal.

For jumps in the house, make a point of noticing how your dog handles the pole, whether he trips on it, tries to go under, or overjumps it. You may need to spend more time practicing with him, in the house as well as outside, or improve the traction on the floor in the jump area. But don't go on to Step 2 until your dog is happy and accurate with a single pole at half his height, inside the house and out.

STEP 2. Raise pole one-half inch at a time for small dogs, one to two inches at a time for big dogs, until height of pole is two-thirds height of dog at withers. Introduce wait. Send your dog.

Woody's low jump develops confidence, timing, and coordination. It's just a cardboard cylinder threaded with string.

Fig. XII. Give plenty of slack in the leash, or your quick dog will be brought up short. Let go if necessary, or use a retractable leash.

HINTS: Depending on how easily your dog takes to this, how many times each day your dog is jumping, and the size of your dog, you should raise the pole anywhere from every few days to every few weeks. Using a single pole for most of your dog's jump training is best. It's lightweight, portable, and makes noise without causing damage if knocked down. As the bar gets higher, the space under it beckons louder. Many dogs, even those who love to jump, will run under a single bar at their regulation height. By introducing a pole low enough that the dog always goes over, and raising it very gradually as his habit becomes ingrained, you are increasing the dog's tendency to jump over even if he could easily go under.

When your dog is comfortable with low single-pole jumps, use your wait training to help your jump training. Beginning with a jump set at half your dog's height, have your dog wait on one side while you step over and turn to face him from the other side. Stand very close to the jump and entice your dog over, trotting backwards as he commits to the jump. Reward him with great enthusiasm as he arrives.

If your dog needs more wait training, work separately on that rather than interrupting him for not waiting during an early jump lesson. If you need some extra control early on, you can do this on leash until the dog seems steady on the wait and fully in charge of the jump. A helper standing behind your dog, holding a loose leash, can also make your dog steadier.

Remember to interrupt your dog's mistakes without dampening his enthusiasm for jumping. Once you're ready to call your dog, hold out your enticement and call him at once. Holding out the enticement is part of your dog's learning the arm signal to jump, and you'll need him to respond to that immediately as you begin running courses together, so don't demand that your dog sit still and stare at you while you are holding out your arm at the jump. Send the dog over as soon as you extend your arm. Trotting backwards as he gets to the jump helps keep him hurrying to get to you.

Jumping with your dog, even on leash, is often the easiest way to teach him the arm signal for jumping. It's quite straightforward; he just has to learn to jump whatever you throw your arm at. You can practice teamwork and sending your dog on signal by having him wait beside you a few strides from the low jump. Then hold out your arm to the jump as you tell him to jump, and run with him. As your dog learns to take charge when you signal and send him, begin to run around the jump and let him go over by himself. The right time to begin doing these jump lessons off leash is when your dog is happy to jump and has the habit of coming over the jump and then to you.

When your dog is comfortable with this, begin raising the jump just a little at a time, depending on his ability and size. It's tempting to think that an extra couple of inches won't make any difference but it often does, so know your dog before you decide to raise the jump. Do this gradually so your dog can adjust his effort a little at a time, honing his ability to judge his jumps. You have completed this step when your dog waits with bated breath for you to command him, starts forward as soon as you command him, jumps comfortably at two-thirds of his height, and then comes to you to be congratulated. Don't raise the pole any higher than two-thirds of your dog's height on this step.

Because the jump is low and the dog has been going over it matter-of-factly many times a day, it's not likely he'll try to go around the jump. But if he does, do this exercise in a hallway or doorway, or any other indoor or outdoor location where both sides can be blocked, so the dog has no option of running out on the jump. Make sure you've provided good traction before and after the jump. If your Yorkie's eyes are five inches from the black slate floor and you're using a black plastic pole, he might not see the pole well enough. Putting some contrasting tape around it every foot or so would help.

Don't assume your dog is recalcitrant or thick-headed when he messes up with these simple jumps. Check out your set up from the dog's point of view; there may be a good reason for his resistance. As long as he's healthy and doesn't have any physical infirmity hampering him, your dog will learn to jump, and jump well, if you let him begin where he is comfortable and gradually increase the challenge. If he's just not a natural jumper, there's nothing to be ashamed of in that. It's one of many things he can learn. And he may prove to be more controllable on the course and more reliable about touching his contact zones than a jump-happy dog, so perhaps with a little work you can have it all.

Although I have worked with many big dogs who are naturally good jumpers, and I own one, my better-known Rottie was nothing of the sort. It took several months of working at it step by step to help her become a good jumper. Since then, although we mess up now and then, she has often drawn applause from the crowd for her handling of jump sequences, and as long as I don't accidentally short-circuit her confidence she truly enjoys jumping. Those of us who knew her when still call her the flying pig, but we have to admire her.

For dogs who are not inherent jumpers, I recommend positive drilling on low jumps after Step 1 is completed and the dog has happy feelings about jumping with you. Have the dog wait right in front of a jump that is half his height at the withers. Straddle the jump. While inviting the dog to jump, tempt him with a favorite enticement held just on the other side. The instant he lands on that side, give him the reward. It doesn't matter if he raps the jump because it's his effort you're rewarding at this point. Back the other way too, with the enticement in your other hand.

This exercise would not be a good idea for dogs who love to jump; it's for dogs who need more practice picking their feet up over the jumps and pushing off with their hindquarters. As he gets more proficient and eager, begin to reward him less than every time, and only for clear jumps, but don't chastise him for mistakes. This simple exercise has turned many a nervous jumper into a happy one.

By starting with the jump very low and keeping your attitude light and supportive, the dog doesn't feel pressured. Raise the jump much more gradually than you think you need to. Remember you're doing this because your dog needs extra help. The obedience utility bar jump with increments of two inches is gradual enough for some dogs, but not for all. Drilling some extra holes or bending a long nail in at one end and out at the other will allow you to raise the bar more gradually.

You can make your own jump by resting a bar on bricks, blocks or buckets and adding fillers to raise the bar gradually. By starting your dog very close to the jump, he learns to propel from the rear and pick his front feet up quickly. By enticing and rewarding him each time and not scolding his mistakes, you keep the dog interested and pleased with himself. His confidence and ability improve and his attitude is enhanced. It bears repeating that this exercise is designed for use with low jumps, up to two-thirds of your dog's height. It is not the way to train him for anything higher, as this would lead to stopping in front of the jump and popping over rather than taking it in stride.

Although I love to use all kinds of strange-looking barriers for backyard jumps, I tend to concentrate on jumps with just a single pole or any type of bar across the top, even a tree branch, once the dogs are fairly good jumpers. It helps ensure that your dog really understands that "jump" means to go over, and it requires more concentration to negotiate a single bar than a more clearly defined solid jump. Just make sure that your bars are easily seen by tying some bright tape or cloth strands across a dark branch if, from the dog's eye level, it could be lost against a dark background of woods.

STEP 3. Introduce multiple jumps. Begin at one-half to two-thirds of your dog's height and work up to his regulation jump height.

HINTS: Now that your dog enjoys a working understanding of basic jumping, this practice should improve his timing and skill on the run. Start with just two jumps, anywhere between one-half and two-thirds the height of your dog, depending on whether he had a hard time mastering jump fundamentals or took to it naturally. If your dog finds jumping to be hard work, you need to start this step with the jumps low and use extra enticement.

Most experts agree that a dog generally ends up jumping better if he is allowed to train himself. You should not be pulling his head up or yanking him forward, and you shouldn't set up any jumping problems before he is confident and has his basic timing worked out.

Agility is a sport in which the dog must learn to think and plan his jumping for himself. There is no anticipating where jumps will be placed on a competition course, what kind of obstacles will come immediately

Willie meets two in a row, first on leash, then off. Work both left and right sides.

Tessa works at regulation height. Leash is loose and held out of the way. The plank under bar stops thoughts of ducking under.

before and after, and what sort of turns and spacing will appear between them. And it's quite common to face four different jumps in a row, so it's most important that you give your dog ample exposure and practice to work out a personal jumping style that works jump after jump.

If you are comfortable jumping with your dog, on or off the leash, that's a great way to introduce each longer sequence. Make sure you stay to either side to give your dog the middle of the jumps. When he is comfortable with his job, let him jump while you go around. As you become a team, begin to introduce wait and arm signals again. Some dogs do better if you gradually bring their skill to regulation height on the run with one jump before returning to sequences with lower jumps. Keep thinking, and you'll come up with an approach which brings out the talent in your dog.

If your dog has a habit of trying to go under or around a single jump at two-thirds of his height, you shouldn't be on this step yet. He needs more confidence. Try drillwork over low single jumps and gradually raise them, as in Step 2. On the other hand, if your dog is fine with a single jump but suddenly balks at two, use lower or solid jumps at first and jump with him, on leash or off, until he's relaxed about going over two jumps. You could use a helper for awhile, and certainly use a strong enticement for your dog.

A popular technique is to drape a long line loosely over the jumps from dog to you before asking him to jump. The Flexi-leads are great for this use because they reel in the excess line as the dog comes toward you.

Seeing the familiar leash helps many dogs understand to follow its path. For better or worse, it will correct the dog for darting under or around, since that would catch the lead on the side post or jump pole. This will not hurt him but will make him think twice before going that way again.

If this happens to a self-assured dog who is simply inventive enough to try the wrong path, this self-correction is likely to help the dog accept the job of going over, always over, the jumps. But if you haven't taught him thoroughly at the earlier steps, and this correction happens to a dog who is unsure of his jumping ability, it will hamper his progress by unnerving him further. And remember that this is a self-correction, not to be accompanied by your scolding the dog. Let him figure it out and decide for himself to go over, smart dog that he is. A sensitive dog would be overwhelmed by your reprimand and a rude bopping by the equipment at once. And a very confident dog would accept much more readily a solution he discovers for himself.

If your dog is ready for this step but you think he might try to duck out as the work gets harder, one good idea is to start with a jumping channel or chute made of natural or set-up barriers that block the way around the jumps on both sides. If your dog can't go around the jumps, he can concentrate on his jumping instead of wasting mental and physical energy trying to get out of the work.

Using a favorite enticement will often make going over the jumps seem like a great idea. Whether you use a jumping chute, the "wait" command, a helper, or any combination of training aids, it also helps for you to stand close to the second jump, even reaching over it with the enticement toward your dog as you command him to jump, and then trot backwards as he comes toward you over the first jump. That helps to keep him coming straight on over the second jump. The instant he arrives, he should be rewarded for his effort, even if he's knocked down both jumps on the way. You'll be more particular as he becomes more advanced, but attitude comes first.

The only reason for not rewarding an early jumping effort would be for going under or around. If your canine student surprises you at this step by avoiding a jump, don't punish him but do interrupt him and return him quietly to the start. Use one of the many steps designed to prevent it from happening the same way next time. If you just assume your dog won't make the same mistake again, you'll probably be mistaken.

Take advantage of what your environment offers in the way of jump supports, poles, side walls, etc., and isolate your dog's jumping problems in specific lessons designed to help him work them out. Two jumps can look like a lot more than one jump, and some dogs will feel discouraged at first when they see an extra one. The same thing may happen when you add a third jump, whether or not your dog was taken aback by two jumps. Just be ready to help rather than to punish. Punishment now will

Stoner and Corene practice with angled jumps and tight turns. Dogs must develop responsiveness before working full-height jumps.

dampen his resourcefulness as well as his enthusiasm. Choose an approach which will make the sequence seem like fun and games while heading off the mistakes you know he's most likely to make.

Don't introduce a third jump until your dog is willing and smooth over two jumps at two-thirds his height, both single poles, with no side walls or long line required to keep him honest. When you add a third jump, most dogs will benefit from your lowering the jumps a bit. Repeat the process of making his decisions easy for him until he is relaxed and assertive about jumping all three in a row. Then begin to give him more freedom.

Once he's jumping smoothly every time, but before you work the jumps up high, begin to introduce angles from one jump to another. Do this first on leash, jumping with your dog and calling him toward you into the turn.

This is a variation on jumping which I neglected with Jessy until I had patterned her too strongly for jumping what was straight ahead. We had worked so hard at her jumping that I was thrilled to see her normal confidence surface when she began charging jump sequences the way she charged through the rest of her life. I didn't want to damage her new enthusiasm, but I should have put her on leash, lowered the jumps a bit, and begun positive control exercises right then. She is a very strong character and a very accomplished agility dog, but as of now she is quite unpredictable on the course and we have remedial work to do in this area of jumping.

Early in jump training, I introduce the idea of turning to an unexpected obstacle rather than completing what appears to the dog to be the right sequence of jumps. This is easy to set up at home and should be done with a great deal of encouragement and enticement to help him accept willingly that he must be heeding your directions as well as getting over the jumps.

As your dog becomes comfortable and proficient with jumping, begin to raise the jump heights. I like to raise one jump at a time because it sharpens their ability to judge each jump independently. Some dogs may do better if all the heights are kept uniform for awhile. It just depends on whether or not your dog likes a surprise.

An agility dog needs to jump well, but in order for him to keep on loving Agility course after course he has also got to love jumping. So don't be in a hurry to get him up to his competition jumping height. First get him up to his competition jumping attitude.

Cutting the corner saves time but requires a bigger jumping effort. Jessy came from the left and flew for the finish line.

Spreads and Long Jumps, Introduction (spreads are also called oxers; long jumps are also called broad jumps)

A spread jump has both height and length. A long jump is low with more length. When you ask your dog to jump a spread or long jump, you are asking him to reach out further and stretch his body longer. He has to use his rear muscles more forcefully to propel himself up and over a spread jump, and he should lengthen his running stride and extend his body flatter to take the long jump smoothly.

Magic breezes over a double spread at full speed.

It takes more skill and a lot more strength, but once your dog can judge these variations and coordinate himself accordingly, he will begin to bring that smooth, powerful movement to all his jumping on the run. He will be able to jump solid and bar jumps from a greater distance away, flattening his arc a bit and landing further past the jump on the run. When this speed and style are brought to all the dog's jumping, it will give him a faster time. That is what I mean by taking the jumps in stride.

From the beginning, Agility has incorporated spread jumps similar to those seen in equestrian jumping events. As the sport became more fine-tuned for dogs, interesting variations were introduced, such as the wishing well. The dog must jump over the bar above the well housing without putting a foot down on the obstacle. This jump was first defined in the English regulations, and is commonly used in agility tests in Great Britain and Europe. It appeared in the U.S. regulations in 1990.

Another jump popular in the equestrian world and adapted for Agility is the water jump. The dog must clear the water (often simulated water) the way he does a long jump, without putting a foot down in it. A hurdle is generally placed over the middle to cue the dog.

The sport is starting to see more wall jumps, some of which look so much like sturdy walls that the dog is apt to hop onto them rather than jump them. Since all agility jumps must be displaceable, the top of the wall should fall off when the dog pushes off. Some wall jumps have a displaceable single pole set above the wall itself at regulation jump height.

In the U.S. and Canada, a triple spread jump unit is part of the basic equipment, with supports positioned to accommodate poles at all jump heights. Formerly, small dogs jumped only the lowest pole, medium dogs the lower two, and large dogs all three. Now the U.S. prefers proportionate spacing to accommodate a real spread for all four of the new height divisions. A simple and inexpensive unit design is shown in the Appendix.

Jumps that have provision for only the standard regulation heights encourage pushing newcomer dogs too fast by going abruptly from one standard height to the next. Many clubs are building individual jump units, combining them to form doubles and triples. These individual units are great for training spread jumps. If they have enough peg holes in them and can be raised an inch at a time, you can create spreads of gradually increasing difficulty.

Handler straddles a low spread and entices Anchor over...

...for a cookie. Gradually a signal replaces enticement and action becomes the reward.

You needn't wait until your dog is jumping his regulation height before introducing some spread down low. Once your dog's attitude and timing are well in place over low poles, it's good to introduce some easy spread and long jumps. It will teach him to notice and gauge the depth of a jump along with its height, before he has to have the extra strength and confidence required to clear tall jumps. He just has to enjoy jumping single poles at half his height or more, and be judging them accurately in order to meet this variation on the theme successfully.

Spread Jumps, Progression

STEP 1. Higher section is set about half the height of the dog. Contrasting panel or pole is set in front at about half the height of the taller one, with a spread between them of about half the height of the dog.

HINTS: Please remember that these are only general guidelines. I know that one-half and one-fourth the height of a grown Jack Russell Terrier isn't much of a jump for a Jack Russell Terrier. It doesn't hurt to start simply, even if your dog is a good jumper. Let your dog have his first introduction to oxers down low while you puff his ego up, even if you think his ego is already too big to handle. If he needs extra work, begin using spreads in the control exercises above.

As with the single jumps, it's best to jump with your dog for a few lessons to enhance the spirit of fun and acclimate him to having you run beside him. Let him figure out for himself his timing and the need for a slightly elongated effort. As soon as he is successful, begin to use your jump command each time over. Always congratulate the dog's first efforts, even if they leave you scratching your head. Then learn from them and set about helping him improve his skill. The goal is to make your dog comfortable, as gradually as he likes, with a simple spread jump of single poles only.

STEP 2. Gradually raise the bars and increase the spread between them.

HINTS: Some dogs come to Agility having an advanced background in obedience. If your dog understands the obedience broad jump and doesn't seem to take to these spread jumps, set broad jump boards beneath the spread jump poles for awhile. This could help your CDX dog see the similarity and apply the skills he knows to this new challenge.

Keep the poles low, and set your broad jump at less than his normal competition length. Build understanding and confidence first, then begin to raise the poles bit by bit. When you're ready to begin removing boards, lower the poles at first. In other words, get your dog interested in the game and make him successful. Then start upping the ante, but don't make him want to fold. Keep him a winner.

STEP 3. Introduce a wide variety of spread jumps. Gradually use familiar spreads in jump sequences.

HINTS: In the U.S. and Canada, a so-called "double bar" spread is

Dizzy collects himself for the spring...

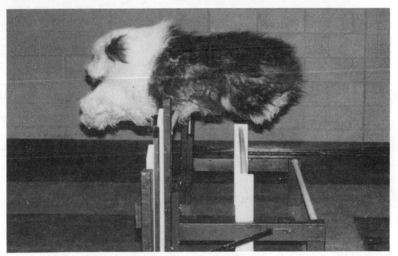

...and clears the spread even though the mat slipped. Indoor jumping at full height can be dangerous, especially for big dogs.

used. Like the triple spread jump unit, it is made in one piece and poles are placed at the regulation jump heights. But there are two columns of poles, about 12 inches apart. It can be difficult for the dog to determine in time that this is a spread. It's common for big dogs to knock the second top bar on the way down and for little dogs to land on top of the second bar. The new practice in the U.S. of lowering the near bar will help. Your dog needs specific exposure to this type of spread.

Fig. XIII. This talented Terv has jumped over the wing of the triple spread rather than the poles, so he has not completed the obstacle. This is considered a refusal.

A homemade version can be made by using two of your low single-pole jumps close together. This will get your dog to study his jumps more closely and put forth a bigger effort when the jump spread is questionable.

Both the wishing well and the wall jump, popular for years in Great Britain and Europe, are now being used in the U.S. and Canada. They each present the dog with an invitation to bank, or put a foot down on the jump. Banking the jump is penalized by five faults, so your dog needs to be trained on jumps that have some solid width at top. A shorter hurdle in front of a wishing well or wall obstacle often helps the dog understand that he should clear the structure in one jump. The feeling of jumping between the well housing and the roof can be approximated by introducing your dog to a low jump set crosswise under a stepladder.

Tire-jump practice helps as well. Try teaching your dog to step through two large tires attached and wrapped together, and then to jump through. This will really help him stretch his body out when he does spread jumps. In fact, the tire jump performed correctly is much like a spread jump. I included it in the tunnel section (Ch. 5) because the trickiest part of training for it is to have the dog always go through the tire's aperture. As you work to perfect your dog's jumping technique, think of the tire as a spread jump, very similar to the wishing well. They are handled with a long leap, body extended.

The tire jump frame can also be used without the tire and made up to simulate wishing well challenges. Be sure to do some impromptu decorating of your equipment, and move it around a lot to be sure your dog doesn't need things just so. As always, you can find things in your backyard that will improve your dog's skill on regulation equipment.

Long Jumps, Progression

STEP 1. Introduce long jump using one to three boards, depending on the size and natural ability of your dog. Begin with a total span about equal to your dog's height.

HINTS: Many handlers who use one jump command for all other jumps choose to use a different command for long jumps. I feel that my dogs are looking up at other obstacles rather than taking note of this one laid out low, so by giving it a separate name I hope to call up a quick change in their focus on the run. By contrast, I could never hope to keep straight all the different jump commands that some quick-thinking handlers use on the course, and I know that, for better or worse, my dogs will jump what I signal them to even if I call it by the wrong name. They would surely jump the long jump just as willingly on the same command if they saw it in time. I happen to call the long jump "over" and all the other jumps "jump."

There are three standard countermeasures most commonly taken to help dogs who put a foot down on or between the boards rather than jumping them. You could put the boards closer together, or put them on their sides, or you could set a bar jump over the middle between the boards. The goal is to get the dog jumping the upright boards early in his long jump training, before the jump approaches his full regulation length.

Using a pole jump as an early aid, for example, as soon as the dog is jumping nicely move the bar back a bit at a time, so eventually it's over the last board and no longer in the middle of the span between the boards.

Chaucer and Hazel include some simple long jumps in an impromptu obstacle course.

This seems to make it easier for the dog to make the transition from having the bar across the middle to having the space between the boards open up again.

I do not advise doing recalls across the long jump. Many dogs put a foot down between the boards that way who are happy to jump across when the handler runs beside. In Agility, the handler will generally be running too. We can take advantage of that momentum as a training tool by encouraging the dog to jump with us. We will be approximating that same motion even in competition for some time. It's another personal decision. Your dog might do better with one method than another.

STEP 2. Lengthen long jump, and add additional boards as required.

HINTS: To minimize long-jump problems as the length is increased, turn the middle board on its side at first, or put up your single pole hurdle again for a time. With each increase in length, jump with your dog at first if at all possible, or ask a friend to do so. This helps many dogs get the idea immediately, and it's fun.

Hannah didn't care for the long jump at first, but cookies, patience, and ingenuity changed her mind.

Many dogs can be taught the long jump beginning with two boards that are gradually pulled further apart without adding any additional boards. As long as your dog is not put off by seeing extra boards in the middle unexpectedly, this is an excellent way to teach long jumps. It assures that the dog understands that he is to clear the entire length, no matter how inviting the middle might look.

It's unusual for a dog who is progressing well on the spread jumps to have much trouble with the long jump, but if it happens go over your dog's jump-training history to select the best course for improving his understanding. Because the tallest long-jump boards are often quite a bit taller than they are wide, turning them on their sides lowers the jump quite a bit. This can be just what your dog needs, or for him it might be better to prop up a few planks to your regulation long jump-height at first instead.

Another helpful system is to set up a "long jump" made of two or three single pole jumps, like those you set up early in his high jump training. Set the poles no higher than the standard height of the long jump for your country. Space the pole jumps close together at first, to be sure the dog jumps them as a single unit. Then gradually spread them apart. As the dog understands, add your long jump boards underneath so he can make the association. Then remove one single pole at a time, beginning with the one closest to the dog. A simplified version can also be set up in a hallway indoors.

As your dog progresses and you lengthen the long jump, make sure the traction around it is good. Unlike jumping a higher single jump, the dog's front feet don't land as perpendicularly after a long jump. His landing force is as much forward as downward, so his front feet will tend to skid forward if the footing is at all slippery. On a positive note, it's easier on his shoulders.

Bear clears the 36-inch long jump. Extra board at side reminds him not to cut the corner with handler at a distance.

STEP 3. Introduce some variation in long jumps. Introduce pole markers at four corners. Gradually use familiar long jumps in jump sequences.

HINTS: Water jumps present an obvious distraction to many dogs. It comes back to the consistent practice of teaching your dog that when you tell him to jump he must clear the obstacle without touching it. Don't use the same command for telling your dog to jump into the car that you use for telling him to jump over things. How about "hup" for hopping onto something and "jump" for jumping over?

If your dog is afraid of water or especially fond of it, get his long-jump training well in hand before introducing water in tubs or fake water under the long-jump boards. As things progress, a helper who will splash gently while the dog is working is useful. As you work with more water and fewer long-jump boards, you might want to put a few low raised single poles over the water jump to help your dog remember to jump. This helps whether the dog would rather go around or jump in. As you're ready to begin removing the poles, delete the one nearest the dog first. You need him to focus on the far end of the jump.

In competition, long jumps are often marked by some sort of tall post at each corner. It's a good idea to be ready for anything, including streamers on the marker poles, or metal poles which reflect sharply in the sunlight. The dog must jump between the poles and clear the entire length of the jump to avoid faults. He's got a better chance of success if he's not staring up at the poles.

When you're ready to begin including a long jump in your jump sequences, give a little extra room between jumps at first. It will take some practice for your dog to get the knack of stretching long and then immediately coiling for a taller jump. It's very helpful to set up a downscaled series closer together specifically for working on this flexibility. Once he's comfortable, it's time to incorporate turns as well, both left and right, also using simplified jumps at first.

Whatever combination of teaching aids your dog needs, you can find a trick that helps make it click for him. Keep your agility eyes open and find a solution both you and your dog will enjoy. People have used everything from chicken wire between the boards to yanking their dogs through the air to get them to jump a long jump cleanly. It's a lot more fun to put your mind to work on invitations to jump long rather than punishments for jumping short.

Jumps, Summary

Use your dog's favorite enticement every time at first to alleviate stress. As the dog becomes more confident and proficient with each step, use enticement less often on that step. Always praise your dog's first efforts, and keep the training sessions lively and fun.

Switch sides with your dog regularly to keep him accustomed to taking direction from either side. Change your jumps often and move them to different locations so your dog can get used to variations.

STEP 1. Practice solid jumps at half the dog's height, inside and outside. Jump with dog and/or use helper for training sessions. Gradually switch to pole jump.

STEP 2. With single jump, raise height bit by bit as dog's ability improves. Introduce signal and send your dog. When he is confident, introduce low spreads with highest bar at half his height. Long jumps no longer than the dog's height may also be introduced.

STEP 3. Introduce multiple single jumps. Gradually raise heights of spread jumps and length of long jumps. Introduce angles and improve signal and voice control.

STEP 4. Incorporate all types of familiar jumps into multiple jump sequences. Further improve control work.

Melissa Lee Harris

Strong and proud, Zebedee clears the 20-inch long jump. His friends call him the "dash" hound.

Fluffy and Brian get comfortable on the pause table.

8

THE PAUSE

Genius is eternal patience.

–Michelangelo

Each competition agility course contains either a pause table or a pause box, but not both. Handlers are required to have their dogs lie down on the pause obstacle. The pause table is a sturdy three-foot-square structure with a nonslip surface. The height of the table varies with the jump heights. In Canada, three heights have been used, the same as their jump heights. The U.S. has preferred a 12-inch table height for the small dog class and 21-inch height for the large divisions, but now a 30-inch table height for dogs jumping 30 inches is also used. Table heights do not exceed jump heights.

The pause box is not literally a box, but consists of any four-foot by four-foot clearly delineated area within the course. Many clubs use PVC pipe or a border of upright boards nailed together to define their pause boxes, but well-anchored strips of sturdy tape sometimes serve the purpose. Corners are sometimes marked by tall poles, just as the long jump is, to make the obstacle easier to spot.

All dogs perform the box in the same way, as if they were atop a table. Although the dog may leave a paw or a nose outside the defined area, if an elbow or too much of the body extends from the obstacle the judge must indicate this, and the handler must have the dog reposition himself or accept penalty faults for not completing the pause obstacle. The dog is considered to be out of the box if the judge feels the dog would not be balanced atop the table if he were to assume the identical posture there.

The pause must be maintained in competition for five seconds. The judge begins with "5" as the dog assumes the correct position, then counts down aloud in a cadence, "4, 3, 2, 1, Go." Any dog who breaks position must put himself back correctly before the count resumes or, usually, begins again with "5." If a dog leaves the obstacle before the count is done, he must be brought back to start over in order to avoid penalty faults for failing to complete the obstacle.

The one concession to being "almost done" is called "uncorrected anticipation of end of count." If the dog leaves the obstacle a split second before time, the judge may mark five faults for anticipation instead of the full (usually 20 faults) penalty for failing the obstacle. A dog will be apt to break too soon during the rushed spirit of competition, so it's better to train for steadiness on the pause obstacle well beyond five seconds.

In the excitement of competition, a dog often finds it difficult to put up with this sudden interruption of the course run, and the handler often reminds him several times during the exercise to hold his place. A dog may need his handler to stay beside him to remain steady; a dog who will stay put while his handler looks away and even moves away makes it much easier for the handler to be in place to direct him accurately on the next obstacle without loss of time.

Pause Table, Introduction

When a dog performs the pause table perfectly, it's done in one smooth motion; by the time the dog is completely onto the table, he is already lying down. A dog can learn from the beginning to work the table this way, with the handler commanding "table," running with the dog to the table and encouraging him to hop up, then immediately having him lie down.

Gradually, the handler helps the dog learn to take more of the responsibility. He commands "down" earlier, so the dog has it on his mind while he's jumping up instead of after he's atop the table. Eventually the dog's performance can be shaped into one smooth motion, and the length of time spent in that position can be lengthened. But it is the unusual dog who can learn the whole job at once and learn it well. A dog who is expected to put it all together too soon may become patterned for a slow and deliberate performance, not at all what you want.

Don't teach the table all at once unless your dog already enjoys hopping up onto anything and is happy to perform an instant down anywhere you ask. If you try to put the whole picture together when either of these elements is less than foolproof, you create problems that will cost you a lot of time and extra work to reshape. The steps outlined here are perfected separately, then brought together.

Competitors with large dogs will find that the taller table actually makes the job easier for taller dogs. Though we will always see an occasional dog of any size go flying onto the table and off the opposite side (generally penalized by five faults), this happens less often when the dog has to jump up as well as forward to the table.

Pause Table, Progression

STEP 1. Make dog comfortable with the table. Name the obstacle and teach him to hop onto it with you when you say the name. Introduce release word.

HINTS: Before introducing a command for the table, let your dog get comfortable there. Even if your dog is apt to hop onto strange things before checking them out, it doesn't hurt to introduce the table by getting up there yourself and inviting your dog to join you. Being on the table with your dog helps prevent a tendency for him to jump on and off and on again. Right from the beginning, he will tend to hop up and stay there if you are up there with him, so it's for the overeager dog as well as the hesitant one. Just make sure you leave him enough room.

A dog who doesn't enjoy being atop things, a very big dog who overlaps the table when he lies down, or a dog who is used to being boosted up has good reason to hesitate at the table. Let him use a step or ramp at first and don't issue any discipline up there yet. If your dog needs to start with a low table or a larger platform, that's OK. Or perhaps he'd do better to meet the pause box before the pause table, then come back to try the table at his own speed with a little more confidence. Just work your way gradually to the real thing.

Once the dog enjoys the obstacle (you should spare no tricks in helping him associate pleasure with it), begin to use the table command when enticing him to join you. As soon as he's up there and has enjoyed your heartfelt praise, say your release word and get off the table yourself, coaxing him to hop off.

This step is completed when your dog is happy to pop himself onto his regulation-size table and stay there with you. Don't put any emphasis on making him lie down on the table just yet. Once he loves this silly table game, it's time to teach him to hop on and off by himself, and from further away.

STEP 2 (See also Step 3 for concurrent exercise). Have dog get onto table alone, with you right beside. Begin to send dog to table on command.

HINTS: Once your dog loves the table, just your patting it and saying the name will be enough to get him up there. Be generous with your praise when he does this, and don't ask him to stay there yet. As soon as he's taken in your congratulations, release him. Don't forget to work sometimes with your dog on your left and sometimes on your right. Also don't feel compelled to wipe off the table if it's wet. If your dog hates water you need to wait until the training has progressed somewhat before surprising him with a wet, slippery surface, but keep in mind that he has to get to it sometime in order to accept it and to learn to judge wet footing accurately.

Now is a good time to introduce a toy or other enticement on the table, if you haven't already done so. As soon as your dog is completely onto the table, play with him, keeping the toy or cookie down on the table. Keeping the enticement down patterns the dog to focus down when he gets onto the table. If your dog is apt to grab the toy and take off, do this step on leash, but practice recalls and other obedience exercises regularly (Ch. 2) to help him learn to stay close.

After he's learned this part and is hopping up quickly and bending down to get the reward, begin to emphasize an arm signal at the table and de- emphasize the patting of the table until you no longer need to touch the obstacle. When your dog is ready for an additional piece of the puzzle, try putting the toy or cookie on the table, making sure your dog notices it, and send him to the table with your cheerful command word and arm signal. Run there with him from a short distance, perhaps only a step away at first.

Pat the table only if necessary, and put a hand on the enticement if need be to focus your dog on it and prevent him from snatching it without jumping up. As he learns and takes over the whole task, run with him less than all the way. Keep your dog accurate and fast with enticements on the table and gradually make your guidance less obvious. Increasing the distance too much at a time can result in the dog stopping short or misjudging the landing pad and going off the other side.

As soon as he's up on the table and has the toy, release him. Even if he would hop off on his own without your releasing him, say the word first anyway. Because he will have to learn to wait until he hears it, let the release word become part of his table experience early. Likewise, it's important not to pattern your dog for hanging around on the table, since you will soon be requiring the instant down whenever he's up there. Since attitude is paramount now, time the table command and release words to imprint them without forcing the issue.

Your student hops on for a coveted reward, hops off when you release him, and struts with the prize while you praise him. Repeat this exercise a few times each session. As your dog becomes quick at it, begin to vary the angle from which you send him. Gradually increase your distance from the table. If all is going well and you think he could wait just a second longer before being released, it's OK to do that at this point. Work on leash if necessary to prevent your dog from taking off too soon, but don't reprimand him.

STEP 3. Away from the pause obstacle, perfect your dog's instant response to the command "down." Once he is quick as a wink, introduce distractions and practice everywhere.

HINTS: The dog who argues with his handler about assuming the down on the table is the dog who needs separate work on assuming the down anytime and anywhere. Begin by reviewing the basic commands in Ch. 2, both at home and in public. Teach your dog what the word "down" means, that good things happen when he lies down on command, and that he must lie down when you tell him to, no matter what and no matter how long. This is all part of the necessary groundwork.

Don't combine practicing the down with a pause obstacle until your dog really enjoys the down command and is quick about it. Many handlers who use the pause table for early training sessions with the down find that they have inadvertently patterned their dogs for resistance and slow responses there, even after the dogs become quick at responding to the command elsewhere. Better to perfect a fast response off the table first and then transfer that familiar skill to the table.

Continue to entice your dog before he obeys as well as rewarding him after. When you bring the instant down to the table, your dog will soon be ready to do the work first, then see the treat. Some dogs readily accept drill work for treats, and speed up just for food or a toy, ready to practice the down exercise on the pause obstacle in only a week. Other dogs need a more well-rounded approach, making some favorite activities of each day contingent on responding to your command to down.

Through your quick response to the dog's correct action when you say the command word, you help him teach himself how to train you to give him the reward faster. Hold the enticement out to the dog, either literally by having it in your hands, or figuratively, perhaps by having the dog on leash and the car door open for him. The very second that he lies down you reward him, either by popping him the goodie or by inviting him to hop into the car.

The reward has to suit your dog and it has to be immediately available at first. If your dog barks and dances around and tries every trick in the book to get the goodie without lying down, ignore the antics in a good-natured way, without getting upset. Repeat the command. Let him figure out how this new job works. He's not used to being the trainer. If he's wild, he needs to be on a leash to keep him around, but not to make him comply. You shouldn't be doing this until he is very familiar with the command through all your groundwork. This is for speed.

The first few sessions may take a long time, but as he realizes that the reward comes immediately on his assuming the down position, and that nothing else will get him the reward, he'll suddenly begin to get very good and very fast about it. Humans are so painfully slow by comparison, you may need to practice to improve your own reflexes. Get that reward in there at once.

Training your dog to be the trainer is a different sort of job, and it requires a different mindset. It will prevent you from intimidating a sensitive dog or from setting up a power struggle with a tough dog. Many sensitive dogs are also quite independent. If you escalate force training to combat his so-called stubbornness, you may set up a sullen passive disobedience. Where a more confident dog would actively resist, the quieter dog withdraws. In either case, letting the dog control the more advanced fine tuning of this exercise brings out a cooperative spirit.

When your dog is hitting the deck with speed on your command to "down," make him start waiting a second longer before you reward him. It's a gradual process. Begin by interspersing immediate rewards with slightly delayed rewards. As with early training, a hand on his withers may help steady him while you say "stay" and praise him, then offer the reward. For some intense dogs it's better not to touch them but to repeat "down" or "down, stay" a couple of times before giving the reward. By association they learn what "stay" means. Remember to give immediate rewards often, too.

Alternatively, you would not have to use the word "stay" for this exercise at all. It is just as useful for you to repeat "down" or to teach your dog to recognize an arm signal for the down command. If your dog has been trained that "stay" is a lengthy exercise, or that he should flop over onto one hip or tuck a paw, you might prefer a different command because you will want your dog to remain ready to run while in the pause position. In Agility, commands and signals can be repeated and used together. Even if you train your dog in practice to be steady with a single command, you should plan to repeat the command during competition when nerves are tighter.

Good signals can be much stronger than words. An upraised arm or a palm outstretched toward the dog can help keep him steady. Although you need to keep eye contact with the dog in early pause training, you do not ultimately want the dog to rely on that to keep him steady. You will need to focus momentarily on the next obstacle, prior to the judge's release, in preparation for continuing on the course.

Many intent dogs will pop up in anticipation when their handlers look away from them. You need to train your dog to stay down while you move your head and even walk away. Here again, a hand on the withers or the command repeated as you begin to look away can help at first. Once your dog learns the signal, that will also help maintain continuity while you introduce movement.

STEP 4. Introduce the down command on the table. Use the table only with the down command from now on. Send your dog, and begin to command him down earlier.

HINTS: When your dog is happy to go to the table on command, and also happy and fast with the instant down, it's time to put the two together. This step is much like Step 2 except that you will have your dog lie down each time as he hops onto the pause table. Use a toy or cookie held down on the table to help him if he likes, but now couple that with helping him all the way down every time, assisting physically with your hand or arm on the withers, if necessary, to help him incorporate this variation into the pattern. You could also practice Step 3 on the table at first if that helps your dog understand the job better.

Ultimately you'll need your dog to stay still in the down position, so it's OK to start delaying the release word just a second or so sometimes, but please don't keep him there for a full count yet unless he is blindingly fast leaving the table and is leaping off too soon every time. Concentrate on keeping him fast on the departure by releasing him quickly to dissuade

---

After the instant down is learned, it is used to teach the dog to land on the table in the down position. By the time Kari's feet are on the table, she is already lying down.

him from settling down too comfortably. Keep this up until he completely understands the job of getting on and lying down at the same time, then begin to lengthen his down time on the table. In general, crimes of action are easier to correct in Agility than are crimes of inaction.

As he gets quicker with this, begin to command him down earlier and touch him less. Accentuate your arm signal and touch the enticement less. To help your dog put the pause puzzle pieces together and take over the whole job, you will have to taper off gently on all the various kinds of help you've been giving him, including enticement, physical assistance, touching the obstacle, using a leash, running all the way to the table with him, and any other personal ingredients which have served you in teaching this obstacle. You need to begin weaning your dog from these helps. But wean too abruptly and he'll become confused. This process of putting it all together, progressing from a handler-centered interaction to a dog-centered interaction, takes a long time. Don't try to do everything at once.

STEP 5. Lengthen down to down-stay. Introduce distractions and odd approach and departure angles.

HINTS: Just as you increased very gradually the length of time your dog had to wait for his reward when you were teaching the instant down, incorporate a brief extension of time now between down and release on the table. Your dog might do well with a hand on the withers and a cookie to his nose at first, or you might want to repeat your command word.

Distance is gradually increased and eye contact and hand signal are weaned, but it takes time. For now, signal reminds Val as Ron looks away.

(Some dogs will wait still as can be just by holding them with your eyes.) Use any combination that gets and keeps the dog down without making him unhappy. As he accepts the challenge, start weaning him from your ideas for helping him. Every once in a while pull out a motivating idea or two and toss them in again just to keep things lively.

Because you've maintained a kinetic pace at the table, never making your dog stay long, he should be patterned to expect a quick release, which he demonstrates by remaining fully prone, looking at you. If you see him lean back and get comfortable, you're increasing the stay time too much at once or losing his attention. If you have a dog who finds it impossible to lie still on the table, start practicing some long downs up there (see Ch. 2) until he does settle back a bit. The trick is to keep your dog's interest while you keep him steady longer and longer. Work up to 10 seconds or more, and it doesn't matter how many weeks it takes you to get there. Your dog's attitude and accuracy have come together now, and lengthening the time he can hold position will be a matter of reading your dog correctly and keeping him motivated.

When you're ready to vary the direction and distance from which you send your dog to the table, begin again to run with him and use your tricks to help him get it right, then gradually use them less blatantly and less often. Don't forget to work your dog on both the left and the right. The more he learns about working the table, the more quickly you can dispense with the extra help.

With his handler at a distance, Farley contains himself, ready for the next assignment. It's hard to walk the line between patience and impatience.

Pause Box, Introduction

The pause box area is four feet square, quite a bit larger than the pause table, but it can still be very difficult to stay in bounds. A dog is apt to run in one side and out the other before he can stop. Sometimes it happens so quickly and the timing of the handler's command is such that the dog ends up lying down completely outside the designated area.

If your dog already understands the pause table, you can move through the first three steps of the pause box quickly. If you are starting with the box, that is fine, but first read through the table section before you begin training here. The two obstacles have many similarities.

Casper hops into the box, where his toy is waiting. Introduce signal early, and work both sides.

Angled approaches and greater distances help the dog learn to find the box for himself.

Pause Box, Progression

STEP 1. Help dog recognize the pause area and feel comfortable there. Have him join you there. Name the obstacle.

HINTS: As with the table, get into the area yourself and encourage your dog to play and relax there. When using a toy or food, hold it down on the ground.

Don't name the obstacle until the dog is relaxed about it. Most people use the word "box" for this obstacle. Many handlers tend to keep the dog with them while approaching the box to prevent the common problem of dogs going out of bounds before lying down. In this case, the command "heel" or "come" en route to the box, and arm signals close up along with verbal encouragement to get the dog in and down correctly, are used. Sending your dog ahead to the box is risky but can save a lot of time once it's learned.

There will be a great variety of pause-box-perimeter materials in your dog's career, so it's wise to set up several makeshift ones of your own, and it doesn't hurt to make them just a little smaller than regulation size to give your dog a wider margin of error in competition. He needs to recognize different-looking pause boxes.

Get your dog used to the rain with this obstacle. If your dog hates to lie down on wet grass, practice his long downs when there's dew on the lawn and use your strongest enticements to keep him happy. Make sure you dress for the wet grass, because if you're not comfortable you will have difficulty making your dog believe it's fun to be there. Work up to practicing in a solid drizzle. It takes a real downpour to cancel an agility competition, and some judges decide that a pause box will weed out some less committed dogs.

STEP 2 (See also Step 3 for concurrent exercise). Have your dog enter the box without you being in it. Begin to send your dog.

HINTS: When you can coax your dog into the box while you stand beside it, you're ready to help him learn to get himself there on command. Begin by trotting with your dog to the pause box, carrying a toy or treat. Let him see you put the enticement down in the middle of the box, then walk him out of the box a step or two and turn around. Point to the enticement and command "box." Run with him, help if necessary, and release him as soon as he's in the box. Gradually, help less until you can send your dog alone from only a few steps away. Then, as you increase the distance further, be prepared to help again and taper off as before. Once your dog is going quite a distance on his own to the box, you could go back to shorter distances and introduce some complications, like odd-angle approaches, practicing in the rain, etc.

It's a good idea to introduce marker poles at the four corners of your practice pause boxes now. In competition, these markers are about four feet high. On many agility courses, the box perimeter is difficult to spot from a dog's eye level. To find it quickly, the dog needs to head for the poles, then look for the box. Sometimes use plain dowels or rods, and other times decorate your marker poles using streamers or hanging a blouse that flutters in the breeze. Your dog needs to be accustomed to extremes. When marker poles are not used, plan to accompany your dog closer to the pause box to be sure he spots it.

STEP 3. Away from the pause obstacle, perfect your dog's instant response to the command "down." See Step 3 of the pause table exercise for a fuller description of this work. See also Ch. 2 for remedial work and Ch. 10 for advanced work pertaining to "down."

HINTS: Step 3 accomplishes the transfer of the enticement from a lure, which is held out to the dog to induce him to perform a task, to a reward, which is presented after completion of the task.

When you first make this transition, your dog may question whether food is available. Soon he learns that the prize will appear immediately when he lies down. It then becomes a little easier to convince him that the food will appear soon enough even if it's tucked into a pocket and not held in the hands at all when the command is given. Just let your dog watch you put the goodies in your pocket at first and he will soon figure this step out.

It's necessary to wean your dog from a lure system to a reward system. The lure system is a wonderful motivator which can make difficult new tasks stress- free and fun. That makes it a very good tool. But it's only the first step in the dog's learning by a reward system. If you were to try to abandon the use of food all at once, or wean too quickly from lure to reward, your dog would be apt to lose faith that he will be rewarded.

Advance gradually to less blatant use of the reward until your dog can run an entire agility course and know that he'll get a big reward after the finish.

STEP 4. Combine the down command with pause box work. From now on, have your dog lie down whenever he's in the pause box. Send your dog, and begin to command him down earlier.

HINTS: Repeat the playtime of Steps 1 or 2 with an enticement held down on the ground. The kicker is that now you will not be releasing your dog until he is completely lying down; being in the box and playing down low were enough for the introduction to the new obstacle, but not any more.

Another variation that may help your dog put it all together is to practice Step 3 in the pause box, keeping the enticement in your hand instead of on the ground. Gradually keep the reward hidden until the dog is down. This is good preparation for delaying the reward longer and longer, which you will soon be ready to do.

Once your dog has combined the skills of getting into the pause box and lying down at once in it, repeat the process of sending him to the box from gradually further away. Now, though, he is not released until he is completely lying down in the box. This step is completed when your dog recognizes the box and views it as an instant down obstacle.

STEP 5. Lengthen down to down-stay. Introduce distractions and odd approach and departure angles.

HINTS: If your dog has been working with the enticement in the box,

---

Arrow is sent to the box and ordered down as soon as he gets there...

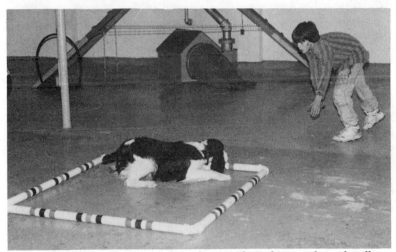

He is kept there only a second at first, to keep him ready and willing. Gradually the time is lengthened. Handler has to walk a fine line between steadiness and motivation.

it's time to make the switch. Stand close to the box, holding the enticement, and send your dog into the box. Present the reward as soon as he lies down. He'll catch on quickly to the new rule, and then he'll probably be faster than ever with it since he already likes training you and already knows how to do the box correctly.

Now you can stand further and further from the box when you send him. This will automatically lengthen his down, as it will take you longer to get to him with the reward. Begin to change sides and vary your approach and departure angles. Remind him to stay down as you avert your eyes before releasing him. It's time to help him get steady no matter what you do, so when he's ready you should start practicing jumping jacks and turning around before you release him. Be inventive with your distractions, and bring his reliability along at a pace he can handle.

Start having your dog catch up to you for his reward, although you will also return to him with it sometimes. Eventually you'll want to direct him to the next obstacle from the box, so he needs to learn to watch you walk away and be ready to charge off to wherever you like when you release him. Keep up the games with the pause, because it helps balance the "hurry up and wait" extremes required here.

Pause Table and Pause Box, Summary

Use your dog's favorite enticement. Entice the dog every time at first to alleviate stress. As the dog becomes more confident and proficient with each step, use enticement less often on that step. Always praise your dog's first efforts, and keep the training lively and fun.

Switch sides with your dog regularly to keep him accustomed to taking direction from either side. Work from all sides of the pause obstacle, and move it to different locations so your dog can get used to variations.

STEP 1. Make dog comfortable on the obstacle with you.

STEP 2. Make dog comfortable on the obstacle without you. Introduce signal and send your dog. Introduce angled approaches and departures. Introduce wet conditions.

STEP 3. Away from the pause obstacle, perfect instant down. Introduce distractions.

STEP 4. Combine instant down with pause obstacle.

STEP 5. Lengthen down time with the pause. Introduce distractions. Review various approach and departure angles. Improve control work.

9

THE WEAVE POLES

The greater the obstacle, the more glory in overcoming it.

–Jean Baptiste Moliere

No obstacle calls for pure Agility like the weave poles, which consist of 5-12 poles or stakes of approximately one-inch diameter, spaced 18-24 inches apart. The dog must enter the row of poles from the right and weave back and forth, slalom fashion, down the line. Any deviation, including beginning on the left side of the first pole, weaving to the wrong side of any individual pole, or skipping any pole, is incorrect.

In the more advanced classes, anything less than a smooth and accurate performance with no back-ups will result in a penalty, so train with the perfect picture in mind as you go through the all-important beginner steps.

The better approaches to teaching weave poles, first used extensively by the English, pattern the dog for attitude and speed early, and give him an unabashed enjoyment of this nonsensical task we call weaving. The fastest dogs are weaving 10 poles in well under three seconds.

I will focus on two approaches to teaching the weave poles: the chute method and the leaning-poles method. The leaning-poles method assumes that you have read through the chute method.

Speed, one of the first things you need to pattern, comes more readily when the dog is happy, so use all your tricks to keep him working tail-up. Later, at the advanced stage when the dog needs to flex sharply, the familiar fast pace is easily resumed once the task is mastered. So make the extra effort on each step to keep the work fun and snappy. Don't assume your dog will understand tomorrow because he seemed to understand today. This job is a lot to remember, so you must always gauge your dog's current frame of mind and level of competence. Bolster his speed and confidence by reviewing well-learned previous steps often. You should plan to take several months to bring the whole task together.

Libby snakes through the poles with grace and style.

Chute Method, Introduction

This approach calls for the dog to run a chute– a column formed by two rows of individual weave poles. It requires a supply of 8-12 individual poles, which can be custom made or improvised. Introductory poles should be taller than your dog, but short enough for you to handle a leash over them with one hand.

Wooden stakes or dowling makes inexpensive poles. Individual lengths can be nailed onto wooden X-shaped bases, or a long spike can be driven into one end for sticking them into the ground. Lengths of PVC pipe on wooden bases are lightweight, durable, and very portable. The thin white reflector stalks that stick into the ground are also fine. Some people have cut PVC at an angle to make a sharp point for easy hammering directly into the ground. My Canadian friends, the Legers, made indoor poles from small plastic traffic cones with white balloon sticks tucked through the top hole.

Chute Method, Progression

STEP 1. Arrange two rows of individual poles to form a chute at least three times the width of your dog. Helper holds dog by collar. You run down the chute, turn and entice your dog to follow.

HINTS: In each row, poles are spaced three feet to four feet apart. The two rows are staggered, with the first pole on the left closest to the dog. This is very important for helping him learn the pattern of always entering a line of weave poles with the first one on his left.

First walk, then trot up and down the chute with your dog, so he's comfortable on either side of you in there. Then start running it. Your helper holds your dog by the agility collar, watching you run down the chute. Turn around to face your dog, crouch and call him down the open path formed between the two rows.

Don't make this a recall because that puts you in the position of having to correct him if he's wary of the poles and doesn't come. It's just as easy to use other sorts of cajoling and enticement until your dog is sure of himself (widen the chute initially if need be). Then introduce your weave pole command. I use "Poles" because it has a strong sound and doesn't sound like any other obstacle name.

A short chute, using four to six poles (two to three on each side), is enough to start with. Use any trick, like running the other way or holding out a cookie to get him coming in fast with this game. As he gets good at it, position yourself a little further from the chute's exit.

Some dogs run a chute faster if there's an enticement but no person at the other end. If so, get your dog interested in the food or toy, and walk him down the chute to place the object down, on a white paper plate for visibility. Return through the chute and turn around, then get him excited

Fig. XIV. Although this dog is weaving happily, he is too keyed in to looking up at his handler, which will slow him down immensely. It's important to pattern your dog from the beginning to focus straight ahead. When you do add hand signals, keep your hand low.

Handler runs chute to place toy and excite dog...

...Anchor is revved up and released...

..."Got it!" The same sequence is used if the handler is holding the enticement and helper is holding the dog.

about the prize before sending him. If you start the chute this way, use only four poles at first.

If your dog is a "monkey-see, monkey-do" dog, leave him at the entrance end while you run the chute and grab the reward a time or two. This strategy is a good substitute if you don't have a helper. When he's caught on, leave the enticement a bit further past the exit. My dog, Anchor, was taught this way (see photos), as he's very keen on sighting his toy and grabbing it fast, before the other quicker dogs nab it. Although he loves to come to people and was willing to work the chute that way, he has been trained because of his size not to throw himself at us, so he tended to dance in the chute, with a lot of sideways antics as he approached. He worked the chute with much more intensity and a straight path when I switched to his beloved ball.

STEP 2. Gradually lengthen chute. Switch from enticement to reward. Begin to narrow the chute.

HINTS: Be sure that you're using your weave pole command word each time now. That will help him continue to understand what his job is as you gradually make it more difficult. Continue to use a helper if possible. The helper can keep the dog eager to run the chute while preventing him from leaving before you give the command. For all but the most wild workers, this is much better for early pole work than leaving the dog on a wait command. You're trying to encourage speed and even impatience on the dog's part.

Don't begin to narrow the chute until your dog is flying fast and comfortably down a wide channel of 8-10 poles. Then narrow the path by bringing the two rows a bit closer to each other. Working two sessions each day, with a few repetitions through the chute each time, you'll have your dog fast and happy in a pathway only slightly wider than his body in only a week or two or three, depending on his size and his sensitivity to the chute. Don't be in a hurry. You'll probably find that you can bring the rows closer together by several inches at a time at first, but that rate is short-lived.

The closer the poles come to the sides of the dog, the more gradually you need to adjust them inward. An inch a day may not seem like enough at first, but it could easily be too much by the next week. At the completion of this step, the dog is still moving straight, close to but unencumbered by the poles. He is not yet weaving.

Your dog should not slow down or take any particular notice of the poles. If he does, you have moved them inward too rapidly. You want him brazen about them, so that when he has to bump into them later when learning to weave, he will not hesitate.

To switch from lure to reward, gradually hold the prize closer to your body, then hide it behind you or in a pocket to delay the dog's gratification a bit longer. You could also turn and run away from him as he runs down the longer chute; when he catches up, he gets the reward. Another

Max works a short snug chute expertly, so...

...she's ready for a longer chute, then back to a short one when it's narrowed a bit more.

favorite is to throw a toy as your dog exits the chute. This helps him keep running forward even as you begin to stand in different locations when you send him down the chute.

If you are using an enticement without a person at the exit end of the chute, adjust the rows in toward the dog extremely gradually. You don't want him to cut out and grab the prize unfairly, and you don't want to have to chase him or yell at him. You will not be switching from enticement to reward just yet, but it will not be difficult to do so later, since the dog has already learned to send himself down the chute with you behind him. It's just a different order of details.

STEP 3. Shorten the chute, and run beside dog. Work from left and right sides. When he's back to fast and snappy, begin to lengthen chute as before.

HINTS: Keeping the chute just a bit wider than your dog, remove all but four to six poles for a few days. Practice on leash if necessary to help the dog learn to do this same job with you beside him, and don't hesitate to widen the chute a bit at first if he needs it. Now is the payoff for having taught him the command word, because this will help keep the continuity of purpose for him as your position changes.

Continue straight past the exit for a short way to help the dog pattern for always finishing the whole row of poles. Since you have already switched from enticement to reward, it shouldn't be difficult to get the dog to chase after you as soon as he's exited the chute.

Soon enough you'll be charging off to the left or right, but for now run a few steps straight ahead before changing direction. If you're working on a leash or tab, keep it straight up in the air through the chute, taut but not tight.

If you are sending your dog to an enticement, shorten the chute and run beside him, then run forward and play with him when he's grabbed his toy. Don't take the toy away yet. This step is usually easy for these dogs, since they were not dependent on running to you from the beginning.

STEP 4. Back to four to six poles, and begin narrowing the chute again. A smidgen a day or an inch a week is plenty. Use enticement and teach hand signal. Use leash as necessary.

HINTS: This is the most important step, the transition from running to weaving. You've only got inches to go before the poles are in a straight line, but these last inches will take many times the work of the earlier steps. Although at some point in this step your dog will have to slow down and think more about his job, this is not the same as dwindling motivation. His speed will return as his coordination improves. Don't ever add more poles or move your poles closer together until your dog is reliable and fast off leash at the previous width.

Keep your chute short enough that your dog only has to flex a few times to complete the job. This will speed him up quickly once he learns how to make his body weave. Keep tuned in to how he is taking this each session, and be prepared to make adjustments accordingly. He may need the poles a bit wider one day than the previous day. Once you start working with your poles narrower than your dog, the dog's job begins getting difficult. Keep him motivated with quick success, enticements, and lots of praise and excitement. Don't punish mistakes, just issue more guidance next time.

Practice separate flexibility exercises (see Ch. 3), and play games each day that encourage twisting and turning in motion. Following an enticement during practice helps your dog flex left and right around the poles, patterning him for the work and heading off mistakes. It also helps him focus on the hand signal you'll be giving him with your left forearm.

At this stage, the signal with the forearm may be what prevents him from staying at your side when he should be weaving left, going away from you. The arm blocks his forward progress and physically directs him to his left without punishing him. Then the enticement draws him back to his right. It's important that the left hand not contain an enticement, because you don't want the quick dog to back out following the withdrawal of that hand.

Instead, the right hand, holding the enticement, takes over between the next two poles as soon as the dog has crossed the median. This keeps him moving forward while weaving smoothly, and is not difficult to

Anchor can no longer run the chute without bending. Use leash and enticement at first, then allow more freedom as your dog's speed and confidence resume.

Fig. XV. A sideways pull on the leash throws the dog off balance and causes him to pull the other way. Don't use the leash as a substitute for raising poles very gradually so the dog can teach himself to flex.

coordinate, even at considerable speed. As the dog's speed increases, the enticement may be presented less often, but continue with the left hand signal for some time.

Use your left forearm to signal the dog away from you every other pole. You and your dog will soon have worked out a positive understanding of weaving and a system that is available the instant you need it. The left forearm is used to send the dog away from you just as you do with other obstacles, so he can learn this system quickly. As the dog becomes more proficient, make your signal less obvious until your hand no longer crosses the plane of the poles.

Eventually your signal should become so subtle the dog doesn't need it anymore. This is a system that allows the handler freedom of movement, so you are more apt to be able to keep up with the dog as his speed increases. It can also be used to maintain continuity for your dog when you begin to guide him from the other side of the poles, with the dog weaving on your right.

F.L. Corden Sr.

Arrow follows a strong signal through regulation poles. Keep your hand low to keep dog's head low. Gradually eliminate signal.

Whether it takes two weeks or two months, this step is completed when your dog can negotiate quickly, with your guidance, a row of six poles about half his body width. Stay at this point and enjoy it for awhile, adding another pole sometimes to vary the dog's exit direction. Never change the entrance direction.

Anchor weaves with hand signal not crossing the line of poles. Enticement is ready in handler's right hand if it is needed to bring him quickly back around the next pole.

You will be able to work the poles down one side and back the other only when you have an even total number of poles. When you have an odd total number, coming back the other way would put the first pole on the dog's right side, which he must never be allowed to do. When he's fully trained, he will understand that he must enter the line of poles from right to left between the first and second pole, no matter where his handler is.

STEP 5. Use narrower and longer chutes, without losing speed. Use leash as necessary, as above. Keep using hand signals, gradually making them less obvious as the dog takes over. Switch from enticement to reward.

HINTS: This step is so much fun. Don't rush it, even though your dog may sometimes ask you to rush it. It's exciting to see his confidence soaring and his body flying. He should work poles very quickly and full of power now, with or without a reward. The only reason to use rewards often is to help him through tough times to come.

Don't hesitate to put your dog on leash occasionally because, although it slows him down, it helps him concentrate and gives you an opportunity to prevent mistakes and reinforce the guidance he needs to accept. It's fine if the dog is intent on catching the enticement. In addition to encouraging him to weave faster, that chase reflex will help him keep going when he bumps the poles. You want him to work close to the poles, pushing them as he goes from side to side. He'll make considerably faster time this way.

As before, don't make the chute any tighter until your dog is fast and comfortable off leash. Another common plateau seems to occur when the rows of poles are just a few inches apart. It's a good idea to stop here for an extra week or two. You might see some regression here, which is simply met by an appropriate combination of widening the chute slightly, putting the dog on leash, using a favorite enticement and shortening the rows of poles, etc. Don't put yourself in the position of having to punish your dog, especially for enthusiasm.

From setting the rows of poles at only a few inches from each other to getting them in a straight line takes anywhere from two weeks to two months. When your poles are finally in a straight line there will be 18-24 inches between poles, depending on whether you began with your poles three feet or four feet apart in each row.

The leash is not for pulling the dog left and right; it is held up out of the way and tightened if the dog veers too far or skips a pole.

Enticement helps keep Anchor moving forward quickly and close to the poles.

Working with a single row of only four poles, get your dog up to the same speed and confidence level you have kept as your standard all along. Your dog should now be pushing every pole to one side or the other as he weaves. Be sure to keep him excited and motivated. Only a couple of times through, perhaps twice a day, complete with all the hoopla and treats he prefers, is enough. Don't ever work until he's tired of poles.

Even though you'll need your hand signal less and less as your dog's ability matures, the use of the hand signal gives you an unobtrusive extra precaution for your dog's competitive career. It takes a long time, even years, before a dog is really ready to take complete responsibility for the poles no matter where his handler is.

STEP 6. Introduce regulation poles. Improve understanding of correct entry.

HINTS: It's time to introduce your dog to as many different versions of weave poles as possible, in short rows and with all the help your dog wants. Your weave command word, the familiar hand signal and enticement routine should have him accepting any sort of material, surface, and reasonable spacing.

Even though your dog may be whizzing down rows of eight or more individual poles now at regulation spacing, you should limit yourself to five or six regulation poles when you first make the switch. Regulation

The ball is thrown just as Libby crosses the plane between the last two poles – this keeps her charging forward.

poles are often attached to wooden bases in sets of five or sometimes six poles.

The bases feel differently underfoot and might make your dog hesitate. Begin regulation pole training by using only one base at a time. Very small dogs need extra practice on poles with bases under them, as they have to step on the base continuously in order to weave fast.

The poles are attached to the base in various ways, and some designs permit the poles to lean more than others. Most flexible are the rubber cups made of crutch tips into which weave poles made of doweling or lightweight PVC pipe are placed.

Rubber does not last well outdoors or in cold climates, and it tends to weaken and let the poles fall out too easily. Least flexible are the metal sleeves onto which larger widths of PVC pipe are slipped. These have a few inches of give in each direction at the top, and next to none at the bottom. Individual poles stuck into the ground permit give in any direction according to the soil type, and also allow for variation in number of poles and distance between them. Your dog needs to be exposed to all sorts of weave poles.

Make sure to use both odd and even numbers of poles to keep your dog comfortable exiting to the left or right. Try weaving down a short section, then immediately back the other way. If the dog is on your left weaving an odd number of poles, he exits toward you and is kept at your left side (your "heel" or "with me" command) while the two of you make a quick left-about turn and immediately begin weaving again. With an even number of poles, the dog exits away from you. Call him close and meet him just past the poles, then pivot right-about and immediately begin again. Reverse the procedures when the dog works on your right.

To improve your dog's understanding of correct entry, arrange a row of four individual poles about 21 inches apart. Run your dog through once, with enthusiasm and a big reward. Then move the poles slightly so the second pole is only 18 inches from the first pole, and the other poles are still 21 inches apart.

Unless your dog thoroughly understands correct entry, he will try to start with the second pole. If you put your eye level at his, you will see how much more closed the opening for the correct entry looks than the more inviting second opening. But he has to learn to enter after the first pole every time. Plan to help him get it right the first couple of times at this uneven spacing. Using your hand signal and encouraging him should be enough. Twice through with help and a big reward is enough for the first lesson.

After you have assisted your dog in getting it right, a couple of times through each time, send him normally and interrupt him with your stop sound if he enters incorrectly. Tell him it's all right, you know he can figure it out, as you bring him back to start again, and guide him once

There's plenty of room for Moulty to gallop through the poles. It's not unusual for poles to be tilted, even in competition.

more, giving extra praise as you get him to enter correctly. If your dog is sensitive to weave poles, this would be a good place to end the lesson for now.

If he's tougher, immediately try letting him make his own decision again. Use your stop sound if he chooses the wrong entry, and show him twice more with a big reward each time. That's enough for now. Repeat the lesson several hours later, beginning by guiding him through and rewarding generously. Then let him try it without so much physical guidance. If he gets it right, go inside out with praise and end the lesson.

The next time you repeat this exercise, show the dog correct entry and reward him generously the first time through. Your dog is not stupid, he is a thinker, and his resourceful mind tells him that the larger opening makes more sense.

When your dog can't be fooled any longer by skewing the first pole, it will be that much easier for him to learn to get it right under other variations. In separate lessons, work out problems with having a middle pole slightly too close to another, or a pole slanted slightly to the right or left.

I have seen very loose rubber cups which made it impossible for the poles to stay upright, and warped wooden bases which tilted half the poles one way and half the other. In cases like these, it's best to stay near your dog when he weaves the crooked line and use your hand signal to help him get through without mistakes. He's learning a lot, but you are still the captain.

Arrow is sent from a distance to weave on his own as the handler walks away.

Another common pitfall to correct is the dog's dependence on the handler's position. Don't be surprised if your newly competent weaver suddenly begins on the wrong side or with the wrong pole if you suddenly stand in a different place. Most dogs have become patterned on their handler's habitual starting point. I see nothing wrong with developing this kind of dependence as your dog is putting the job together; it can help him get it right for you to trot to the poles with him as you say "weave," and stand at the place where you want him to begin weaving.

But once he has learned the task, shift your start position, being subtle at first, and keep a ready wrist for signaling him if he begins to guess incorrectly. He has no way of knowing whether the first pole or your body is the more important cue, and it is likely that he will choose your body until you educate him on that point. Do so with guidance, not criticism.

Start training for this new twist using about half your usual number of poles. Send him to the poles in your normal pattern, but hold on to his agility tab. This time, instead of standing opposite the first pole, stop a foot or more prior to the poles (still on the dog's right at this point), and help him enter the poles correctly, then continue down the line with him, giving extra praise. Graduate from the tab to your hand signal alone.

The choice is more difficult when you trot with him to the poles but stop opposite the second one rather than the first. Again, be ready with any combination of tab, hand signal, and enticement to help him begin correctly without inhibiting him. After your dog has regained his

Robby's ability to weave on the right and on his own helped J.C. Thompson earn the ultimate compliment: It was said the judge took more steps than J.C.

correctness and speed with this sort of challenge worked out, begin sending him while you position yourself in line with the poles, as if you were the new first pole.

Again, begin with your dog on a tab and show him the correct entry, then go with him down the short line of poles, giving him extra credit for his work. Then begin in the same position, but go down the short line of poles on his off side, guiding him on your right. When you have it smooth as a team with a short line of poles, try the same thing with more poles. Only after he has that worked out, use a few poles and stand slightly off-center to the left before you send him, etc.

Many agility dogs are taught the weave poles always on the handler's left, but it's not necessary. It just takes extra time and effort to begin making him comfortable on either side from early on. When the course layout curves to the left around the poles, the dog who can be sent off to the right to weave on his own allows the handler to follow a shorter path, making faster time. It also provides an extra cue to the dog about which direction and obstacle are next. Because of its difficulty, it represents a well-respected, agility ultimate in teamwork and control.

Weave Poles, Chute Method Summary

Use your dog's favorite enticement every time at first to alleviate stress. As the dog becomes more confident and proficient with each step, use enticement less often on that step. Always praise your dog's first efforts, and keep the training sessions lively and fun.

Switch sides with your dog regularly to keep him accustomed to taking direction from either side. Use different homemade and regulation weave poles and move them to different locations so your dog can get used to variations.

STEP 1. Use two short rows of individual weave poles to form a wide chute. Walk and trot dog through chute. Helper holds dog while you run chute, then turn and call dog through.

STEP 2. Gradually lengthen chute. Switch from enticement to reward. Begin to narrow the chute.

STEP 3. Shorten chute and run beside dog. Work both sides. Gradually lengthen chute.

STEP 4. Shorten chute and begin to narrow it further. Stop for awhile at dog's flex point. Introduce signal, using enticement at first.

STEP 5. Gradually use narrower and longer chutes. Make signals less obvious.

STEP 6. Use regulation weave poles. Improve accuracy from either side. Further improve understanding of correct entry.

Leaning Poles Method, Introduction

This method is becoming a popular approach and, although it may look strange, it makes good sense and it works. In the U.S., Will Koukkarri of the Minnesota Agility Club designed a simple piece of equipment that makes this method very easy to employ. It consists of a base that supports dowels that are easily adjustable, eliminating the time-consuming task of changing the angle of the dowels by pulling them all out of the ground and repositioning them. It also lends itself to indoor use and makes the approach a viable one for group work, in which dogs will be at different levels of expertise.

Leaning Poles Method, Progression

STEP 1. Poles are flat or nearly flat on ground, bent alternately left and right outward from a straight line. Entice your dog to trot down the length of poles, stepping over them.

HINTS: The dog can be held by a helper as with the chute method, or walked or trotted through on leash or off, using an enticement to increase motivation. As soon as he understands the job, start building speed. Keep the lessons short and exciting.

As with the chute method, it's most important that the first pole the dog must pass is leaned to his left to establish a pattern for him to enter the line of weave poles with the first pole on his left. For this reason, the apparatus should be built in units of four or six poles, so you can work them in both directions. Once your dog is fast and snappy over one section of leaning poles, add a second, and later even a third if you like.

STEP 2. Gradually raise poles an inch or two at a time over several weeks. Switch from enticement to reward.

HINTS: Each time you raise the poles, begin with only one section, and add another after your dog has resumed his quick pace and confidence with the first. Begin delaying the dog's reward, running away and having him catch up to you, putting the reward in your pocket, throwing a toy for him as he completes the poles, etc.

Ivan prances down the line. Now is the time to start working from either side. As soon as he's ready, off with the leash.

On with the leash at each new step. If poles are raised very gradually and the dog's happiness is kept up, he gets faster and faster even at difficult levels.

If your dog wants to run out the side or hop over more than one pole at once, you are raising the poles too abruptly. Put him on leash for several times through until he is in the habit of mincing quickly down the line, picking up his feet for each pole. It is amazing that dogs can keep track of all their feet and all those poles, but they learn this rather quickly, and it will make the added effort of flexing around the poles assimilate that much more readily later.

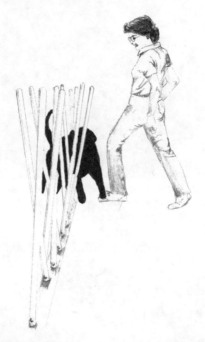

Fig. XVI. Excessive legwork used to prevent dog from weaving incorrectly is slow and cumbersome, and can be penalized five faults for handler interference.

STEP 3. Once your dog has to begin to bend, raise the poles much more gradually. As poles approach the upright position, introduce hand signal, as with chute method.

HINTS: It's always tempting to try to get the poles upright as fast as possible, but don't. Plan to spend months going from flat to upright.

With this method, a big dog has to begin doing some flexing as soon as the poles cramp his upper body, so big dogs will begin to weave when the poles are still quite tilted. Small dogs will begin weaving when the poles get too high at the base for them to step over.

In either case, there are only two factors that keep the dog happily going down the baseline through the tilted poles on his own rather than cutting out the side: he has become comfortable there through his

Although he could still step over, Hawkeye is already starting to weave. Build up speed and confidence at your dog's transition point, wherever it is, with fewer poles and strong enticement.

Candi zips through with the poles at about a 15-degree angle on ever it is, with fewer poles and strong enticement.

extensive practice at the lower pole heights, and you make him feel so proud to do this. Don't think he doesn't know that there's an easier way to get there from here.

Again as with the chute method, your dog will have occasional set backs and need the poles lowered a bit for review now and then. It's a good idea to pause at the point at which he first needs to flex, because that changes how he needs to use his body through the poles. Remain at that level for some time, building speed and comfort with the new requirement. This will also build his strength and coordination for more advanced weaving.

Introducing the hand signal as the poles approach the upright position will help your dog get comfortable winding around the poles. It also provides that all-important backup assistance that can prevent mistakes after the dog has learned the job.

STEP 4. Using regulation poles, improve the dog's accuracy from any start point. Improve understanding of correct entry.

HINTS: Even when your dog is weaving fast and steady with a full

These poles are upright on one side, slightly leaned on the other. Lisl winds through on leash.

line of poles straight up, work shorter sections of poles now and then just to keep him very fast, and introduce your dog to other weave poles that look and feel differently from your own. Many clubs now have a set of metal poles, and these feel so differently from wood or PVC that many dogs literally don't want to touch them when they weave.

Make sure your dog can handle an odd number of poles as well as an even number. As always when introducing a new twist, begin with fewer poles.

Begin to introduce the exercises to teach correct entry (see chute method, Step 6). The end goal of any weave training approach is a weaving wizard who loves the poles and knows the obstacle inside out from anywhere.

Weave Poles, Leaning Poles Summary

Use your dog's favorite enticement every time at first to alleviate stress. As the dog becomes more confident and proficient with each step, use enticement less often on that step. Always praise your dog's first efforts, and keep the training sessions lively and fun.

Switch sides with your dog regularly to keep him accustomed to taking direction from either side. Use different homemade and regulation weave poles and move them to different locations so your dog can get used to variations.

STEP 1. Poles laid alternately left and right outward from the center line. Entice dog to trot over them.

STEP 2. Gradually raise adjustable poles inch by inch over several weeks. Switch from enticement to reward.

STEP 3. Stop for awhile at dog's flex point. On leash as necessary and using enticement, help dog learn to weave. Switch from enticement to reward at each new height.

STEP 4. As poles approach upright position, introduce signal and other control work as in Step 6 of chute method.

Panther is comfortable with poles nearly upright. A short row of poles, a signal and an enticement will increase his speed.

BRINGING IT ALL TOGETHER

When love and skill work together, expect a masterpiece.

–John Ruskin

"Sequencing" and Run-throughs

"Sequencing" means completing two or more obstacles in a row. The term "run-through" is used to mean a practice run. Helping your dog learn the fine points and particulars of running an agility course is done by designing specific sequences to expose him to all the tricky elements, one by one, then two by two, and so on. It's a preparation process – getting ready to put it all together.

It's beautiful to see a dog spring from the ground and reach up in a graceful arc over a brightly decorated jump. In midair he takes in the next instruction, then becomes riveted to the next obstacle, and he lands on the run. To carry this off well jump after jump makes the course look fluid, even easy. The dog and handler are giving a lesson not only in physical ability, but also in timing and teamwork. Watch all the course runs you can. The flawless ones will give you a better feel for what you want, and the faults will help you learn to recognize and prevent some of the many things that can go wrong.

"Sequencing" helps build confidence, stamina, and mental sharpness. For beginner dogs, sequences are the building blocks of course running. For experienced dogs, isolate specific course problems for extra practice.

As your dog's ability develops with individual agility obstacles, sooner or later he'll be ready to go from one obstacle to another before being rewarded. Don't wait until your dog is able to do all obstacles at regulation difficulty before beginning to use simple sequences, on leash at first if necessary and off leash as soon as he's ready.

Tom begins indicating the next jump before Keeper lands; no guesswork, no hesitation. Working dog on the right lets handler take shorter route on this sequence.

Begin with two of his favorite pieces and keep it simple for awhile by jumping with him, compressing the tunnel, lowering the A-frame, or using your low dog walk. Design first sequences that will introduce your dog to the feeling of completing one obstacle after another without him having to think about whether he can handle any obstacle you include.

Nicole introduces Astro to his first sequence; through the weave poles chute...

...and left to the low double bar. Vary the obstacle and direction, and work from both sides.

A good first sequence consists of an open tunnel followed by a low jump. Since the dog expects you to play with him when he exits the tunnel, he may trip you up as you move on to the jump, slow down before the jump, or may appear to be refusing the jump. It's different from the pattern he's used to, so don't be upset if he balks.

Coaxing him to continue to the jump and using a strong reward on completion may be all it takes to convince him of the new idea. Once he understands, he may speed up through the tunnel because to him the jump will now represent completion of the task. That's the kind of thinking you want. In the future, his big reward will be gradually delayed until the end of a complete course, so the whole course will be the task.

Once your dog understands the sequences, his performance will accelerate unless you have met his mistakes harshly. The dog realizes that the second obstacle, not the first, marks the completion of the command, so he rushes to perform it. If your dog works slowly, whether because he's methodical or because he's unsure, work on speed before you add more obstacles. Get out the toys and treats, the kids, or whatever gets him going. Most dogs get revved up over one or the other of the great motivators – food and fun.

Don't take the attitude that since he knows the obstacle now you can make him faster just by pressuring him to go faster. Sometimes the extra urgency in your voice translates to an alarm for the dog. You might need to isolate work on a slow obstacle, or break the short sequence down into subtasks that can each be speeded up separately.

Speed is secondary to accuracy on the agility course as long as your dog finishes under SCT. But if you have given your dog the impression along the way that fast is not fun, you need to change that.

If your dog is slow, you might be smart to ignore an accuracy error when he first does a job quickly. I remember trying to speed Jessy up through the weave poles after training her with a method that patterned a slow and careful pace. The first time she tried to rush that stocky body, she missed a pole, and my reflexes blurted out the stop command. How sorry I felt. She had been so pleased to be going fast, and the stop rudely burst her bubble. It was a long time before she tried dancing through the poles again; she didn't want to risk it.

You can't always get everything at once right away. Speed up individual obstacles, then combine them to complete two in a row, but don't lengthen your dog's sequences until he moves briskly through the first obstacle and speeds right on to the second.

It's important to vary your sequences as soon as the dog is ready so his mind can be kept open to include any obstacles you name. Letting him decide for himself what is next will not teach him the names of the obstacles or to pay attention to you while he's working. Many courses call for turns away from the obstacle straight ahead, or another obstacle placed near the one that is next. So when teaching your dog to handle obstacles in a series, incorporate turns, recalls, signal work, and the names of individual obstacles.

Steve Hooper

Stoner is down the A-frame and into the tunnel.
This is a sequence often seen in competition.

You don't need regulation equipment to learn the basics of "sequencing." There is much you and your dog can learn from a column of three low makeshift jumps. Start by interjecting recalls between jumps. Call your dog as he's in the air over the first jump, and entice him to you (trotting backwards helps) as he lands. Practice your handling here, too. You have to be saying with your body language "go around the obstacle when you are called to me." Next time, call him after the second jump and before the third. If either time he jumps the next jump in spite of your call, ignore him – no praise and no scolding. Put the treats away and quietly bring him back to the start. Now cheer him up and try again.

If you've practiced single jumps followed by recalls as part of your early jump training, the dog should make this adjustment quickly. Separate this lesson from distractions as much as possible at first. Keeping the jumps low and in a straight line helps, so the dog doesn't have to spend extra physical and mental energy applying a jump strategy just yet. As he learns, gradually introduce some variety by angling the jumps, putting some distance between his start point and your start point, etc. Be sure to work both sides.

With a very strong-willed dog, or one that jumped all three jumps in spite of your calling him after the first, do the sequence on leash and jump with him. This will also improve your recalls in general, since the eager dog is rewarded for coming by active play and being allowed to jump again.

Begin to call him while he's still in the air over the first jump, and guide him to you with the leash as well as enticement. Make him very happy that he came when called. Next time, call him in the air over the second jump in the same manner. Then jump all three jumps. Then do the same exercise with the dog on the other side of you, calling him to the other side. Soon you'll be ready off leash.

Teach your dog to jump the next jump when you say so, whether you are standing in front of him, to either side, or behind. Then teach him to jump back over a jump on command. You could name this "back" or "again." Or call your dog's name; then, when he's facing you, indicate the same jump as you tell him "jump." You must work out a way to tell him to return over a jump. He should go around unless you direct him over. Put him on a leash at first if he doesn't believe you. Intersperse jump-agains with come-arounds. Keep your patience and exaggerate your body English to help him.

As your dog gets the idea, introduce complications. It's time for sequences that involve a choice of obstacles. At first, put your dog on his agility leash. It's inhibiting to yell at him as he's choosing the wrong object, and it can take years for a dog to get all the obstacle names straight while under pressure. Better to guide him with the leash now as you name the correct obstacle, so you can praise his choice. Using signals also helps, and makes the transition from on leash to off leash go more smoothly.

A few obstacles in a row with an extra one to each side offer many sequence possibilities. Here Daci takes the cue from A-frame to pole jump.

When your dog is ready for another complication, send him from different angles and begin to station yourself in different spots. With each new twist help him succeed in making the right choice, using as much positive guidance as he needs. Don't forget to keep your equipment simple, and vary the obstacles often to keep your dog working with his mind open.

Practice your own timing so you can call your dog before his mind is set on an incorrect route. How independent your dog and how fast he moves through the obstacles determine how early you need to command and signal him. Your command should be given before your fast dog is finished with the previous obstacle. It may be that your same command only a second later is not in time, even though he's not off course yet, for he is already committed to the obstacle he believes is next. Likewise when this dog is ready for more involved sequences you will need to name the next required obstacle very early in order to help him focus on it and continue directly to it without being sidetracked.

Conversely, if your dog does not move fast, or if he is uncertain, a very different approach might work best. It might be discouraging or confusing to him if you call before he has completed the obstacle he's working on. These dogs usually do their best agility work if you refrain from exercising extra control over them. They still need guidance, but no extra restraint.

When you feel that you and your dog are ready to try a full course, walk the course carefully first and evaluate it with your dog's training background in mind. Are there combinations he hasn't tackled before? Is he still hesitant sometimes about one obstacle or another? Is any of this equipment different from his own? Might he skip a pole? The strain of a run-through is cumulative from one sequence to the next, so your job is more than calling out the next obstacle; you have a lot to do with the outcome.

Help your new agility dog and give an extra measure of guidance on

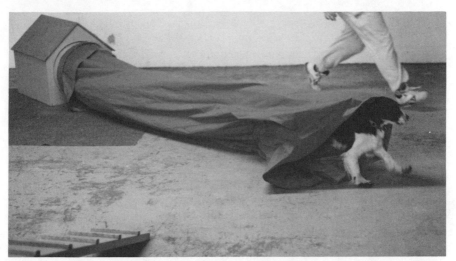
Hannah is already headed left on the next command. If she had been called too soon, she would have become tangled in the unanchored chute.

every obstacle, for this is just another opportunity for furthering his education. You can blend sequences with run-throughs by skipping an obstacle or section of the course that is apt to give your beginner dog trouble. Look at your dog's agility courses as a series of sequences and decide which ones are good for him to try right now.

While you work the course with your dog, stay tuned in as you see him handling it, and be prepared to take whatever steps necessary to help. Your desire to see if he can do a certain something today is not worth the risk of demoralizing him at this critical stage. Many dogs with exceptional talent and good early training have had the fun of Agility pressed out of them by too much pressure at this stage.

"Sequencing" brings out your dog's rhythm and helps him think ahead without losing the ability to listen to you. Make sure to switch the obstacles often as soon as he knows what he's doing. The less he loves a particular obstacle, the more you should work on it individually, with big rewards, before including it in a short sequence. Interject recalls and unexpected turns into simple short sequences. After your dog can handle a variety of short sequences well, listening while he works, work up to longer and more difficult ones.

I'm an advocate of entering new dogs noncompetitively in their first few agility trials to prevent us handlers from putting an extra measure of pressure on them too soon. Otherwise, even though I might come to the competition thinking that we are there for experience and not to win, I have a lot of trouble keeping that priority first when he's doing well.

It's especially difficult not to press too hard the second round when the newcomer has turned in a brilliant performance on the first. Entering "noncomp" (called "for exhibition only" or FEO) can prevent that selfish syndrome from taking hold. Knowing that your new hopeful will not be considered for a placement will keep you light and relaxed with him. You can handle the extra nerves and pressure together after you have bonded as a team in competition.

Advanced Basics

Your dog's education in the basics will begin to be more important in Agility once you feel ready to start running courses. There's a world of difference, for example, between coming when called and always coming when called. It's one thing to have a leash between you, quite another to control your dog by voice and signals only. But from there it's another quantum leap to the point where your dog can be in competition, running full tilt at his favorite obstacle, no collar, no treats, no nothing, and the word "come" stops him in his tracks and spins him around to return to you at a dead run.

All along you've been using and refreshing your dog's positive acceptance of basic control and basic obedience. You've done exercises off leash and from either side. You've gradually reduced his dependence on food and toys, leash, collar, and hands as each challenge became familiar. Though you may need to review some of your dog's basic obedience training as a prelude to more advanced control, you should be well on your way.

Here are some ideas about improving your dog's understanding of some of the more advanced agility requirements: control, heelwork, recalls, and down, and lastly some hints about the advanced mindset.

Control

You will hit snags as you make your agility sequences more difficult, and some of them are a tribute to the positive thinking you've instilled in your dog. The more he loves the work and feels confident about it, the more he is apt to take matters into his own paws whenever he sees his favorite obstacles. He has to learn to resist, to watch and listen, in order to avoid penalties for going off course. But you don't want to inhibit that wonderful funloving attitude toward his work.

Try to think of ways to turn a negative lesson into a positive one. It's more helpful in the long run to give your agility dog something to do rather than to concentrate overtly on what he shouldn't do. Although there will be times when you will have to speak sharply to him and correct him strongly, don't make this your automatic answer to all your control problems.

I have a dog who likes to decide her own course route. Jessy has often felt she could run it better without me, and consequently we have turned in a few performances that looked like we were on opposite teams. Neither of us enjoys Agility much if our control lessons are reduced to punishment sessions, but early in each competitive season we have to do serious control work.

What helps us most are lessons that let her make most of her own decisions. My favorite is a 5-10-minute, quiet, leashwalking session on the course because it is extremely hard for Jessy to walk and trot past the equipment. During these leash lessons I don't say much except for praise when she goes past an obstacle. This is not a lesson in heeling or coming when called, it's a lesson in leashwork, to keep her attention by choice. It helps her decide for herself to pass the obstacles when she would rather jump on.

This kind of lesson might help your overeager dog, or any dog who is unsure whether to refrain or not. It's nice to help him decide to pay attention without badgering him to pay attention. It lowers everybody's stress level.

Basic control can be improved with exercises you can do in a small space with makeshift equipment. One of the most popular is "take two, skip one." Arrange four obstacles in a circle and practice sending your dog to take the first, then the second, and then call him to you. Then you

Missie is congratulated for turning on command away from her favorite, the tunnel.

skip the third obstacle, send your dog over the fourth and first, skip the second, take the third and fourth, skip the first, etc. Work both directions. Keeping obstacles easy and relatively close together keeps the pace slower, good for working out your timing and cooperation. Practice sending your dog ahead, emphasizing signals, changing direction quickly, even instant downs. Try doing three of the four, then calling your dog across the circle and begin with number one in the opposite direction.

After your dog has done some choice-making work as in the "sequencing" section, use obstacles in a circle to practice your dog's ability to recognize the equipment by name. It also lets you practice sending your dog away from you and having him check in again after completing the command. Stand beside your dog in the middle of the circle and tell him with word and signal to go perform, for example, "tire." Dogs well versed in go-out obedience exercises may benefit from the command "go tire" or "go jump" as you signal to the correct obstacle. As your dog learns the game, make your signal less obvious until he can choose correctly on the word alone. As he gets good at it, vary the obstacles.

You shouldn't need a leash for this work, but you might want to use a short agility tab on your dog in case you need to guide him, and it's smart to use rewards after each success. This is not easy work. You may be disappointed to discover that your dog didn't learn all the obstacle names because he was tuning in to other cues as well. You need him to read your body language too, and that is more natural to dogs. It does take a long time for the dog to understand which name belongs to which piece of equipment, especially since the pieces look different from one course to another.

A simple way to help your dog key in to signals is to use them around the house. For example, when you open the door for your dog, hold your index finger up and command "wait" (wait training is covered in Ch. 2). Give an arm signal to the opening as you say "OK." Soon your dog will know the wait signal and will watch for a signal to follow. Play the same game at mealtime. Gradually introduce distance.

You can bring that skill to Agility using a sharply bent tunnel. Have your dog wait facing the tunnel, and you face the dog. Then give an exaggerated signal to one opening or the other. Praise his correct decision and reward on completion.

"Tunnel!" Tiger gets an exaggerated signal in an early lesson about directionals on the course.

Try two obstacles in a horizontal line (low jumps work well for this). With your dog on one side and you across from him, have him wait until you signal him to one or the other. When he's good at it, do these exercises with your back to him. You'll need that versatility in competition.

As your dog learns the game, add a third obstacle to the row. Now he has to refine his discrimination of the signal. When he's very good at it, start mixing recalls with jump commands, and introduce an arm signal to direct him between the jumps to you when you call him. Mixing words and signals will sharpen your dog's listening and visual skills.

At large competitions like the U.S. nationals, signals can sometimes be the only way to communicate with your dog on the course. Several thousand appreciative fans can render your voice unintelligible to the dog just when you need it most. Agility fans are happy and supportive, and every dog is apt to be applauded for his efforts, but any dog who does something outstanding or something cute can bring the house down. Handlers often need signals more than voices. It's all part of keeping your dog tuned in to you as well as to the work.

Basics like zone training on the go-up obstacles can be sharpened to help your dog handle difficult course arrangements. In competition, the course layout sometimes presents an angled approach to a go-up obstacle. More often than not, a dog who tackles the climb from the side spends more time scrambling than he saves by cutting the corner, and often misses a zone in the process.

One solution is to teach the dog to climb always from the end. This is more fun for both of you if you devise a way to help the dog decide for himself to go around to the end. Teaching the dog to go through hoops at either end is helpful, as is using a training chute (see Appendix). One student set a large traffic cone beside an up ramp in class to dissuade her dog from cutting the corner. It worked beautifully.

Introduce angles progressively, beginning only slightly off center and perhaps using your downscaled obstacles at first. Exaggerate your signal, pointing and guiding the dog around to the end. As his habit develops, send him from sharper angles, letting the cone or hoop keep him accurate. Work both right and left sides, gradually increasing the angle of approach until your dog will go around to the front even when sent from a parallel position.

As with all tricks and trappings to improve performance, it takes more than a week or two to develop the habit you're after. Don't grab onto a new idea as a quick fix. When your dog is very sharp with this and you decide to try angled approaches without the props, don't forget to begin nearly straight on again, exaggerating your signal and guiding the dog around to the end. The props can help your dog develop the correct habit. When you remove them you need to show your dog that the habit should remain. Otherwise you are setting him up for failure. While the failure might appear to be the fault of the dog or the prop, it's really a basic training error on your part.

Control problems in Agility are usually problems of commission. The dog doesn't do what is asked because he is doing another agility task that is not being asked of him. This is not to be confused with problems of omission, which stem from a basic lack of confidence or enjoyment.

Control problems are frustrating, but they are more encouraging than problems of omission, which include lagging, running out of the ring to get away from agility work, fear of certain obstacles, confusion about what is wanted, etc.

Problems of omission indicate that something basic and important is missing from your dog's repertoire. The dog who suffers badly from problems of omission needs an objective review of his agility foundation, from basic soundness of body (a common cause for jump refusals in an otherwise happy working dog) to his background and education on each obstacle. In many cases, he should be brought back to square one and restarted, with motivators that are more attractive to him and an emphasis on positive experiences to help him associate each problem obstacle with pleasure. His foundation, for some reason, is unsuitable, so it will usually take a change of approach to change his feelings.

Control problems may warrant an evaluation of your dog's training, but this work is designed to hold your dog's attention, improve his self-restraint, and redirect his energy. It would not be fair to emphasize strict control measures as a means to force your dog to do what he is insecure about doing.

Heelwork

On an agility course you need a command such as "heel" or "by me," any word to keep your dog close to you while you get past an inviting obstacle or two placed to lure him off course. Heelwork is popular because so many dogs learn it for general use anyway, but it may be better to use a variation like "by me" or "come" to mean stay close to either side, rather than the traditional "heel" which means to the left side. Call it what you will and define it as you wish, but be consistent so you and your dog can develop the same interpretation. Teaching your dog to stay at your side while you negotiate a crowded sidewalk is good advanced practice for heelwork amid distraction.

The more your dog loves both heelwork and Agility, the stricter you can be with these lessons. But it's a shame to see a dog subjected to drillwork in something he resents. In obedience competition, heeling is one of the most kinetic parts of the test and should be a motivating exercise. This attitude can transfer beautifully to the agility course. In Agility, though, heeling becomes one of the least active parts of the test and is not required. If your dog dislikes heelwork, use another word and another approach to help him stay close for several strides. Your first assignment is motivation, no matter what the job.

A tunnel under the A-frame can make the handler work at a distance from the dog. Voice control is necessary to slow the dog down for the contact zone.

Steve Hooper

"Got it." Bruno is already fixed on the jump ahead.

Steve Hooper

Handler recalls Jessy and begins to motion her around the tire jump. A different word and position are used when calling the dog back through.

Recalls

Recalls on the agility course are a must, but they are easily abused. If you've been interjecting recalls into your sequence work in a positive way and your dog comes happily when you call, you're ready for recall work past the obstacles. It will go more smoothly for you if you didn't use your recall word to entice your dog to go over jumps or through tunnels, etc. This recall means that no obstacle is to be taken on the way.

Have your dog wait beside a favorite obstacle, positioned so it would not be convenient for him to perform it on the way to you. A *Flexi-lead* can be good for this work since it automatically takes up excess line as the dog approaches. Make this a very happy and high-spirited affair. Repeat the game a few times, gradually leaving the dog in good position for taking the obstacle on the way to you. Be sure to position yourself and use body language to direct him around to the correct path.

Be prepared to stop the dog if you see him decide to take the obstacle. If he takes it anyway, correct his mistake according to his confidence level. For example, with a brash dog who has gone over a jump when he should have gone around, try holding the line, keeping it tight, walking to him and quietly untangling him with no apology. Then call him from up close, guiding him around the jump with lots of praise. For a very sensitive dog, you might choose to ignore the mistake and let him figure out from your silence that it wasn't a great choice. Don't risk making him suspicious of the obstacle by punishing him.

After a failure by any dog, bring him back to a start point slightly less inviting and try again, perhaps using an extra bit of body language to encourage success. Greet that success with an extra measure of enthusiasm. As your dog becomes adept at these tricky recalls, vary the obstacles by calling him around to either side and introducing more obstacles, motion and variety on the course to distract him. Work up to sending him over one obstacle, then calling him between obstacles and sending him to another.

Down

Don't try to force your beginner dog to assume the down position on the pause before he has learned to enjoy the obstacle and the instant down. It's important that the dog like the contraption and understand how to get there from some distance before complicating his performance. The best way to keep the performance fast and happy is to introduce the fun and action first and add the hard stuff and compulsion later.

As you ready your agility dog for advanced course running, you are bound to go through a period of thinking he is incapable of staying down for the count. You have practiced varying the number of seconds he has to wait to reduce predictability, and you have worked to make him steady for much longer than five seconds. But the more eager he is to run the course, the harder you will have to work for reliable stays on the pause obstacle.

If he finds it impossible to lie still at the pause, start doing some long downs there. He needs to get so steady that you can turn your back and walk away without him lifting an elbow. Teach your dog to lie down on command even with your back to him. Then give the command while you are lying down. When he's really tuned in to lying down, no matter what, whenever you tell him to, I have three favorite exercises for improving steadiness on the down without dampening the dog's love of the pause obstacle.

The first exercise can be done anywhere. Once your dog is quite steady on the down, remind him "down" or "stay" as you slowly and deliberately lower a much-anticipated enticement to him. If he begins to rise, remove the enticement while making your stop sound. Command him again and begin again with the enticement when he is settled. Remind him of his job all the while you lower the goodie. Help him succeed, although it may take several tries at first.

The second exercise is a "down" in motion. During a play session with your dog (or just walking along beside him not while heeling or recalling) interject a quick down. Be ready to use your hand over his withers to ensure a quick response. Give an immediate reward, anything from a cookie to a lively OK and a quick roughhousing. Over the next few weeks, let your dog come to expect the command at any time. The more you need to use compulsion, the more desirable the reward should be to balance that. Once he's fast and proud at this game, add an arm signal.

Most people use the right arm, quickly raised and lowered again. Eventually, the signal from start to finish lasts about one second. Begin by holding the arm up longer and pair it with the verbal command to help your dog make the association. The dog who can work on signals is the dog who knows how to watch his handler.

The third exercise is useful in a class setting or on a practice course. It uses "conspiracy training," meaning that others take part in the correcting of your dog's mistake. The down command should be thoroughly understood and accepted by the dog under normal circumstances with the handler close by and watching before progressing to this stage. This is for steadying the dog who cannot stay down when the job gets a little tougher.

Used with the down on or off the pause obstacle, this approach can convince your dog that a correction will come even if you're not looking at him or not there. Have your dog down, wearing a loose, lightweight line which is held by a helper standing inconspicuously behind him, as far away as necessary for effect. If the dog breaks his down command when you look away or move away, the helper jerks the line, giving the dog an appropriate correction. You respond by replacing the dog and trying again, perhaps making the job slightly easier this time to ensure success.

A similar conspiracy can be arranged off leash by enlisting helpers to watch your dog. If he rises from the down position when your head or your back is turned, they scold the dog from the sidelines. You wordlessly put him back into position and repeat the command and the exercise. Much praise should be lavished upon him for holding still.

In short, many dogs cannot tolerate being chastised severely by their handlers without losing their enthusiasm for the obstacle. It's better to separate the down from the pause table and box. If you still need help steadying your dog at the obstacle, think of a way to use conspiracy training. There's always a way, and where there's a way, there's an agility dog.

The Advanced Mindset

The two major factors that decide your success are being thorough with your dog's basic education and not considering him "trained" until the two of you can work as a team anywhere amid strong distractions. Don't abandon simple things like short tunnels, low jumps, enticements and silly stuff in your agility work now that you have lofty goals. Keep rekindling that excitement that made your dog thrive on this great confidence builder. You're never done with the basics, because you always have to keep polishing the three As: attitude, accuracy, and action.

Once you start bringing your dog's agility talents from the individual obstacles up to running complex courses, it is likely that many of your previous shortcuts will come back to haunt you. No one is free from agility gremlins. There is a saying that education tries to replace an empty mind with an open one. Make sure your mind stays open to your dog.

How well a certain approach suits him will be told soon enough. Your dog can give you some wonderful custom training ideas. Reexamine your efforts often. Be sure you're not training this dog by habit. Don't let yourself expect this dog to be like another dog, especially like "good ol' Motley," who "never needed much work."

Advanced lessons can be hard work and very stressful. Break difficult work down into manageable chunks without losing sight of your ultimate goals. You are the one to define your ultimate goals, but let your dog, not you, decide what is difficult. Each of you will feel more like going away than trying again sometimes, and both of you will feel completely drained now and then. In planning your approach, anticipate this and balance the necessary difficult things with the fun stuff that made you and your dog fall in love with this sport in the first place. When you mull over your goals and your progress, ask yourself an honest question that can keep the necessary balance in your teaching: "What is it like lately, being trained by me?"

Nickie pays attention and prepares to head left. This set-up is good for advanced "take two, skip one" exercises, over-and-back jumping, recalls, and signal work.

Tangents of Competition

Interested in agility competition? It's great fun, although the butterflies in your stomach can make you question that as your turn in the ring approaches. Each competition is an adventure, and, like any unknown, the waiting is usually much harder than the work. Once it's your turn, you just do the best you can.

Traveling with your Dog

It's unlikely that any competition will afford perfect circumstances for you and your dog. There will always be peripheral aspects that challenge you both to maintain normalcy. Training for competition means preparing for the unexpected on the course, but often the preparation has to include training for traveling as well. What you bring to the competition, the routine you follow there, and some useful travel skills can help you do your best.

You'll want to bring your dog's own favorite toys and treats and his collar and leash. Many dogs do better with their own water from home. If you'll get home well past your dog's mealtime, you might want to bring his food. His regular food dish would be nice too, and so would his crate, so he can rest in his own familiar space wherever you are.

If you'll be spending a night or more away from home, plan to crate your dog in your hotel room. If he has not been taught to rest quietly there while you go out to dinner, then take him with you or don't go out. It's irresponsible to allow your dog to vocalize his loneliness to the world. It's unfair to other paying guests, to all dog owners who want to travel with their pets, and it's unfair to your dog who is experiencing stress instead of rest. Teach him to relax when you leave him, but teach him at home and practice at a friend's home and in your car before you expect it in a motel room.

It's very important to travel with provisions for keeping your dog's body cool enough or warm enough, whatever the season warrants. The troupe from my club brings a small wading pool and a garden hose to every summer competition. More than once it has been borrowed by nearly every competitor there. When you set your dog's crate in the shade, make sure to check it often, as shade often changes with the movement of the sun during the day.

Many dogs have their own cool-down coats, and many owners have effective tricks for keeping dogs comfortable, using wet towels, freezer packs under plywood in the crate, ice cubes to eat and frequent wet-downs with cool water. Although dogs cool their bodies differently from people (primarily by panting and by sweating through the pads of their feet), they need extra water in hot weather just as we do.

Keeping dogs warm in winter ranges from unnecessary for some heavily coated dogs to impossible for some sparse-coated ones. Sweaters and coats are available for every size, but they can't be worn on the course for safety's sake.

Dogs who mind the cold can be bundled up between course runs, kept in heated buildings or cars, kept moving and in the sunshine as much as possible, crated with another dog or in a crate covered with blankets, given warm water to drink, etc. Past a reasonable point, though, a dog who is uncomfortably cold should not run a course because the risk of injury is high when muscles are tight, and very cold muscles cannot relax.

Most dogs love riding in cars and get very excited when they see their things being packed for a trip. That's a nice way to start. Understandably, a dog who dislikes riding in the car will have a hard time enjoying the trip because to him it means being upset and sick. It takes some time to help your dog get over fear of riding in the car, but it's not usually difficult. You just have to begin at a point where he can succeed, and work gradually from there.

If he's afraid to jump into the car, start with all doors open, motor off, and entice him into the back seat with you. Just sit there and feed him treats for a few moments, then hop out. Make a big deal of him while he's in the car and be quiet when he gets out. Taking it from there will involve several intermediate steps, like shutting doors and windows, moving further away from him, starting the engine, and moving back and forth in the driveway. Find what helps him, anything from crating him to having a helper sit with him.

It's a good idea to take your dog for short rides at first, but the way you do that can make all the difference. Rather than taking him away from home and returning quickly, plan a very short excursion to a place your dog will love, and get out there to enjoy it. If there's a nice place to play near your home, drive there. Make the car ride mean something great away from home, not something to endure to get back home. Enjoying the ride together is part of enjoying competitions together.

Many of us take airplane travel for granted these days, and many dogs do, too. Gail Levering of Pennsylvania told me of some very upset airline baggage handlers who thought her dog, a laidback veteran traveler, was dead in his crate. Bentley had slept, on his back with four feet in the air, through the entire process of being unloaded with the baggage, transported by cart to the terminal, and carried by the concerned staff to the pick-up area. Gail woke him up and reassured everyone.

Most dogs do not take airplane travel in stride that well, but it can turn a trip of a few days by car into one of a few hours. The most important details of your dog's comfort and safety are up to you. Use any distinguishing feature, such as colored strips of tape, to identify your dog's crate, and tape your dog's travel plans, your name, and all pertinent phone numbers securely to the crate in a clear plastic bag. A strip of tape over the front door with the dog's name on it makes it easy for the baggage crew to report what dogs are on board. Clear plastic tape over this protects the ink.

Depending on your flight, you should secure a water dish to the inside front corner of the crate, so attendants can water your dog from the outside in case of emergency. Emergencies are unlikely, but whenever you hand your dog over to strangers some extra precautions are in order.

You should get a direct flight, preferably nonstop. In the U.S., you can't buy your dog's ticket ahead of time, so you will need cash or a credit card at the ticket counter. You can usually buy him a roundtrip ticket then, so you don't have to repeat the procedure coming home. Fares for dogs are quite reasonable if you are traveling on the same flight.

A few more things to remember: a veterinarian's health certificate is required. Allow about an hour to get your dog and your baggage squared away. Always carry some of your dog's food and a few essentials for your dog (and for you) onto the plane with you rather than checking everything through as baggage.

Speaking of baggage, I have never had to hand over my dogs with the baggage at the ticket counter, but that often seems to be the expectation of the ticket agent there. They should call an employee to pick up your dog. I am told that some small dogs have been sent down the baggage conveyor belt, but I have never seen that. I certainly wouldn't recommend it; just request a skycap, and don't relinquish your dog.

Check that the proper destination tag is securely attached to the crate. Then go politely with the pick-up person to the dog's point of departure in the terminal. Stay with your dog until the person loading him has to take him to the plane. You should plan to tip anyone who is assigned to handle your dog's crate, and also tell the person who takes him from you that you'll have someone at your departure gate radio down to be sure he's on the plane.

Often you can get to your gate and see your dog be placed aboard. If not, just ask the gate check-in to call down and get the names of, in my case, "a large dog and a small dog with blue tape on the crates," when they are being boarded. Mention that the baggage crew is expecting the call.

Sometimes other waiting passengers may have seen your dogs boarded and will tell you the names. An excellent review of major airlines and their dog policies and track records is compiled and updated annually by the American Dog Owners' Association. Contact ADOA, 1654 Columbia Tpk., Castleton, NY 12033. This organization does a lot of important work for responsible dog care and ownership, and has been instrumental in upgrading conditions for dogs on many airlines. Membership is $10 per year.

Anyone who travels with a dog can appreciate the value of teaching your dog to eliminate on command, on leash, and away from home. Whether you are preparing to drive for several hours, to have your dog boarded on a plane, or to go into the ring at a competition, there's nothing like knowing that your dog is comfortable. And it's awful to know that he's uncomfortable.

Practice at home first using a very long leash, and say your chosen word as your dog eliminates. First thing in the morning is best to start, as you know he has to go. It's not necessary to use two different words, since you won't always know what he needs to do. Gradually gather the leash a little closer, until he accepts you up close.

I have one dog who had trouble with this. Since we travel so much, it's a necessary survival skill. It took one whole day of keeping him in a crate and taking him out often to a certain spot. When he didn't relieve himself after 10 minutes I offered him water, then calmly put him back in the crate until next time. It couldn't last forever! When he finally succeeded, he enjoyed a playtime, still on the leash until he had emptied completely. Then the leash came off until the next morning. After two days, he had no hesitation even on a six-foot leash, and he knew the cue word as well.

By the way, if you have a male dog and think it's necessary for him to walk half a mile and spread his urine drop by drop on every blade of grass, reconsider. Again, home is the place to teach him that, on leash. He gets one squirt and then comes inside. Use the crate again at first if you think he might try to cheat in the house. Before long, he'll lift his leg and stay there until he's finished the job, which makes traveling with him a lot more pleasant. Some female dogs enjoy marking territory also, and the same rule can apply.

When you travel with a dog you are responsible for picking suitable places for him to relieve himself, and for picking up after him. Always have plastic bags handy when you walk your dog (we save our bread bags for this purpose). Put your hand inside the plastic bag, pick up the deposit with the outside of the bag, then use your other hand to peel the end of the bag up over the mess, thereby turning it inside out and leaving the mess inside and your hands outside. Knot the end of the bag for good measure.

There's no need to get dirty and no excuse for leaving your dog's droppings. If we all do this, dogs will be better received by the general public. If we don't, we deserve to have dogs banned from public places.

There are other details, like eating and sleeping in strange places, that your dog needs to learn to be a happy traveler. The more he is comfortable with new things, off the agility course as well as on, the more he can tune into the challenges of the course with all his energy when it's his turn. What comes of that time is always a reflection of his personal comfort as well as his training.

Competing Under Adverse Conditions

Rain, wind, snow, heat and cold have each made appearances with a show of force at agility events which went on as planned.

Have your agility club schedule some practices to include nasty weather, and learn to keep your dog from succumbing to it. If you practice working in all kinds of weather, you will learn a lot about what affects your dog and what to do about it. So the next time you think you'll postpone a walk because of rain or snow or heat, think Agility and enjoy your walk anyway. The more you and your dog get out and learn about staying comfortable in less-than-favorable conditions, the better prepared you will be to compete successfully in them.

Agility under adverse conditions requires extra dedication, preparation training, and a generous measure of good humor. I don't know who has the harder lot, competitors or judge.

If you're open to it, there's a certain camaraderie among competitors, judges, well-wishers and volunteers who are crazy enough to go to all that trouble on such a day. You and your dog can have some of your best fun, and certainly a day to remember. Good sportsmanship is the rule.

Sportsmanship at the Event

Although it's tested more directly in nasty weather or with substandard course conditions, good sportsmanship is part of the fabric that makes Agility strong. You can be either a positive or a negative competitor; it's up to you.

There's nothing wrong with trying to win. There is everything right with encouraging others and congratulating a fine run by someone else.

Being a positive competitor doesn't mean you don't mention things that strike you as unsafe or improper on the course. It means telling the appropriate person rather than complaining to your friends outside the ring. If you notice a problem, bring it up to the judge or steward (who should report it directly to the judge) during your walk-through. The judge should examine the situation and decide whether to make a change at that time.

The judge may not see the situation as you do, so don't take it personally if a change is not made. It's important that you feel free to mention what you see as a problem without crying "unfair" or feeling sorry for yourself, even if you feel it may hamper your run. Try to handle your dog accordingly. No course is without its inequities, and they even out in the long run.

If something is slightly troublesome and you want to warn the other competitors, fine. Don't bother the judge with trivialities. But if you feel that something is unsafe, you are within your rights and good judgment to advise a ring official, politely and matter-of-factly, about what you view as a hazard on the course, and ask that he inform the judge.

The same applies if you personally note an instance of cheating or bad sportsmanship which you feel requires an official action. If you see an action in or outside the ring that requires the judge's attention, inform a steward immediately rather than after the class is complete. If at all possible, it should not come as a surprise to a competitor at placement time that he has been eliminated.

When reporting a serious infraction, you must be prepared to put what you saw in writing. This is the only way to distinguish between who actually saw what and who simply believes that so-and-so would do such a thing. You don't want to be part of an effort that will be more damaging to the sport than the infraction you are reporting.

Developing a Competitive Strategy

Competitors wait for the call to walk the course in Pennsylvania.

I have some excellent students who can't imagine why anyone would want to spoil the pure fun of Agility by turning it into a competition. What is it about competition? Except for money, which I hope will never be among the prizes at agility tests, why would anyone want to turn a pastime into a contest?

I love the preparation and the traveling with my dogs, seeing the people and dogs who have come to be my friends through our mutual love of this sport, meeting new people and seeing new places, sharing ideas about equipment and training, getting the news of everyone's latest travels and doggy details. But that's not all.

Competition is what keeps me trying to refine skills and learn to work always a little better with my dogs. It pushes me to keep in the habit of practicing even when it might be more fun to take the week off. It provides a format for agility people to come together to appreciate the sport, and these exchanges upgrade, enhance and expand the sport.

Virtually any physical skill, your dog's and your own, can be improved by practicing in your yard or in your house. It becomes second nature to work on stamina, timing, coordination and teamwork. But the mental preparedness to do your best in competition is not so easily simulated. There are many good books available about developing the will and mental ability to succeed at anything. Success does indeed produce success; the expectation to succeed is an important component of doing well. Skills like visualization, positive thinking, biofeedback, concentration, etc., all help lower the test anxiety that interferes with so many of us when our brief turn arrives.

Keep thinking of Agility as a team sport. When you give in to your nerves, you are tuning out the job at hand. Your job is your dog's success, and it's helpful in competition to lose yourself in that.

Find out, perhaps through trial and error at competitions, whether your dog needs to rest quietly in his crate while you work out the pre-performance jitters. I found that I need to spend time with Jessy on my lap before a big run. It seems to help us find grounding in the teamwork we've built over the years.

If you're handling very different dogs over the same course, your task is more complicated. No two dogs work alike, so try to give each dog a separate walk-through. Take notes if necessary so you can review for each dog. I find it difficult to show my little Springer and my big Rottweiler over the same course because my own job is so different with each one.

In one major tournament, thinking of the big dog, I called for a quick spin to the right, and my little dynamo gave me so tight a turn I sent him up the wrong obstacle before I knew what happened. Looking on the bright side, except for my handling error the youngster went clear, with style and delight, exceeding all my personal goals for him. That's a great day.

When you walk a competition course, take your time and tune out the people around you. You need to be comfortable with the order in which you'll be taking the obstacles by the time you finish your walk through. Those individual markers are helpful to spectators, and they can help you as you walk slowly through the course, but don't count on them when you're running and watching your dog. Know the sequence of obstacles, and imagine you and your dog tackling each one without hesitation between them.

That's what it takes to plan a strategy for your run. Anticipate where your dog might have problems. Know where you want to position yourself, and whether you want your dog to be working beside, in front or in back of you at each station. Plan your commands, your timing, and even your praise. Most people find it useful to walk the course once methodically to familiarize themselves, then begin again and trot through to test their ideas.

After you have finished your walk-through, stand at ringside where you have a good view of the equipment. Now visualize yourself with your dog at the starting line. Mentally go through the process of leaving your dog and going to your own start point, and then take yourself in your mind obstacle by obstacle through the run. Imagine yourself encouraging your dog, bolstering his performance. Picture your dog sailing over the jumps and performing each obstacle well, and see yourself running your pattern smoothly and directing your dog surely. See the smile on your face. Feel the support and confidence going from you to your dog and back again. Do you want to do well? Then train to do well, plan for it and you can do it.

There is a war veteran in New Hampshire who takes problem teens rock- climbing, and before he sends them off the edge to rappel for the first time he asks them if they're afraid. Most admit to real fear, some don't, and he tells them it's OK to be scared. Those butterflies in the stomach are normal. He tells them not to try to get rid of the butterflies; just get in there and make those butterflies fly in formation.

Agility Clubs

All over the world, local agility clubs provide a network of news and information to enthusiasts of the sport. Most countries now have a governing national organization (see Appendix) which serves to keep member clubs up to date and focused in the same direction.

Joining a club is a great motivator to get people and dogs out practicing who otherwise would have too many other things to do. There are all kinds of clubs with all kinds of reasons for existing: to hold weekly run-throughs for competition practice; to enjoy the fun and games of one or more dog sports including Agility; to promote the enjoyment of Agility in the community; or, to instruct agility classes, sponsor trials or workshops, etc.

To start an agility club takes a few dedicated people with a compatibility of purpose. Attracting additional members and promoting the sport outside the group requires more time and energy than maintaining the original group. It's a good idea to discuss two central options before formalizing a club. Does the group want to: 1. enlarge its membership, and/or 2. align with a national organization.

These options define a general framework in which the club can begin to function. Enlarging the membership requires a certain commitment to public relations work, outreach via agility demonstrations and information booths at dog shows, civic events, etc. Becoming a member club in a national organization generally carries some concomitant requirements which you need to learn about and discuss before making a final decision.

First come up with a concensus of what the original members want from this effort to organize, and then develop a strategy and perhaps a rough timetable for nailing down the particulars.

When your club is ready to decide the nitty-gritty details of its existence, it's wise to get input from other clubs who have similar goals to broaden your ideas about what your club would like to stand for and how you'd like to run it. You can also learn a lot about formalizing your club by studying the structure of other kinds of successful clubs, like civic organizations in your area.

In the U.S., nonprofit status is important for tax reasons. Many clubs also incorporate for insurance reasons. This is not as complex or expensive a process as it can be for companies seeking profits. Details may vary from state to state, but the required form can be obtained through your state's Secretary of State's Office. With the completed form you will need to submit the club's slate of officers, a copy of its bylaws, and other details, such as what will be done with the club's assets if it is disbanded. These issues should be formalized by your club regardless.

Applying for tax-exempt status is done through the IRS, using Publication 557 as a guideline. Like most such booklets, it looks more complicated than it is. A nonprofit club with a healthy budget should probably apply.

Most clubs tend to start small, and in a sport like Agility that means every member has to pitch in to get the work done. It takes several members just to keep equipment serviceable, and the camaraderie of doing these tasks together makes cooperation the rule rather than the exception. The club evolves through many hours of conversation among friends who get together to share the hobby. Here is a brief description of different start-ups represented by some of USDAA's member groups:

By 1986, the agility clubs begun by Sandra Davis (Agility Dogs of El Paso, Texas, or ADEPT) and Kenneth Tatsch (Dallas Agility Working Group, or DAWG) were very busy introducing the sport in local demonstrations. These first two groups are more than 600 miles apart.

In the northeast, the first USDAA member club was the New England Agility Team (NEAT) begun in 1988 by Jean MacKenzie and others. This small group traveled thousands of miles in giving more than 50 demonstrations and seminars its first year. The club was working so well and was so busy promoting Agility that an official structure and slate of officers wasn't proposed for six months.

The Minnesota Agility Club (MAC) was organized by a steering committee headed by Sharon Anderson. Over the course of a year, the committee guided the group through the difficult process of focusing and becoming a cohesive club, with a very strong 85-member unit emerging.

The Spokane, Washington, Agility Team (SWAT), led by Sharon Nelson, took shape as a subset of a larger dog obedience training club.

Many agility clubs, especially in the midwest, are also active in the sport of flyball. Canine Combustion, from the Detroit, Michigan, area, is one such club active in both sports. Darlene Woz and other founders were introduced to USDAA by Mary Jones when she moved from Dallas to Michigan.

In Danville, Virginia, Bev and Burt Franklin built on their property one of the nicest agility courses anywhere and started inviting friends and students to come and play at the BB Agility Center. They had previously built small-scale equipment which they now use for puppies.

Alaina Axford from Pennsylvania took on a big job after participating in the USDAA Agility demonstrations at the Radnor Hunt International Horse Show. She and Gail Levering started the Keystone Agility Club on a shoestring. Their equipment was made by two NEAT members, Ron Pitkin and George McLaughlin, incorporating many of the improvements they had pioneered.

In 1988, Art Weiss of Long Island, New York, built a quality set of equipment based on downscaled agility guidelines. As soon as he saw the original version in action, he started over and built another complete set of obstacles, this time to USDAA standards. The Long Island Agility Club hosted its first USDAA Pedigree Grand Prix qualifier in 1990, showing us some new motifs in their "hydrant" jump, "castle" closed tunnel, and arched pause table. (See Appendix for details of some of the equipment ideas these clubs have introduced.)

In Canada, the ADAC has worked tirelessly under the leadership of Art Newman of Ottawa, helping Agility catch on in spite of the inevitable problems of promoting a developing sport in a very large country. Mr. Newman and his wife Edna dedicate much of their lives to activities that help people and dogs enjoy each other. ADAC sponsored the first agility nationals for Canada in 1990. The event was held at the Guide Dogs for the Blind training institute in Manotick, Ontario, and all profits were donated to that organization. More than 1000 spectators attended.

In NEAT, outreach efforts are part of our club's charter, as is the policy not to provide agility demonstrations at events that prohibit mixed-breed dogs. Like many USDAA clubs, we have a significant percentage of members who come just to enjoy some extra fun with their dogs. NEAT

Phoenix and owner, Pierre Lalonde of Cornwall, Ontario are the first Canadian national champions. Art Newman is in middle of back row.

originally required three visits before accepting a new member, but this has now been revised to incorporate a combination of more "working" visits and a lengthier process of participation and application.

In the Long Island Agility Club, Art Weiss keeps records of visits and he has a great system. Before an individual may join the club, he must have logged 12 working visits. That means that he must help with either the set up or the take down of the club's equipment. Anyone who comes to practice and does neither is not checked off or credited with a working visit. This sounds like an effective way to make sure that members know how to be contributors.

Clubs that want to be active can gain a great deal of experience by putting on public demonstrations at any level. If you design a schedule to fit the occasion, you can benefit the sponsoring organization, your parent club, and your club members who get to practice working with different distractions and often in unusual locations. As a club, you gain extra recognition, interest more people in your activities, and have an opportunity to practice organizing and running an event.

Stay in touch with the host organization and check out particulars like the site, convenience of your demonstration area for loading and care of dogs, if your members will be offered a meal, if there's a sound system and announcer, if you can have information booth space to set up an agility video, etc. To avoid misunderstandings, be sure both sides make clear what they expect.

Set up an agility information station at your demonstration and keep it supplied with fliers and information about Agility, your club, and any upcoming agility events. Take down names and addresses of those who'd like to be on your mailing list.

On a larger scale, the diversity of background represented by a country's member clubs adds to the richness of the sport. With every opportunity for competition comes an appreciation for another club's agility eyes and another group's talented dogs. As long we keep our rules and obstacle guidelines compatible on an international level, we will be able to enjoy other cultures and sharpen our agility eyesight that much more as the sport continues to prosper all over the world.

If you are thinking of starting a club, it's easier than setting up agility courses all alone, and it's a great way to give yourself a steady opportunity to practice with others. Round up a few more dedicated individuals, and start collectively breathing life into your club.

Sometimes when a club takes off and starts growing rapidly you might get a sinking feeling that it's not what it used to be, and that is inevitable as a club gets larger. Just in case your club starts taking itself too seriously, remember these words of the great comedian Groucho Marx: "I wouldn't want to belong to any club that would have me for a member."

SECTION III
Agility for the Very Young

- *Agility for Children*

- *Agility for Puppies*

AGILITY FOR CHILDREN

When Joe Carraclough came out of school and walked through the gate, he could not believe his eyes. He stood for a moment, and then his voice rang shrill. "Lassie! Lassie!"

–from *Lassie Come Home*, by Eric Knight

Kid Meets Dog

There are so many kids around that a dog is not well equipped to live in harmony with his environment if he cannot tolerate them. And there are so many dogs around that a child who grows up afraid of dogs will suffer a great deal of unnecessary fear and trauma. Raising a child to appreciate dogs and raising a dog to enjoy children are important responsibilities of our stewardship.

If your dog happens to dislike children, or is annoyed by uninvited approaches or by having his food or toys touched, you need to get help from a professional trainer, especially if you have young children around. The correct line of resolution here depends on your dog, your lifestyle, and yourself. Although a book can offer good ideas, it probably won't match your situation exactly, so get help from a professional also.

Assuming that your dog is trustworthy about children, let your young child help you feed the dog. At the same time, you will be teaching your dog not to feel threatened about food when the child is near. This simple exercise involves having your child put small amounts of dog food into the dog's dish. Measure out the dog's total meal and help the child scoop food to the dog's food dish. As they both get used to the arrangement, let the dog start eating as the child is adding more. Don't let the occasional spills spoil the positive interaction. Cleaning up can be fun, too.

If you want your kids and your dog to get along and to have confidence, you need to supervise and guide their early interactions by helping each of them feel successful.

"Some of my best friends are kids," says Arrow. This furnished playhouse/tunnel is made from a galvanized culvert.

It takes confidence for a child to relate well to dogs, and a child's confidence is nurtured the same way a puppy's is – by our ensuring success in the early encounters. The child cannot feel successful when the dog knocks him down, rips his pantsleg, steals his sneaker and runs around playing keep-away. Though the dog may be saying "I love you, wanna' play?" it puts a damper on the interaction from the child's point of view.

Teach your exuberant friendly dog not to jump on people, and keep him on leash around people until he has mastered basic manners. Teach your exuberant young child not to jump on dogs, and keep close tabs on him around dogs until he has mastered basic manners. Judith "Miss Manners" Martin makes an observation about children which is equally applicable to dogs: "We are all born charming, fresh, and spontaneous and must be civilized before we are fit to participate in society."

Kids Training Agility Dogs

A universal link between kids and dogs is food. To the canine world, a kid stamping his foot and crying represents an underling. Dogs are not programmed to respect this, although they are generally more than happy to lick the jelly off a face and extract the cookie from the stubby fingers.

In turn, the understandably frustrated child gets a negative early imprint and finds it difficult to enjoy the dog. There are several steps you can take even with young children to start them on their way to a happy coexistence with dogs.

The dog's trainer has to be ready to discipline the dog before he steals a child's food. It's not fair to punish the dog consistently after he's devoured the food; that's a mixed message at best. As with any other obedience training, when you don't have the time to be on guard you should take steps to prevent the problem from arising. Either crate the dog or tie him to you, put the child in a high chair, or confine the dog and the kid to separate rooms. Take a measure that suits your situation, but don't let your dog continue to get away with stealing food from kids.

This lesson will come easier for the hapless dog if you teach him the command "leave it" (see Ch. 3). There are two most important benefits of this training: the dog learns to answer to you in the face of one of the world's most tempting distractions; and, your child begins his education in dog training by learning that this problem, perhaps one of his most important aggravations, can be solved.

Help your child learn to praise the good doggie for going away from the cookie. Because you make a habit of praising your dog when he ignores temptation, many kids will begin to do this by way of imitating you, and that's good, even if their timing is not quite right yet. Happily, as long as you're consistent it will all come together in time. Your dog can get used to accepting treats from children by invitation only.

If your child enjoys feeding the dog, it would be fun to include him in simple agility lessons which let him give out the rewards. Since this is seen by the child as the teacher's job, and since the dog already knows that Agility is great fun, it's easy to make both child and dog feel very smart and important. The adult needs to play a lot of backup here, being both helper and coach.

Agility is a great way for kids of all ages to begin learning how to work with dogs. It doesn't take a lot of instruction for a three-year-old to learn to show Lassie the cookie and call her. Once the dog has learned the exercise and the kids have watched you do it a few times, go ahead and serve as helper while your child assumes the teacher's motivational role at his own level of ability.

Young children are happy offering treats in an outstretched hand. But older kids want more responsibility and can be a great help introducing the dog to tunnels, A-frames, jumps and weave poles. They can crawl through, climb over, jump the low jumps, run through the weave pole chute, and think of all kinds of ways to entice the dog's first attempts with their antics. It's very helpful to the dog when the owners laugh and enjoy the obstacle themselves. Kids are a great asset in my agility classes. They help us to loosen up, and they bring to the obstacles an energy and a sincerity of pleasure that inspire dogs and adults alike. Kids are fun.

Jessy takes possession in a backyard soccer game.

Once the dog is happy and familiar with the obstacle and his job, the enticer can be very young, just old enough to offer a treat. Then an older child might enjoy being the helper and holding a gentle dog while a younger child holds out a goodie and calls. Sometimes older children prefer to work with the dog alone or with friends, and certainly without parents. Although their interest is to be encouraged and it's natural for them to want to step right into the boss's job without any help from you, you should stay on as helper until everyone's role is well rehearsed.

Although children can take part in many basic agility exercises, before establishing a leadership role with the dog there are many things that they should not attempt until they have done some general obedience groundwork with the dog. This will help them avoid the frustration of being ignored as an underling just when they want the dog to respect them and take direction from them. With your help, your child can learn to give orders effectively, see them through, and reward the dog immediately so as to make himself worth listening to from the dog's point of view. At the same time, the child improves his timing, his confidence, and his ability to coordinate demand with motivation and reward.

The adult's role in the following obedience exercises is to provide physical follow-through to backup a child's command. But keep a low profile. Whenever possible, your physical corrections and placement of the dog in the position the child commands should be done without your saying the command word yourself. Let your child command. If you reiterate each order when you have to enforce it, the dog will continue to wait for your instruction rather than acting on your child's. Many dogs ignore commands by children, but you can help your dog and your child tune in to each other. It's good for both of them.

Don't worry about your dog being confused by other children if he

Misty loves the tire and three-year-old Jessica, but has never put the two together. Mom coordinates...

...Viola; "mutualism."

begins to take orders from your kids. He'll quickly learn whose commands are meaningful and whose are not. That's how so many dogs come to ignore children's orders in the first place. To establish the dog's interest and the child's power in a positive way from the beginning of this effort, the child should have the fun and responsibility of rewarding the dog.

Before you get your child directly involved in your dog's obedience, you should make some major inroads yourself (see Ch. 2). When a lesson seems to be well learned, you can let a child as young as three play a part. My favorite obedience lessons for young kids to join are "sit," and, separately, "wait." The older your child and the more naturally he assumes a leadership role with your dogs, the more responsibility he can learn to coordinate in your joint lessons.

Don't be in a hurry to let go of the leash since you may quickly need to enforce the child's command if the dog ignores it. As long as you keep your verbal interference to a minimum, the child will be more apt to accept your backup.

The dog who has been trained to "sit" on command can easily transfer that response to a child's order when the kid is holding a treat. It may be necessary for you to tuck a big dog into the sit position for the first few times, but since the child will then give him the treat he will soon decide to do it on the child's command to get the treat faster.

If the child can reach over the dog's head, he can entice the dog to follow a treat, as in Ch. 2. Little dogs are good at jumping up and nabbing the goodie from little hands, and big dogs can nuzzle it away, so be ready for that. In any case, you will need to prevent the dog from stealing the treat without sitting, so keep the dog on leash and don't let child and dog go it alone until they each have their parts memorized.

To practice "wait" with your child's help, begin with the dog sitting and have your child command "wait" as he puts a treat or toy on the floor. You need to do any necessary correcting with the leash, but try not to say anything. Since the dog already knows the exercise, he can make the transition to listening for your child to say "OK." Kids usually love this one. You may find yourself reminding the child to say OK, but don't be hard on him.

The sensation of power just makes kids giddy with pleasure sometimes, and they're reluctant to let it go. Just gently say something like "That's great. Now would you like to tell Lassie OK or shall I?" Then go ahead and free the dog if need be, and tell your child he may be the teacher again next time. If your dog doesn't care for physical enticements, you could do this exercise just prior to going for a walk, with your child opening the door while he has the dog wait.

The same technique can be used to transfer the important commands to lie down and to come when called. If your dog likes treats or toys, he will easily learn to follow the enticement down when the child lowers it.

Four-year-old
Colton reminds
Lynn to wait...

...“OK! Mom
is teacher,
coach, and
enforcer
without
stealing the
child’s show.

You should be ready to press on his shoulders to help if necessary, but let your child give the command and the reward. Recalls can be practiced first with you holding a short leash, then gradually working up to a long line, so the child can call the dog from longer distances. Older children can assume control of the leash once the dog is well adjusted to the routine. Gradually work off leash when the dog is ready.

Some dogs are gentle enough for a child to use play as a reward, but in general food offers far fewer drawbacks starting out. Wean the dog from dependence on tidbits later on, just as you would yourself, when the child has more control. Gradually, the enthusiastic praise which accompanies the dog's efforts becomes a more important part of the reward. By contrast, it is quite unnecessary and really difficult to train the dog to work happily with a child by using punitive measures. The child needs to know from the outset that the reward is as important as the command.

Astro works a wide weave pole chute with eight-year-old Nicole. 12-year-old James is the helper.

Both child and dog need you to guide early lessons in a positive way, heading off mistakes and praising initial efforts. You may tend to be hard on your children after working so persistently yourself to help the dog understand these commands. It just hurts to see anyone perform these hard- won rituals imprecisely.

But, if you accept the approach that attitude comes first, you need to bring your patience and positive thinking to every lesson for your children as well as your dog. Presumably, you have put the dog on the right track with your own work already, so a mistake in the child's timing will not cause irreparable damage. I would rather see the dog rewarded inappropriately and both child and dog grinning at each other than have the youngster chastised for poor timing. Just think ahead for next time, and try to prevent the same mistake in a positive way.

Another difficult but helpful point to remember is that it's much more useful to suggest something to do rather than repeat what not to do. So rather than yell: "Not that way for goodness sake! Stop him," just say something calm like: "Good. You got him past the tire. Maybe next time he'll go through the hole. Try holding the cookie right here."

Although it's painful to see mistakes happen, it's worse to demand that your child stop the dog physically when he's unable to do so. Perhaps a helper is needed for awhile longer so the dog can be interrupted from behind, wordlessly if possible, if he still tries to go around. Just remind yourself of the good things that are being accomplished between your dog and your child.

In my obedience classes, I encourage adults to bring an older child to watch and often include the child in some classroom work. I advise parents to invite an interested child to read instructions out loud from the homework sheet while the parent follows those directions with the dog. This is much harder on the parent than on the child. What I usually find is that the kid is really tough on the adult, ordering and criticizing unmercifully. Resist the understandable temptation to shut the child up or hand him the leash.

You're doing wonders for your child's confidence and his understanding of the exercises. This process will help him work very hard to succeed when it's his turn. The child who comes to class with a parent and is a part of the progress in a positive way at home gets a well-rounded and supportive start in training his dog.

Without having to handle the dog physically at first, he has more opportunity to watch, listen and learn from what others do and assimilate the information. And his attitude toward training his dog can be nurtured without letting him feel the frustrations of failure too soon. As a result, this child will be better prepared to handle the dog effectively himself than a child who is uninvolved with the lessons or one who is given more responsibility than he can coordinate.

Children are welcome in my agility classes, and there they can be completely involved from the very beginning. Kids can bring out wonderful things in agility dogs, beginning with a sense of fun. Many a dog will follow a laughing kid through a tunnel and over an A-frame where grown-ups have failed.

I don't clamp the lid on spontaneity in Agility, and I don't underestimate a dog's tendency to relax and have fun with children. Some very quiet dogs will be happier watching the action from the sidelines at first, and all but the most introverted will do so with unabashed curiosity. Arousing interest is the first step to arousing cooperation, in both species.

So let your child call the dog through the tunnel for a cookie. If he's old enough and wants to, let a child hold the dog until you call him to jump. If the child lets go too soon, just call out the command immediately so you don't have to correct anyone just yet. The child should not be blamed for being weaker than the dog. Perhaps next time you'll want to switch places and let the kid call the dog and you hold him, or support the child's effort to hold your dog back by reminding the dog to wait. Depending on your child's age and interest, ask what he thinks and let him help plan a short lesson.

The children in my life have given me many good ideas for helping dogs accomplish things that are difficult for them. There have been many lessons around my house that were put off until the neighborhood kids came home from school, and there have been many afternoons when the neighborhood kids all seemed to live at my house. Agility attracts kids and they are terrific assets to bring to your dog's education. When you brag about your dog, tell friends about your child's contributions as well. Think of something nice to say about both of them.

With one foot securing the plank, seven-year-old Heather practices zone work with Arrow on the downscaled seesaw. Many of the how-to photos in this book feature children who have training skills and dog savvy.

The most important skill for a child to acquire while young and transfer from one sport to another is good sportsmanship. When a child puts real effort into an accomplishment, he feels good. "I did it!" is a spontaneous, heartfelt pronouncement. And when the child tries and fails, the disappointment comes equally naturally.

When young children meet their problems with a loud show of displeasure, we can help by showing them the fun of problem-solving at their own level. Instead of feeling powerless, an older child can learn to reexamine a problem, tackle it from another angle, see it through, learn from failures and improve as a result of them. Then he won't need that intense defensive reaction because he will not be unduly afraid of failure.

Later in life, the world of competitive sports opens up a whole new set of opportunities for frustration, and for handling that frustration constructively. Those who have not yet learned to handle failure are quick to blame their failures on outside forces – the judge, the equipment, the competitors, the spectators, the weather. Though at any time any one of these factors may present a problem, it is self-defeating to dwell on it.

The most counterproductive reaction is one I see most often dragged into adulthood, that of complaining loudly at ringside without informing the person who could effect a change. This shows not only a lack of sportsmanship but also a lack of initiative. A problem serious enough to warrant extended discussion should be calmly explained to a ring steward, who can bring it to the attention of the judge.

In small classes, a child who doesn't understand his score should be encouraged to have it explained to him by asking the judge afterward for particulars. The judge can't be expected to remember each competitor personally, but he may remember some points, and he can look up the scoresheet for that run, or have a steward do so.

Children who lack confidence have a hard time doing this, but it's a skill they should develop. They may not like the answers, but at least they might learn what the judge thought instead of what they assumed he thought. Those two things are usually quite different. It's worth asking.

If the kid isn't pressured to place too much stock in winning, then it won't be so difficult for him to approach the judge. A child will be nervous about competitions, and you will make a child feel more nervous if you admonish him to do well. It is more useful to the child for a parent to say: "You and Corky have fun." It's a given that he doesn't want to do badly, and what he now needs to know is that your love doesn't depend on him having an excellent round or winning the competition. This is something your child should understand before he ever enters a competition. Teach him from the beginning to be a positive participant.

A positive participant has learned good sportsmanship. It shows up especially in the words "congratulations" and "thank you." When a child says "congratulations," he is saying that he can take the good fortune of another in stride. When he says "thank you," he is saying that he appreciates the same gesture from another competitor.

A positive participant comes to each event with a set of personal goals for the day. He tries to help his dog have a good day rather than counting on his dog to give him a good day. Most of all, he is open-minded about things that go right and things that go wrong, so he learns something with every exposure. His participation in Agility is part of a healthy growth process for him, and the sport benefits from him taking part.

A negative participant has not learned good sportsmanship. It shows up especially in the angry accusations made to a third party. If a child grows up blaming others for his mistakes, he will not look to his own training for solutions to his agility problems. Even in practice sessions with no one but his dog, he will choose to blame his dog rather than improve his own skills.

The negative participant expects his dog to carry him through, and if the dog cannot do so he is incapable of recognizing his own responsibility for that. He cannot take the good fortune of another competitor in stride. His participation in Agility is a hindrance to his personal growth, and the sport is not healthier for him taking part.

Agility is for kids, and can be a terrific source of personal growth for them. What they give to Agility and take from it is in large part up to us, the adults who love both the sport and the kids. Along with sound training in agility basics, we need to guide the development of good sportsmanship by instruction and example.

AGILITY FOR PUPPIES

I wish someone would tell me what it is that I've done wrong. Why I have to stay chained up and left alone so long. They seemed so glad to have me when I came here as a pup. There were so many things we'd do while I was growing up... But now the family "hasn't time;" they often say I shed. They do not want me in the house, not even to be fed. All I had, you see, was love. I wish they would explain. Why they said they wanted me, then left me on a chain?
                                        –from Alone Again, Anonymous

First Impressions – The Advantage of Starting Young

Like a new baby, a new puppy changes your life immediately, for better and for worse. But a puppy is young for a very short time, which is also better and worse. What you do with your first several months together can chart a collision course or shape a mutually satisfying relationship.

If you are choosing a puppy, make sure you select one who has had lots of quality contact with other dogs and with humans. A pup who lives in the house and regularly gets the chance to explore new places and meet new people is a pup with a real head start. A pup who lives his early weeks outside the house or in the cellar often finds it difficult to fit in when he suddenly is brought into the mainstream.

Making a puppy live its first weeks without loving attention from humans and without being introduced gently to different environments is to deny it the necessary preparation for life in the real world – and that is cruel.

It is difficult to socialize even a young adolescent dog if he lacked early handling and affection from strangers. So don't judge a pup's potential by whether his breeder has a beautiful home or a lovely kennel. Insist on seeing exactly where the pups have lived and get a feel for how much contact they've had.

A pup learns from his mother, his siblings, his contact with humans

Six-week-old pups enjoy backyard agility obstacles. Tunnel is a cardboard tube; wooden box has holes on both ends. Planks and tube are nailed to supports for safety.

and his physical environment at a phenomenal rate. Whether he learns what is considered to be good habits is largely up to his human family.

A puppy's brain reaches its potential ability to process information at an early age, about seven weeks. But a seven-week-old pup is not ready to be trained like an adult dog; he is still a baby, limited by the short time he has been alive. His mature brain is an asset for training purposes only if the training is presented in a way that the pup is ready to accept.

So here you are with a fast-growing creature who's a sponge for information of all kinds and whose natural tendencies would render him with habits absolutely unacceptable to us. That is why now, while your dog is very young, is the best time to teach him many things about getting along with humans and their ways.

Your new companion is already learning fast. But he can't find out how to deal with life outside his instincts unless you help him. Expose him in a friendly way to the big, wide world. You will find life with your dog much brighter if you teach his quick mind, at his "kindergarten" level, what you would like him to learn.

My puppy kindergarten classes emphasize socialization, manners, and skills for harmonious family living instead of rigorous or formal training. I also introduce downscaled agility equipment because it's effective in building confidence, trust, and teamwork between puppy and handler. It's lots of fun and makes use of the pup's physical prowess, balancing the different and often more demanding efforts of obedience lessons and physical and mental restraint. Every puppy can benefit from agility training that is tailored to his own level of readiness.

In 1989, I began to work with an English Springer Spaniel puppy who showed a more classic aptitude for Agility: he was confident, well coordinated, and curious, like Jessy, but he also trusted people and wanted to please them, a big advantage in Agility.

"Arrow" is easier to train. Fun and games along with positive control work are the strategies. Arrow earned his AD at only 12 months of age, still dancing on the course and years away from reaching his full potential. Puppies mature and bring their skills together at different rates, and rushing their personal development always extracts a heavy price. Keep it fun.

You might find that your puppy falls in love with Agility. It's nearly impossible to predict, and it's not always the athletic pups who show the most aptitude for the sport. You can help your pup improve his coordination, explore new surroundings, develop physical skills, build confidence in himself and trust in you. This may be the start of a career in fun and games.

If your puppy is shy or aggressive, both signs of fear, you need to follow a socialization program to help him understand that life is nothing to be afraid of. One of many tools to help build social skills in such a pup is agility training. Agility skills improve his self-image and give him more confidence, which assimilate readily into his daily life.

Once well established, this confidence is his to keep. He'll retain a good measure of it, even if he doesn't stay involved with Agility as a sport. If he does stay involved with Agility, whether backyard or regulation, he will do more than gain some extra confidence and skill. He will grow to love to see what he can do with various obstacles, because climbing, balancing, jumping, and tunneling will be as natural as breathing. This is a wonderful outlook which will enrich his life immeasurably. It will also get him into trouble.

Your agility puppy will climb "because it's there," without giving a thought to whether his perceived obstacle is safe or secure. I have seen dogs go up a seesaw ramp that was only resting on its base waiting to be assembled. Likewise, don't expect your dog to keep off the dog walk just because the cross-ramp has been removed. If you're going to be around partially dismantled equipment, keep your pup on leash.

Get to know your puppy's strong and weak points so you can give him guidance that suits him. Let him use all his senses to explore equipment. Puppies first need to smell, hear, and see the stuff, explore the texture and even the taste, then be enticed to use the piece in another way, like walking up a low incline or going through a short tunnel. No matter what he does, don't issue any correction.

If he is about to do something dangerous, just scoop him up in your arms while you praise him; then guide him more closely next time. Letting him watch happy agility workers is very helpful. Even if your pup doesn't take note with his eyes, he is taking in the sounds of laughter and praise and the happy feelings of the working dogs and handlers. Attitude comes first.

When it's your puppy's turn, have your enticements ready for even the simplest things because your puppy will soon surprise you, and early frights are the hardest to overcome. The line between introducing the impressions of Agility and beginning the actual training is blurred. I tend to call it training if I'm asking the pup to do something he didn't think of himself.

It's best to begin the training on an obstacle after the pup is so comfortable with it that he doesn't know he's working. For example, before asking the pup to walk up a textured plank leaning on a cinder block, first lay that plank on a hill and play with the pup on it until it's an old friend. Then the incline up to the cinder block (or brick if you want the plank lower) poses a new step but not something difficult.

There are many games you can play at your pup's level that will help him want to try new things and try, try again. Simple problem solving while he's young helps your pup develop a mind for perseverance, sound thinking under stress, the desire and expectation to succeed. These attributes mature into a real work ethic. A dog who enjoys work, enjoys Agility, and enjoys his handler is a privilege to train.

How lucky you are to be one of your puppy's first teachers. Here are a few problem-solving games you can adapt for the age and experience of your pup:

1. Set up a low barrier and encourage your pup to get over it. Use a doorway if he wants to go around.

2. Hide from your pup and call him to find you. Use a helper if he needs a motivator.

3. Walk on leash in crowded places when he's ready, and play hide-and-seek (standing behind a parking meter or tree, or crouching beside a bench can constitute hiding).

4. Work with your pup after dark as well as in daylight, so he has to work harder and use different senses to find you.

5. Practice recalls across wide expanses and crowded rooms, uphill and down. Praise him all the way and greet him with delight.

6. Play with him using a big ball that he can climb on and roll around with so he learns to take a tumble without becoming upset.

7. Set your pup up on a low box or platform in a corner, with a plank down one open side and a stepping block on the other. Encourage him

and let him figure out how to get down. Help him if he needs it, then try again. See if he repeats his success readily. Then remove that dismount and talk him into the other (block the open side if he's too young to jump).

8. Set up a high barrier and lean over it close to your pup. Call him and let him figure out that he has to go around the barrier to get to you. Help him if necessary, then see how quickly he remembers next time. Then block that side and let him discover going around the other way.

9. Set a short length of tunnel or a cut-out box in a doorway, and block around and above it. Entice your pup through.

Help your young pup be successful right away at first. Make sure that he comes out of his early problem-solving set ups with his self-image enhanced; you do this by seeing that he is mildly challenged and that he sees that challenge through to success quickly. Don't make the job harder until he is ready, and don't complicate more than one aspect of the job at a time. Don't ever give him a job he can't do. Soon enough, he will be an independent thinker who trusts your judgment and uses his head to work with you. That's what you'll need to be a team, in Agility and in everyday life.

Basic Skills and Manners

Your puppy will behave with you according to the reaction he expects from you and how that anticipated reaction affects him. When you are consistent and give your pup love and guidance he can understand, you give him habits for a happier life, ones which further a healthy living arrangement.

Try to resist the common advice to get two puppies so they can keep each other company. What that usually means is that neither pup gets an adequate education individually. They generally spend an unhealthy amount of time alone together, and understandably bond to each other more than to their human family. That is no substitute for the input and education each puppy needs in order to reach his potential.

Your puppy needs to develop a healthy way to accept being left alone, and a proper understanding of what is for chewing and where to go to the bathroom. He needs to accept gracefully a few simple obedience commands, especially "come" and "down" (see Ch. 2), including long downs of at least 30 minutes (work up gradually). This will let him be exuberant without being insufferable in public.

It is difficult to be consistent because pups are so resourceful in their wiles and endearing in their antics. But inconsistencies will come back to haunt you, and you are not being fair to the puppy when you let him behave badly one moment and punish him for the same thing the next. Rules are rules, no matter how cute he is when he cocks his head. Yes, who is training whom is often open to interpretation. You can use that to your advantage in your training, but don't let it get the better of your efforts.

There is a game to play with your puppy that will help prevent destructive chewing and will also shape a fun-and-games reward system you can enjoy throughout agility training. Assign your pup just two toys, perhaps one soft and one hard, that are his to chew. Each toy should have a name – ball or bone or sock or toy, whatever. About twice a day, even if for only a minute each time, play with a toy and the pup together, calling the toy by name and encouraging the pup to get it, chase it, chew it. To keep your puppy tractable, you will also need to teach him to give the toy to you on command, but praise as you extract it and give it back as soon as he stops trying to grab it.

Soon he will look for it when you ask him to get it, and eventually he'll think of it himself whenever he gets the urge to chew. Be on the lookout, and when your pup looks like he needs something to do, suggest he get a toy. (If you're too busy to be watching, he belongs in his crate or tied to you.)

The other benefit of this kind of playtime is that you will have an effective enticement and an upbeat game to use with agility obstacles. The puppy who learns to enjoy toys and games with you will take well to the action rewards you want in Agility.

Starting your puppy in Agility at his own level gives him a well-rounded way of looking at education, communication, and problem solving. The youngster needs to explore his physical environment and practice his physical skills anyway, and Agility lets him do that in conjunction with earning your approval and using his head. That kind of first impression, combining fun, work, and cooperation, is an advantage for life.

Favorite First Obstacles

By the time you have played many problem-solving games with your puppy and taught him some basic rules and obedience commands, the two of you should have established a mutual bond and cooperative mindset. This is a good time to introduce some different challenges to round out your background for Agility. The idea is to take advantage of what your puppy is ready to handle, and to stretch his confidence and ability a bit further.

Most puppies do well at this stage with simple tunnels, inclines, and all manner of different mediums and surfaces underfoot. Don't concentrate now on regulation equipment – quite the contrary. Teach your pup to accept variety so he doesn't have limited expectations about agility conditions. The rules are always changing, the equipment list is always growing, and the courses will always vary.

Maria Kalmring

Three-month-old Olympia doesn't have to know that this is an introduction to cleats and zone work. It's all about fun and cookies to her.

Talus trots through to Margaret's open arms. Get down to the pup's level and praise, praise to build confidence.

Now is the time to expose the pup to concepts he'll need to understand and materials and surfaces he'll have to accept. Before he uses regulation equipment he needs to have this intermediate level of confidence building in which mistakes are not costly and new skills are the next progressions of familiar ones.

Here are some of my favorite puppy agility toys for this stage:

1. Planks and cinder blocks. Make a cleated, texture-painted plank, about eight feet long, to incline here, there, and everywhere on appropriately low surfaces. You'll use that plank (or two) right through your dog's advanced training.

2. A-frame. Any wide ramps, set flat, then very low at the apex, will do. An adjustable regulation piece, set nearly flat, is also fine. Don't prop the ramps or the regulation A-frame high enough to require any extra impulsive push from the rear yet.

3. Hay bales & plywood. This calls for a wider ramp, to mimic the A-frame. Hay bales offer a surface which has give to it, so the pup gets a rudimentary lesson in shifting his weight to maintain balance.

4. Tunnels. 55-gallon drums, fiberboard barrels, cut-out boxes, hoops, tires, storebought children's tunnels compressed short, etc. See Ch. 2. Don't use anything long. Enticement and excitement are the rule now.

5. Small pools. Get your pup used to cool-downs with water in preparation for working in the heat. Also help him accept walking through puddles and playing in wet grass, so wet equipment and pause boxes in the rain won't deter him. It's good to pattern him for playing in a wading pool rather than in other water containers. Dogs who tip over their water bowls are difficult to travel with, and dogs who dance around in the water jump draw hysteria from the spectators and faults from the judge.

6. Rocks and logs. Use the elements of the outdoors around you to keep your dog thinking Agility. Playing on uneven terrain and enjoying varied natural obstacles helps fine-tune coordination, climbing and maneuvering skills.

7. Different surfaces underfoot. Plastic, metal, concrete, matting, pavement, grass, leaves, snow, linoleum, fake grass carpet, mud, ice, stones, grating, etc., all provide the pup with different tactile stimulations. Look upon all sorts of surfaces as opportunities to introduce your pup to another sensory experience. Take the time to let him check each new one out thoroughly.

8. Wide weave pole chute. Set a short chute of individual weave poles or stakes, but proportionately even wider apart, several times the width of your pup. Have a helper hold your pup while you run down the chute, then turn and call your puppy with "poles" or whatever cheerful command you wish. This is a terrific opportunity to pattern your pup for a fast response to the poles. If your helper can get the pup all excited, jumping and straining to get to you, so much the better. The poles should be as

wide apart as it takes for the pup to stay in the chute; he shouldn't take any notice of them.

Your pup's agility education is well underway. It's a matter of challenging him further and building on what he already knows. Don't go too fast, and don't assume that your pup should be as advanced on one skill as he is on another. By now you'll probably know what his favorites are, and you should spend extra energy devising tricks to bring his weak points up to par.

It's very important that all this remain a nonregimented game, with no pressure being put on the pup. No corrections for mistakes are allowed. Just think of another approach, a different game, or an easier step that will help improve the pup's concentration or skill. Don't work on more than a few different exercises a day, and only repeat each one a few times. End the lesson while your pup is still eager to go another time, so he can look forward to the next opportunity.

The new climbing effort goes smoothly, thanks to a resourceful young handler and a favorite toy.

Here are some challenges for this stage:

1. A-frames. If your pup is blithely running up and down at lower heights, it's time for steeper and taller A-frames (ones that require the pup to push a bit from the rear along with leaning forward, just a little too steep to walk up normally).

2. Stairs. Practice with short sections of stairs to simulate pushing off from cleat to cleat on the go-up obstacles, especially if you have a small dog. Begin by carrying your pup up all but the last couple of stairs, and gradually carry him less far. This builds up muscles in the rear and the shoulders, as well as improving coordination and understanding of the climbing task.

3. Barriers. Set up lots of interesting barrier problems, using two-by-fours on edge or other very low planks, steps, etc.. You want your pup to get very comfortable with getting over simple obstacles, but you should not be presenting him with real jumps yet. The most he should be doing is hopping over things not even half his height. Climbing over is great.

4. Low dog walks. Your homemade eight-foot plank can be inclined against higher supports (see Ch. 2), perhaps up to two feet high. Another plank down is good for some pups at this stage as well. Pay attention to your pup's confidence level, and don't push it. Taking your time now is what will make him feel secure later.

5. Tunnels. Gradually introduce longer and perhaps narrower tunnels of your own design. Anything goes, as long as your pup continues to run

Cholomondeley enjoys an arrangement of ramp, step, and tunneling obstacles.

through, fast and full of fun. If he starts to slow down, he may need a break, a review of easier tunnels, a different enticement, or something more exciting to do immediately after exiting.

6. Closed tunnel. If your pup is fearless and fast with open tunnels, introduce a closed one with a very short chute (I use a lightweight nylon about four feet long). Introduce it just as you would a long one, folded completely back at first, with a helper holding the pup and you lifting the gathered chute and peeking through as you urge the pup through. It's very common for dogs who run a short closed tunnel quickly to slow down when longer and heavier chutes are introduced, so don't be in a hurry for those. You have plenty of time for that. Gradually let more of the short chute cover the exit and keep your pup motivated to charge through like a cannonball. If you must have more challenge, try a heavier weight short chute, perhaps by folding back a regulation one.

7. Weave poles. Gradually add more individual poles to lengthen the weaving chute. Narrow the chute some, but not so much that it closes in on him. The important things are to keep up the speed and the excitement with which he tears down that path. If you want a variation, teach your pup to focus on an enticement other than you at the exit end, and let grabbing that be his reward. This sometimes makes it easier to transfer your position from the end to the side, and then the beginning of the line of poles. Your youngster should not be flexing around the poles yet.

8. Seesaw. If your pup shows a good sense of balance and no fear of hay bales (which are unstable when stepped on), then you could prepare him for a later lesson on the seesaw by sitting on the fulcrum and holding the pup. Tip the puppy slightly as you shift your weight to tip the plank. Do not put the pup on the regulation obstacle directly. Holding your puppy in your lap while you sit quietly on a swing will also help prepare him for the tippy feeling he'll encounter on the downscaled seesaw.

And Then These Obstacles

I hope my enthusiasm for starting puppies young in Agility hasn't brought you to this section without taking your time with each previous step. It would be a very big mistake to rush a single bit of this. Think of the many years of first-quality work you could easily be throwing away by pushing your youngster too hard now. It would be selfish and unfair to hurry your puppy for the sake of your own pride. There's a lot you can do while your pup is young, but let reason, your conscience, and an honest evaluation of your pup's readiness be your guide. That said, here are a few more advanced agility exercises that are fun for the puppies who are real dynamos:

1. Ladders. Not climbing up, but negotiating the rungs and spaces when it's laid on the ground. This helps the pup fine tune his coordination

and figure out how to handle four feet at once with four different jobs. This simple exercise helps improve your pup's performance on go-up planks and will make it easier for him to control his body when you start having him wait at various points along the ramps. It especially helps large or clumsy dogs get their legs under control. The more nimble pups quickly become very dexterous with this.

2. Children's small playground equipment. My favorites are the very sturdy plastic slides and picnic tables for the pups to go up one side and down the other. The tables are good for all pups. They further improve the climbing and pushing-off skills begun by negotiating stairs and A-frames. The slides require more advanced coordination and should not be used unless your pup loves climbing and you work well as a team. Some pups will follow an enticement up and over without a second thought, and some will need to check out the possibilities more thoroughly. Don't push. Leave it in your family room for awhile until it's been well explored.

3. Jumps. Many puppies are started too soon in jumping. It's completely unnecessary and the risks are great. The pup does not need to push off or land strenuously to learn to negotiate jumps. Youngsters should be practicing with very low barriers, then graduate to bars and poles no more than half their height. At that height, the pup can learn about pushing off, judging effort and timing, landing, turning, continuing to another obstacle, etc. The larger breeds are generally the most susceptible to damage since they bring more weight down on their fast-growing bones and muscles when they land. One-third their height is plenty while they're young. But no breed is immune to complications from straining a young body. Care and supervision should always be applied to see that jumping at a young age is never strenuous.

4. Dog Walk. If your pup is comfortable and eager with your low dog walks, there's no reason he can't continue as in Ch. 6, maybe even progressing to the regulation dog walk and crossover while he is still a small pup. It must depend on how the puppy feels about heights and narrow planks.

You should not be doing any of this without your hands on him for some time yet, as your puppy is unpredictable at best. Part of this unpredictability comes from his spontaneous ideas to enjoy getting on and off the equipment he loves. An older dog would have a more realistic impression of how it feels to hit the ground on one's side from four feet in the air. Keep a hand in your pup's collar for quite a bit longer.

Work on training the pup to walk all the way on from the end and all the way off, feeding treats in the contact zones and following the other safety procedures outlined in the early parts of Ch. 6. Be aware that the pup's confidence is what you want, but that he needs a lot more experience with the real world before he really understands what it means to be up there. It's analogous to your grade-school child feeling ready to drive a

Agility begins at home. This agile eight-week-old has a habit of climbing out of her four-foot-high pen. This is not the kind of "ladder work" we have in mind.

car. He might know a lot of the rules, but you'd be a fool to give him the keys.

5. Closed Tunnels. As long as your puppy loves to run the tunnels fast and is not the least bit hesitant with the short chute lying completely closed, there's no reason not to continue with this training just as the adult dogs do in Ch. 5. Just keep tuned into how suddenly your puppy can tire and how unevenly his confidence and skill will progress. A few times in a row, not more. Go back to review short chutes more often than you would with adult dogs.

6. Weave Poles. When your pup accepts the poles closer to him, stay at that point for quite some time to fortify his impulse to run the chute rather than just trot it. When you think you have to make it more challenging, go back to a very short length and start bringing the poles closer together by the tiniest bit each day. If you are not religiously slow about this progress, you will accidentally teach your pup to run out, in which case you have to widen the chute quite a bit to change his mind. No fair criticizing the pup; he showed resourcefulness in going around.

Chen-yu checks out the slide, then checks out the cookie...

...and decides to go for it, showing her spunk and trust in Bob.

She doesn't yet know what to do with the slide, but she wags her tail and gladly gives it a try. Good girl!

Plan on taking at least six months to teach weaving a short chute of poles. Anything more aggressive is asking for mistakes. When your pup is really ready for advanced pole work, turn to Ch. 9.

7. Seesaw. Using a downscaled seesaw with a fulcrum no higher than 12 inches and with the aid of a helper to ensure that the plank tilts slowly and smoothly, the seesaw can be learned by an advanced pup. The pup should be confident on hay bales and other backyard obstacles that are unstable. He needs to have a good sense of balance and a steady head for novel experiences before being introduced to a seesaw.

Proper handling techniques are very important here, as bad habits are easily formed on this obstacle. Study the training sequence in Ch. 6, and always position yourself beside the puppy with your hand in the collar, to be able to steady his body with your leg at a moment's notice and to prevent him from jumping off.

Throughout your puppy's training, remember to be where you're needed and do what is needed to help your youngster benefit from Agility. Think of positive ways to get what you want from him, without reprimands or harsh tactics. Use Agility in the spirit of fun, as a tool for building confidence and rapport. It can give your pup a giant head start toward Agility for adult dogs; more important, it can give you some of the greatest joys of puppyhood.

SECTION IV

Appendices

- *National Organizations*

- *Sharing Ideas*

APPENDIX A

NATIONAL ORGANIZATIONS

The British Agility Club does not confer titles as such, but bases eligibility for certain classes on placements in other classes. Wins and placements are eligible only through agility classes and jumpers classes at tests licensed by the Kennel Club. Because of the popularity of the sport and the extreme range in the caliber of competition, two new classes, one at each end of the accomplishment scale, were added in 1990, for a total of seven different recognized classes:

Elementary - for those who have never won a third place or better;

Starters - for those who have never won first place other than in the Elementary class;

Novice - for dogs who have never won twice outside of Elementary and Starters;

Intermediate - for all dogs not eligible for the first three classes;

Seniors - for dogs who have won at least two times in Novice or Intermediate;

Open - for anyone; and

Advanced - for dogs who have at least four wins, with at least two of them in Senior or Open classes.

The United States instituted a class system modeled after England's five classes, but began to offer agility titles in 1990. Three titles were established, and it was decided to keep title classes separate from the more competitive qualifying rounds for tournament events. Titles are awarded through their own USDAA-sanctioned classes.

In order to earn the title *Agility Dog* (AD), a dog must turn in a clear round (no course faults and no time faults) in a Starters class. The first Starters class was held at BB Agility Center in Virginia, with six dogs passing the test.

The title *Advanced Agility Dog* (AAD), is awarded to dogs that complete three clear rounds under two different judges in Advanced classes.

The title *Master Agility Dog* (affectionately known as MAD Dog), is conferred upon dogs who meet a combination of requirements including a clear round in a Masters class and qualifying scores in certain novelty classes.

These three titles might be inadequate in a country in which agility competition is very far advanced, but it makes sense where an intermediate range is needed, offering stepping-stone goals to exhibitors who are eager to advance but not making them contingent on defeating other participants.

Although certain aspects of the sport differ according to each country's interpretation and level of involvement, a unity of spirit exists in the worldwide dedication to the fun and vitality of Agility. In addition to sanctioned classes, novelty classes are a popular part of most agility events everywhere. Many have become standard through their steady popularity, and new ones are limited only by the imagination of the individuals involved.

Details, rules, obstacle specifications, upcoming events, etc., may be obtained through national organizations. Here are a few of them, but there are many others throughout Europe and elsewhere.

AUSTRALIA
Australian National Kennel Council
Royal Showgrounds, Epsom Road
Ascot Vale, Victoria 3036

CANADA
Canadian Kennel Club
89 Skyway Ave., Unit 100
Etobicoke, Ontario M9W6R4

Agility Dog Association Canada
c/o Art Newman
R.R. 3 North Gower, Ontario K0A 2T0

Obstacle specifications and construction guidelines are included in ADAC's rule book. ADAC welcomes mixed breed as well as purebred dogs. So far, this has kept the CKC and ADAC apart. The first Canadian national competition, hosted by ADAC in 1990 near Ottawa, was an overwhelming success.

ENGLAND
British Kennel Club
1 Clarges Street
Piccadilly, London W1Y 8AB

British Agility Club
c/o John Gilbert
Keba Cottage, 100 Bedford Rd.
Barton-le-Clay, Bedfordshire MK45 4LR

Since 1989, an elected Agility Council interfaces with and makes recommendations to the Kennel Club, the governing body. Agility in Great Britain is open to mixed breeds as well as purebred dogs.

The Agility Club's monthly magazine, *Agility Voice*, is a first-rate publication recommended to anyone with an interest in what's going on at the forefront of the sport. Subscription cost is approximately 15 pounds per year, 22.5 pounds in Europe and 25 pounds outside Europe. Through the Agility Club Dog Shop, the Club sells books, obstacle construction plans, etc.

IRELAND
Irish Kennel Club
Fottrell House, 23 Earlsfort Terrace
Dublin 2

SCOTLAND
Scottish Kennel Club
3 Brunswick Place
Edinburgh EH7 5HP

SWEDEN
Svenska Kennelklubben (Swedish Kennel Club)
Box 110 43
161 11 Bromma

Sveriges Hundungdom (Swedish Youth Dog Organization)
Box 111 21
161 11 Bromma

Sveriges Hundungdom is a junior organization of the SKC, with its own staff. This active group oversees agility events, answers requests for rules and information, etc. Sveriges Hundungdom reports to and makes recommendations to Svenska Kennelklubben, the governing body.

Mixed-breed dogs are currently eligible to compete in agility events in Sweden, and the sport is quite advanced there. A major annual tournament consists of 10 regional events, with qualifiers advancing to a national competition at the Championship Show in Stockholm. In 1990, more than 100 individual dog/handler teams and 15 four-dog teams qualified to run at Stockholm.

UNITED STATES
American Kennel Club
51 Madison Avenue New York, NY 10010

United States Dog Agility Association
P.O. Box 850955
Richardson, TX 75085

USDAA welcomes mixed-breed as well as purebred dogs. The AKC does not allow mixed-breed dogs on their show grounds, so the two factions cannot easily resolve their differences. One of the most promising venues for agility events is the horse show, a longtime favorite of our English mentors. With plenty of room and often many times the spectators, major horse shows are benefiting from and welcoming agility events in the U.S.

USDAA sells agility rule books, obstacle construction plans, etc.

The "fireplug" jump was designed by Jeanine Dunn-Harmon and Art Weiss of Long Island. It's made from fiberboard barrels, styrofoam and plastic plant pots, and plastic chain.

USE SONOTUBE FOR PLUG 18"

APPENDIX B

SHARING IDEAS

From training hints to equipment improvements, there's always a better way and a strong piece of advice waiting to be discovered. This Appendix is a collection of ideas from all over, dedicated to the hard-working, fun-loving people everywhere who have put their minds and bodies to work for the good of Agility.

Jumps

Attention is now being paid to ensure that jump cups do not seat the displaceable bars too firmly. When closet-pole holders are used they are being sawed nearly flat. Other popular materials for jump cups include small pieces of wood, plastic, or PVC with just a tiny depression carved to balance the pole, not restrain it.

Florence and Byron Archer of Virginia made some simple, clever jumps from square plastic gutter pipe attached with angle braces to three-toed wooden bases of pressure-treated four by fours. Holes drilled through the pipe hold pegs at various labeled jump heights. One jump also sports an inner channel to hold horizontal planks.

Basic pole jumps have also been fashioned from round PVC pipe. For stability, jump feet made of PVC need to be longer than wooden feet.

Canine Combustion's base is designed for doubles and triples. Wings and uprights fit into slits in base made of four-by-fours. Wings are made of one-by-fours. It's simple, inexpensive, lightweight and stackable.

Several clubs have made jumps by cutting and framing lattice panels for side pieces and planks.

Jump planks can be made by cutting a narrow piece from each end of a one by six, leaving a protrusion about two inches long for hanging.

Mary Jo Baldwin of Massachusetts made her wall jump with handles on each section; what a difference!

The Toledo Timebusters have made mock-picket jump wings from thin sheets of plywood, cut with a small power saw. Clever painting creates the illusion that each wing is really all one piece. Slotted bases provide support.

Some basic jumps at Crufts are designed so wings are not inviting to jump.

Hannah and Stoner pose with their bone jump made by Monica Percival of NEAT. Template was traced from picture enlarged by overhead projector. Each piece has a handle on the back.

BB Agility Center's bone jump is extremely sturdy. Bone is firmly seated into jump cups; jump height is measured to top of displaceable pole.

Wishing well jump used at Crufts in 1991 looks like the real thing.

The base design used by DAWG makes for portable, stackable, sturdy jumps. Slot in base supports crosspiece of wing just behind two-by-fours.

Burt Franklin of BB Agility Center modified a tire jump with a PVC insert. The tire slides up and down secured by velcro bands, and height is adjusted via one chain at top. Pulley and cleat system could be substituted for chain.

No chain? NEAT copied this idea from Darlene Woz of Detroit. It uses cleats and braided cotton line from a marine supply store. NEAT secured bottom with line attached to stationary spring on one side, through eye bolts in tire to self-tailing cleat on other side. Top line is marked for regulation jump heights, so changing tire height takes only a few seconds.

Weave Poles

Burt Franklin designed unique individual weave poles from special rigid PVC and machined steel tips. Many clubs have ordered these poles, available from BB Agility Center, P.O. Box 2243, Danville, VA 24541.

George McLaughlin of New Hampshire built a steel base with six-inch lengths of metal pipe welded upright to hold poles. Narrow diameter poles offer little lateral degree of freedom; larger poles have more. Base is heavy and stable, but only three inches wide and one-fourth inch thick, good for indoors and out.

Will Koukkari of Minnesota designed and built this wonderful tool for teaching the leaning poles method. Metal base has feet at each end for stability and holes for staking outdoors. Angle brackets fit into slots cut into dowling. Adjustable wing nuts allow poles to be secured at any angle.

Closed Tunnel

Closed-tunnel chutes are generally fastened by locking lid rings when fiberboard barrels are used. Some are secured by bolts or wing nuts through a flange on the rigid entrance and grommets in the chute. Lesser known and probably the best fastener is a large hose clamp, the kind that is tightened and loosened by a screwdriver.

Although many materials are usable for tunnel chutes, perhaps the best combination of strength, weight, and water repellency is four-to-five once nylon coated with urethane. Chutes of this material, sometimes called pack cloth, are available through Texas Canvas Products (see Ch. 5).

This is the builder's view of the castle closed tunnel, a creation of Art Weiss of Long Island. Plywood facade surrounds entrance to fiberboard barrel. Beware – unless dog focuses on the hole in the wall, it looks like a jump from the front. Chute is nylon net.

Pause Table

Many clubs are using one table top for all table heights. For each height, a good one-piece support consists of four legs of appropriate height, made of wood or PVC, connected by a criss-cross for stability. Table top has a rim which fits snugly over the legs.

Pause Box

Designs using PVC, wood, and metal have all been used; some can be dismantled. An attractive and superior PVC version is available at low cost from Pipe Dreams, 46 Dearborn Rd., Epping, NH 03042.

Dog Walk

Ron Pitkin of New Hampshire has modified several dog walks for extra stability. Longer top and bottom crosspieces widen the base of support, and heavy plywood panels on each face add rigidity. He also uses an angled metal plate in place of hinges. Holes are drilled in the plate and heavy bolts secure plank to metal. The plank rests on the plate during set up and can easily be handled by one person.

Some clubs are fortifying dog walk and crossover planks with an edging of one by twos or two by twos on the long sides for extra strength and rigidity. It helps planks resist sagging.

Mike and Bev Weaver of Kansas built a wooden chute that helps dogs feel secure about climbing narrow ramps. It can be wheeled along the plank, is easy to move and store, and has many simple features which add to its usefulness. For details contact Luv Dogs Agility Club, 5236 Hardy, Overland Park, KS 66202.

This double sawhorse provides a channel for planks. Hooks under channel and eyes on planks can provide extra security.

These dog-walk supports at BB Agility Center have a well- stabilized triangular base.

A-Frame

Canine Combustion has taken rigid edging one step further. It attached two wheels to the edging on one side of each ramp and handles to the other side, so two people can roll the A-frame away without dismantling it.

Many clubs are now using one long metal rod to secure all three hinges at the apex in place of individual removable hinge pins. One end of the rod is bent to form a handle. Shorter rods suffice for dog walk and crossover hinges.

Plywood for ping pong tables comes in a five-by-nine-foot size, stronger and easier for making A-frames, and more expensive than standard size.

Seesaw

Many clubs have taken steps to reinforce their wooden seesaw bases and add more stability, especially side-to-side. A plywood panel or diagonal crosspiece should suffice.

This downscaled seesaw has a fulcrum about 12 inches high. It was made by Monica Percival from scrap materials.

Miscellaneous

Simple hoops for contact zone work can be made by reaming two two-inch holes in a wooden base, bending a five-foot length of two-inch diameter hose and inserting ends in the holes. A nail keeps it secure. It's useful indoors and out, can be tucked under the plank, then positioned further away as dog learns.

To surround an agility ring, colored pennants on a rope define the area inexpensively and decoratively. Available from Dealers Supply, Box 100, Troy, MI 48099, telephone 1-800-521-3870, or Grainger, an industrial supplier with a store in every U.S. state.

SECTION V

Bibliography, Index

BIBLIOGRAPHY

Books

The Agility Dog International, by Peter Lewis. Published by Canine Publications, Southampton, England (1988).

Agility is Fun, by Ruth Hobday. Published by Our Dogs Publishing Co., Manchester, England (1989).

How to be Your Dog's Best Friend, by the Monks of New Skete. Published by Howell Books, New York, New York (1978).

How to Raise a Puppy You Can Live With, by Clarice Rutherford and David Neil. Published by Alpine Publications, Loveland, Colorado (1981).

Making Friends, by Linda Colflesh. Published by Howell Books, New York, New York (1990).

Mother Knows Best, by Carol Lea Benjamin. Published by Howell Books, New York, New York (1985).

Playtraining Your Dog, by Patricia Gail Burnham. Published by St. Martin's Press, New York, New York (1980).

Why Does Your Dog Do That?, by Goran Bergman. Published by Howell Books, New York, New York (1971).

Articles

American Kennel Gazette: "Early Enrichment with Obstacles," by Peter and Nancy Vollmer. June 1989. "Giant Breeds: Building Power and Endurance," by Hazel Olbrich. December 1989.

New Hampshire Times (no longer in print): "Going for the Win," by Peg Boyles. September 7, 1985.

Videos

Dogsteps, by Rachel Page Elliott. Available through the American Kennel Club, New York, New York.

INDEX